MAKING
PEACE

A First-Hand Account of the
Arab-Israeli Peace Process

EYTAN BENTSUR

PRAEGER

Westport, Connecticut
London

Library of Congress Cataloging-in-Publication Data

Bentsur, Eytan.
    Making peace : a first-hand account of the Arab-Israeli peace process / Eytan Bentsur.
      p. cm.
    Includes index.
    ISBN 0–275–96876–6 (alk. paper)
      1. Arab-Israeli conflict—1993- —Peace. 2. Israel—Politics and government—1993-
    3. Bentsur, Eytan. I. Title.
    DS119.76.B49   2001
    956.05'3—dc21   00–032383

British Library Cataloguing in Publication Data is available.

Library of Congress Catalog Card Number: 00–032383
ISBN: 0–275–96876–6

First published in 2001

Praeger Publishers, 88 Post Road West, Westport, CT 06881
An imprint of Greenwood Publishing Group, Inc.
www.praeger.com

Printed in the United States of America

∞™

The paper used in this book complies with the
Permanent Paper Standard issued by the National
Information Standards Organization (Z39.48–1984).

10 9 8 7 6 5 4 3 2 1

Cover photo of President George Bush addressing the participants of the Madrid Peace
Conference courtesy of the Government Press Office of the State of Israel.

Contents

Preface and Acknowledgments

This book was written when I served as deputy director general of Israel's foreign ministry. Its aim is to describe accurately the circumstances that led to the peace process in the Middle East—the efforts, the turning points, the decisive roles played by some participants, all of the factors that brought about the major historic breakthrough known as the Madrid Conference. It was this conference that put us on the threshold of a new era in the relations between Israel and the states in its region.

A watershed event in the Middle East, the Madrid Conference precipitated a revolution in Israel's relations with the Arab states. For Israel, it was the most significant foreign policy development since the peace agreement with Egypt, more than a decade before. Madrid was a major political initiative, and it derived from determination, creative risk taking, and the overcoming of legitimate, deep-rooted differences. The dialogue between Israel and the United States had a part in this transformation as well. Against all odds, an era of peace was reached.

In the final analysis, it was cooperation between a core of Israeli and American statesmen and diplomats that carried the peace process past an initial, historic corner at Madrid. The creativity of this group set the wheels moving, and the peace process got on track.

It was my great privilege to take part in the fashioning and implementation of Israel's political initiative, a plan designed to attain a comprehensive, lasting peace based on a fresh political conception.

Translated into political action, the plan promoted peace negotiations on two tracks—a Palestinian track and a broad Israeli-Arab track. These negotiation channels were followed in parallel, with their point of convergence envisioned as a peace inspired and redeemed by new forms of regional economic development. From the start, it was clear that the road to peace would be strewn with vexing, unresolved issues, each fraught with the power to derail the whole process.

The memory of casualties of the Israeli-Arab dispute, of the many brave men and women who sacrificed their lives for Israel, compels our endless striving for peace. For them and for the future of our children we plod on, so that our descendants can live in a country freed from war. It behooves us to persist in the political process, on the peace route charted originally at Madrid, so that we may, day by day, hour after hour, be able to look into the eyes of our children and say to them: not an effort was spared in the quest for peace.

It is my pleasure to add one final acknowledgement for the English edition of this book. I want to thank Tzion Evrony, Israel's consul general in Houston, Texas, whose persistence, encouragement and unflagging efforts facilitated the publication of this book in English—I am very grateful for his help. My Foreign Ministry colleague in Jerusalem, Dan Arbell, also made a special effort, helping with a number of matters connected with the book, and I thank him. Many thanks also to Matthew Silver for translating this book and to Barry Rubin for his advice. And my gratitude goes as well to Reeva "Gwen" Gorr, who helped with many aspects of *Making Peace*.

1

Los Angeles

In the spring of 1986, as a "national unity" government composed of Israel's two major parties wound down to the end of its term, the director general of the foreign ministry, David Kimche, informed me that then Foreign Minister Yitzhak Shamir had appointed me to serve as Israel's ambassador to Canada. This was the first in what promised to be a succession of diplomatic appointments. I wanted a different assignment; I asked to switch posts and serve as the consul general in Los Angeles. The foreign minister immediately consented. When it was time to part from Shamir, I listed the reasons for my choice—my desire to deal with the second-largest Jewish community in the United States, with its complex political, economic, and media nexus, and to work with a growing community of expatriate Israelis.

I set myself the goal of cultivating political, economic, media, and religious connections, centering on focal points of power and influence. Paramount would be the effort to bridge gaps between Israel and this thriving American Jewish community. I had my work cut out for me: the goal was to improve mutual relations that had been tarnished by the mounting criticism leveled in the American community against Israel as a result of Israel's relations with the Arab states and the Palestinians.

To this, I added another challenge—to act among the growing population of Israelis in Los Angeles, whose number had been estimated somewhere between one and two hundred thousand. This was before the immigration of Jews to Israel from the disintegrated Soviet Union, and the ethos of Israeli state building seemed to be running in reverse. Instead of Jews "ascending" as immigrants to Israel, as the Hebrew *aliyah* implies, Israelis were leaving their home country, "descending" from it, as the alternative Hebrew term, *yerida*, puts it. Among these emigrants were a fair number of young people, veterans of Israel's army. It was imperative, I reasoned, to act resolutely to encourage these expatriate Israelis to come home.

After presenting them to Foreign Minister Shamir, I packed these commitments and goals in my valise. I headed to Los Angeles at the end of the summer of 1986 for a two-year term slated to end with the conscription of my youngest son, Dan, into the Israel Defense Forces.

Endlessly sprawling Los Angeles provided me with an event-filled, challenging term. How easy it would have been to settle placidly in a life of luxury amidst the city's power brokers, in a period of peak financial and economic prosperity! Soon enough, I forged connections with the local plutocracy, the political movers and shakers. Had I wanted to do so, I could have played out my entire term cementing ties with these elements—magnates like Michael Milkin, Gil Glazer, Abe Spiegel, Armand Hammer, and others. Los Angeles supplied a large share of the multimillionaires on the *Forbes* lists of the wealthy. More than once I found myself inviting such a tycoon to a meal at a fancy restaurant in an attempt to recruit him for some cause or another related to Israel, and incidentally spending the best part of my salary in the process.

Los Angeles's amorphous urban contours—six clusters hooked together to make a city—took some getting used to. It was not just the geography: I found Los Angeles to be sprawling also in terms of its power centers. For a diplomat whose habits were related to routine embassy work vis-à-vis the local government, Los Angeles proved to be highly complex. Its power structure featured a number-one man, the impressive and unique Tom Bradley; members of the city council (among them Zaev Yuroslavski, a Hebrew speaker, son of an old-time Labor Zionist and brother of a woman who lived in Israel); and a number of office holders in the state legislature and L.A. municipal council. As to this last structure, I became acquainted with Tom Hayden, Jane Fonda's former husband and an ex-radical turned capitalist, who, it seemed to me, now found it tough to find his place in the intrigue-filled world of politics. All such characters were components of the Los Angeles power structure, and we in the consulate wanted to get close to it, to gain leverage for strengthening ties with Israel.

Also there was, of course, Hollywood, whose flash and glitter, dreams and fantasies, entranced so many in the city. The film industry's impact was evident in the lifestyle and opulence of the Beverly Hills set, with its slew of producers and personalities. During my term I became acquainted with Richard Dreyfuss. He told me at one stage that he was considering taking a year off from the film industry to spend time in Israel and learn its ways up close. Later on, however, when Woody Allen published a scornful, anti-Israel article in response to the Arab *intifada* uprising, Dreyfuss hinted to me that he was thinking of writing a similar piece for the *Los Angeles Times*.

I told Dreyfuss that despite my respect for him as a first-rate screen actor, if he saw fit to write a corrosive article akin to Woody Allen's, I would make life miserable for him. "This is a time to rally around and help Israel, and not join its venomous detractors," I said. Dreyfuss relented. I had better relations with Elliot Gould. We would meet in a Beverly Hills restaurant; I would focus on Israel, and Gould would go on about his exploits raising money to renovate an ultra-orthodox Habad synagogue in Venice, on the Pacific coast. In September 1987 Elliot Gould, Jehan Sadat, and myself were invited to a musical called *Israel, Ho, Israel*, composed by Morris Bernstein and featuring the Denver Symphony Orchestra. This love story between an Israeli soldier and a young Palestinian woman was served up as a metaphor, foreshadowing a future full of peace in the Middle East.

Swept up in the stream of glamorous events and receptions, I came across the stars of the entertainment world, the heroes of my youth—Cary Grant, Jimmy Stewart, and others. Los Angeles revolves around its star glitter, and its celebrities exert a ceaseless gravitational force. The stars were everywhere, from a birthday party that petrol giant Armand Hammer threw for himself to events held at the Wiesenthal Center, a Holocaust research and investigation institute.

At the top of the Jewish world in the city were the fancy occasions sponsored by the Hebrew University of Jerusalem. During my term of service it threw a dinner to honor Steven Spielberg, with Ezer Weizman, today the president of Israel, the guest of honor. Weizman, formerly a pilot and commander of Israel's air force, kept in close touch with the head of the Los Angeles support organization for the Israel Defense Forces, Lou Leonard. Leonard was an American Jew of Hungarian descent, one of Israel's first combat pilots and a founder of Israel's air force.

Naturally, the main thrust of our efforts was solidifying relations with the local Jewish community. We explained Israel's situation, encouraged local Jews to consider living in Israel, sought ways to bring the community's power and influence to bear for Israel's benefit, and generally worked to strengthen ties with the United States. I resolved that the isolation of Israel's diplomatic presence in the city, a by-product of the past, would be overcome at all costs. A bridge to the local community, I concluded, could be built if its circumstances and problems were understood and then attended to. We spread the message of kinship with the Jewish world and fortified the Jewish educational system in the city. We strengthened bonds with Israel among both younger and older Jews in Los Angeles.

The community, led by Stanley Hirsch, the head of the local Jewish Federation, was a rock of support. Also, the Wiesenthal Center unreservedly assisted the consulate's activities, combating skillfully anything it perceived as a threat to Jews or to Israel. The prestige of the Wiesenthal Center rose in this period, thanks to its energetic administrators and managers, Rabbis Marvin Hayar and Abe Koffer; this pair spread the center's influence throughout California and beyond. However dealing with the Jewish Federation and the Wiesenthal Center demanded diplomacy. Working with these two important institutions in the Jewish community, both of whom displayed good will toward Israel, required caution—one could not be preferred at the expense of the other.

With the munificent support of the center, an Israel solidarity march was held for the first time in the history of Los Angeles, following the model of the annual event in New York. Winding along the world's longest boulevard, the pageant boasted participants from all parts of the community's social stratum, demonstrating an impressive display of pro-Israel sympathy. Marching together for Israel were clean-cut, pious church youth and bearded, long-haired, motorcycle bullies, ex-thugs who set aside their abusive habits to ride their bikes in a show of respect for Israel—and this at a time when Israel's stature in public opinion had declined precipitously, its former luster badly marred by mounting criticism of its policies.

Yet conspicuously few onlookers came to watch the pro-Israel pageant. Maybe the reason was the unusually cold weather, or maybe it was the lack of geographical coherence in the anomalous Los Angeles sprawl. Then again this indifference could have been the rotten fruit of the intifada, coupled with the harsh anti-Israel coverage in the media, which was dividing Israel from its old supporters, dampening their will to be counted in public as well-wishers for Israel.

As has been said many times, Los Angeles is a tough town. The reason is not only the lack of a geographical base, or the urban sprawl, or the peculiar, hard-to-discern contours of financial and political power; nor is it only the Hollywood atmosphere, which casts a spell over a large part of the city and its residents. L.A. is a tough town because one's word has so little value. Time after time, I was reminded of Charles de Gaulle's exasperated exhortation: the value of the word has to be restored. More than once I discovered that this person or that could not be trusted, that his or her promises were nugatory, and I had to draw the necessary conclusions. More than many other places, in Los Angeles it is hard to track down an honorable man, one who is not a hypocrite or a pretender. It is a hard place to find a genuine friend of Israel, or people who can be converted into such supporters. Indeed, my contacts brought meaning to the adage attributed to the Greek philosopher Heraclitus: in a large crowd, there are only a few people to be found. Still, we gradually became enlightened as to who our friends were, as to who held Israel dear to their hearts and could be counted on.

This situation applied as well to Hollywood, to its community of producers, actors, and agents. Hollywood is a cruel, thankless world. It punishes both those who ardently seek to succeed in it and those who seem to be at its pinnacle. Nonetheless, despite the tangled skein of artifice and competition, it was possible, with effort, to locate a few people whose bonds with Israel and Judaism had not been extinguished or irreparably mangled. In fact, I was continually amazed by the ways sympathy for Israel was expressed in the film world. Apart from the great impact that an individual can make by donating to a Jewish or Israeli organization or by using influence in the political world to support Israel, I learned, Hollywood can really make a difference: by preventing the production or distribution of films whose plots might be detrimental to Israel and its image. Support in this sense was maintained despite huge film costs and the penetration of foreign influences in Hollywood. Singer-actress Connie Stevens once told me that a group of Saudi tycoons had banded together to produce a pro-Arab film. Though the group had tremendous capital at its disposal, its efforts were to no avail—greed-ridden, money-hungry Hollywood refused to be seduced by elements hostile to Israel.

In hundreds of appearances, lectures, and interviews, I stressed Israel's yearning for peace, its efforts to end the succession of Mideast wars, and the character of its alliance with the United States, which had been founded on a special relationship deriving from shared values, democracy, and more. The idea of Israel and the United States as allies, of a common denominator between Israel and the American government, was a comfort to the Jewish community. Such relief was valued, as the community was taxed constantly by criticism leveled at home or imported from Israel—in opposition to the "unity" government which was headed on a rotation basis by prime ministers from the left (the Labor Party) and from the right (Likud). My goal was to forge a consensus on the basis of an optimal mix of Judaism and attachment for the state of Israel. I did my utmost to keep Israel's internal wrangling and strife from being projected outward. There was no dearth of "volunteers" to try to hitch me to one point of view or another; I had to keep my gaze fixed, knowing that it was forbidden to harm our paramount asset—a Jewish community united as much as possible in favor of Israel.

Briefing the leadership of the Jewish Federation during the last days of my term, I waxed enthusiastic, describing the vision of peace in the Middle East that had always inspired me. One of the Jewish leaders stood and exclaimed: "Finally, in the last days of your stint as general consul, you've finally divulged to us your heart's longings, and your political inclinations. Up to now, we haven't known which part of Israel's government you represent." I responded, "I've represented the whole government of Israel, not just one part of it. I have represented the national consensus in Israel—unifying, not divisive, forces, the binding issues of state and not the partisanship of politics."

Alongside the veritable carnival of frivolity among so many shapeless, insubstantial circles in the Los Angeles area, a few individuals of integrity and true intent were to be found. Dwelling modestly in Los Angeles is a small, intellectually oriented community that remained unpolluted by the Hollywood–Beverly Hills stardust and that stood honorably on one side of the political curtain. One conspicuous figure here was Stanley Sheinbaum, who was married to the daughter of one of the Warner brothers, a founder of the famous film studio that bears the family name. Sheinbaum, a true Renaissance man, a professor of economics and an editor, had special clout among left and center political circles. His home hosted actors and politicians associated with the peace camp. I got into contact with him via the outgoing Israeli ambassador, Ephraim Evron.

During one affair at his house I found myself entangled in an argument with some self-declared friends of Israel who claimed to want to save the country from itself by stripping it of influence in the United States, by breaking down the American Israel Public Affairs Committee (AIPAC), which, they contended, caused Israel to behave arrogantly and dodge compromise with the Palestinians. I wrestled rhetorically with these politicians, actors, journalists, and businessmen into the wee hours of the morning, trying to persuade them that a strong Israel was a prerequisite to any measure of progress in the political sphere. I sketched the devastating consequences that would result from a loss of Israeli power or the negation of its special relationship with the United States. Stanley Sheinbaum himself, though he played host to people who harbored such dubious views, was nevertheless a true friend who was able to help in a series of sensitive and delicate matters, utilizing connections he had crafted with many leaders in the United States and throughout the world.

He was the man who, together with an American politician, Rita Houser, cajoled the PLO into accepting America's terms, thereby enabling talks between it and the United States to resume. At that time, the government of Israel had rejected the signals of conciliation that the PLO had emitted; in retrospect, one can only speculate as to what might have developed, how much trial and tribulation we would have endured had we confronted the challenge of recognizing the PLO at that early date. The government of Israel, however, deferred this decision until the Oslo negotiations. Oslo in fact functioned as a workshop in which the government of Israel was to practice ways of transcending its previous equivocations, en route to a decision acknowledging an inextricable link between the PLO, the political effort, and the Palestinians.

Before departing from Los Angeles, I had told Foreign Minister Shamir that I would concentrate my efforts on a campaign to persuade as many expatriate Israelis as possible to come back to Israel. My estimate was that the majority of them had wandered to California lusting for money but had found only fool's gold, that only newfound routines now anchored them there, along with shame at their failure. I knew that these emigrant Israelis would not be pleased by appeals to their consciences, which would force them to confront hard dilemmas and possibly undermine their attempts to blend in with the local Jewish community while using it as a lever to "make it" in the larger American society. Stated another way, their aim was to achieve legitimacy in the United States, as bona-fide members of the Jewish community and American society; they dreaded being counted as another group of uprooted, drifting emigrants.

The Israeli population in Los Angeles is diverse, and I understood that I could appeal only to one thin stratum of this subsociety. This layer comprised Israelis who had wound up in California due to fortuitous circumstances, not a willful subordination of Zionist values and conscience to a materialist ethos. I focused my efforts on teenagers and children, encouraging Jewish education for the young and service in the Israel Defense Forces (IDF). My colleagues at the consulate general—Yitzhak Eldan, Moshe Pe'er, and Moshe Elezar—assisted this effort, which we called "Looking Homeward." They labored with great ardor and ingenuity. Within a fairly short time, the number of people who were either considering a return to Israel or were in the actual process of repatriation picked up. Soon enough, some two thousand people were being handled by the dedicated consulate staff. Many young people intended to go back to Israel to serve in the IDF; Moshe Pe'er endeavored to persuade the IDF to pay close attention to "lone soldiers" who had come from Los Angeles to serve, and to be sure to honor the various rights to which "lone soldiers" were entitled—return family visits, special allowances, etc.

The Israeli emigré population was not always happy, however, with the campaign we waged to encourage resettlement in Israel. The effort nettled some who craved local legitimacy, and it stirred pangs of conscience among others. Some "expats" vented their frustrations by verbally attacking the Israeli consulate, especially in reaction to one particular public event, which was attended by some two thousand Israelis. I used the occasion to deliver a call for Jewish education and for renewed ties to Israel and resettlement there. I referred to the dangers of assimilation and also to the physical risks borne by an expatriate population dwelling on the edge of a social cauldron that might erupt at any time. My own feeling was that Los Angeles simmered with threatening, possibly explosive, social and economic elements. At any event, the Israeli expat press showed an ambivalent attitude toward this "Looking Homeward" enterprise. One newspaper agreed to run a column under that headline, with pro-Israel themes; this same journal, however, periodically published distortions and defamations to undermine our endeavors.

The campaign to re-settle Israelis was enlivened by a visit by Prime Minister Shamir to Los Angeles. We arranged for him to meet with some three thousand Israelis in a synagogue hall in the San Fernando Valley. The prime minister delivered a fact-filled political briefing, sprinkling his report with an emotional call to return to Israel. His speech was met with a thunderous ovation. Leaving the event in his car, heading out to the offices of Armand Hammer, chief of Occidental Oil, Shamir told me that the night had been one of the most stirring experiences he could recall since Israel's establishment.

"Looking Homeward" was also aided by a group of local Israelis, such as Shimon Aram and Dr. Victor Jura, who boosted the consulate's activities and provided an example for the local Israelis, the vast majority of whom had lost their bearings, having become locked where they were by daily business routines and the sheer struggle to improve their material lots.

The intifada erupted in the West Bank territories of Judea and Samaria, and in the Gaza Strip, at the end of 1987. As the Palestinian uprising flared, Israel was put on the defensive. The woes caused by the intifada increased steadily. The media provided ample coverage of the unhappy events, its access to the flash points guaranteed by freedom-of-press norms maintained in Israel. The media exposure caused tremendous damage. Time and again, our staff at the consulate and pro-Israel elements in the local community pondered how democracies provide abundant opportunity for their own flagellation, while totalitarian societies enjoy substantial immunity from such criticism, by banning media coverage.

The *Los Angeles Times* went on an anti-Israel spree, printing about the intifada news articles, features, and most conspicuously, caricatures drawn by the cartoonist Paul Conrad. These caricatures portrayed Jewish IDF soldiers as Nazi stormtroopers or cruel murderers of women and children. I turned to the heads of the Wiesenthal Center, Rabbis Hayer and Koofer, who always were helpful providing advice and taking action; I asked them to assess the Conrad caricatures from a professional point of view, as Holocaust researchers. The rabbis replied without hesitation that the caricatures were of the notorious "Der Stuermer" (a Nazi, anti-Semitic paper) bent, depicting the Israeli (the Jew) as a cruel, immoral villain. In the Holocaust period, such caricatures had pandered to anti-Semitic sentiment; now they provided a lever for defaming Israel as a reincarnation of Nazism.

I initiated a round of meetings and talks with key figures in the *Los Angeles Times*, while also exposing the newspaper's behavior in public talks and in an article I published in the paper. This activity, however, was to no avail. I took the extra step of appealing to ever-widening circles and groups. I denounced the position taken by the prestigious newspaper, exposing the defamatory tactics upon which Conrad's work depended. My appearances stimulated readers to cancel their subscriptions to the newspaper. The trend picked up steam, causing some concern among the paper's owners and compelling them to ponder whether their journalistic objectivity had gone awry. A large group of Israelis protested, parading with their slogans in front of the editorial offices of the *Times*.

Amidst this flurry of protest, Conrad released a new caricature, one even more infuriating than his past work. The cartoon depicted IDF soldiers as Gestapo troops, with rifles at the ready, burying children's corpses. A new nadir of defamation had been reached. I got telephone calls from dozens of Jews and gentiles venting consternation; some even warned that should Israel not make a drastic response, it would be hard to regard it as a self-respecting country. I consulted with local leadership, including Mayor Bradley, the heads of the municipal council, and a justice from the California Supreme Court; I also conferred with my colleagues at the consulate. I recommended that the new foreign minister, Shimon Peres, expel the *Los Angeles Times* correspondent from Israel in protest. I argued that it was impermissible for Israel, a sanctuary for Holocaust survivors, to refrain from responding to a newspaper that purported to be objective but characterized Israel as a Nazi state.

My recommendation was ignored by the heads of the foreign ministry. They did not furnish an explanation for this rejection; perhaps they did not share my sensitivity, my revulsion at Israel's being depicted in such a fashion. As it turned out, it was President Chaim Herzog who finally attacked the bias, the latent anti-Semitism in the newspaper's criticism, the partisan and nonobjective description of Israel. Herzog spoke out against this coverage in a speech in Israel; we managed to package his comments as an article in the *Los Angeles Times*. Sure enough, the publication of President Herzog's article marked the beginning of a reorientation by the newspaper toward Israel. The consulate disseminated the president's article throughout the West Coast region for which it was responsible, and we managed to extract considerable utility from it.

Relating to the Israeli sector, and also to the local Jewish community, I took care to express myself in terms of the national Israeli consensus. Trends and forces fomenting division within Israel's government at the time were to be avoided at all costs. My approach in this respect differed from that of people who endeavored to recruit particular partisan branches of the Jewish community for campaigns against the other side of Israel's unity government. I had contempt for these leaders, Knesset

(parliament) members and various Israeli functionaries, who were prepared to speak in some opulent auditorium in Beverly Hills denouncing
Israel in order to "score points." I loathed them not only because of the
damage they caused to the state of Israel but also because they were
politicians who betrayed their public trust. Instead of fighting for their
views through the length and breadth of Israel, they chose to luxuriate
in comfortable settings in California and elsewhere in the United States,
to foster bitter argument and incrimination, and to spread denunciations
while denigrating support for Israel.

Contacts with local Israelis were replete with disappointment. More
than once I came across expatriates who had lost all sense of shame, who
had fashioned themselves as righteous prophets praising emigration and
vociferously criticizing Israel. It was these sort of Israelis whom the late
Yitzhak Rabin had in mind when he coined the well-known pejorative
"*Yordim*," for Israelis who leave their homeland. Rabin used a colorful
term, suggesting that such expatriates fall away from their roots in Israel
like withered leaves from a tree. On the other hand, the thousands who
turned to the consulate after hearing our appeals and the hundreds of
young people who enlisted in the IDF reinvigorated my efforts and
strengthened my belief that most Israelis keep in their hearts the desire
to return home and that this longing is ever susceptible to encouragement, even if the realization of their ultimate dream of homecoming is
deferred.

During my term as consul general, the *Jesus* film affair rankled. The
movie was produced by Universal Studios, where Lou Wasserman was
regarded as omnipotent; outside Hollywood as well, Wasserman commanded considerable political clout. Talking with him, I found that this
man of tremendous influence, both in the entertainment world and in
American politics, was terribly frightened by signs of anti-Semitism, to
the point of fearing threats to his own life. His responsibility for the
production of this film prompted several preachers in California to
bandy about accusations containing a coarse anti-Semitic strain, indirectly threatening the Jewish community as a whole. Wasserman doubled his bodyguard protection and turned his office into a fortress,
preparing for the most ominous possible scenario. Time passed, and the
whole affair blew over.

The intifada continued to rage, however, and the unity government in
Israel struggled with the now-chronic public relations problem. As matters worsened, some forces within the government tried to pressure de-

cision makers by projecting its divisive problems outward. I viewed that trend as a genuine danger to Israel's image; it could cause irreparable damage and provide legitimacy to all sorts of elements in the Jewish public and outside of it that were looking for pretexts to attack Israel— even people that had no track record of supporting the country in the first place and therefore lacked any semblance of credibility. Their claim, now being reinforced by elements from Israel, was that Israel should be helped to "save itself from itself." I held that we must not, under any circumstances, toy with our assets; instead, we had to cultivate them. Clinging hard to this view, I maintained that left-wing Knesset member Yael Dayan's participation in a Los Angeles rally held in opposition to Prime Minister Shamir during his visit was inappropriate.

In my dealings with the Jewish communities under my consulate's jurisdiction, from the large Jewish population of California to small, re- mote communities in Hawaii, I stressed the need to confront the forces that diluted Jewish bonds and strength. The numerical decline in the Jewish population had to be halted, and the best instrument to this end was Jewish education of all forms, sponsored throughout the United States, including California. Such education had to serve as a substitute for or supplement to the normal school curriculum.

I believed that many Jewish families would opt for a full curriculum of Jewish education if only they were provided the option. They would choose such an educational route both for the Jewish values it inculcated and also to insulate children from deleterious influences, be they drugs or juvenile crime, which had infiltrated the public school system in the Los Angeles area. I told the communities that they bore an additional burden, namely, to expand organized Jewish bodies. Each and every organization should take up the challenge of adding new members to its ranks. Should every member of each Jewish organization coax one of his or her acquaintances to join, within a short time the power of the orga- nized Jewish world could be doubled. I was gratified when a number of communities in my area of work responded to this idea and started drives to enlarge memberships in their organizations. In contrast, my efforts to encourage Jewish television channels in Los Angeles were in vain.

I also demanded that rabbis in the city show more flair and persistence in spreading the Zionist message. On the date of Israel's Independence Day, which comes after a period of mourning for the casualties of its wars and conflicts, one of the large synagogues in the city omitted the mention of slain Israelis in the traditional bereavement *yizkor* prayer. I explained to the local rabbinical council that this was an egregious omission, from both a Jewish and Israeli point of view.

The issue of immigration to Israel from California and elsewhere in the United States was handled mostly by Israeli emissaries hired by the Jewish Agency, an organization whose world-wide activities include the absorption of Jews in Israel. One of these, Kobi Leket, proved to be an especially dedicated, effective worker in this *aliyah* (Jewish immigration to Israel) field. Now and then I would be invited to attend a farewell ceremony for a group of idealistic Americans who were setting off to start new lives in Israel; I was pleased to give them my blessings, even while knowing that they constituted a small trickle. I was asked often what would be needed to trigger a larger-scale immigration from the United States to Israel. "Peace between us, the Arab states and the Palestinians," I would reply, not missing a beat.

More specifically, I was convinced that the emotional appeal of peace, together with the rise in the standard of living and the major economic opportunities that would follow, combined with the privatization and the liberalization of the Israeli economy, would beget a large wave of immigration.

Housing and Construction Minister David Levy, a Likud politician, visited Los Angeles during my term. We used his visit as an opportunity to publicize the housing terms afforded to Israelis who decided to leave California and return to Israel. We also held a meeting with L.A. Jewish community leaders, including Mr. Stanley Hirsch (a man of unflinching humanitarian character), about a housing-renovation project in Beit Shean, a development town that had become linked to Los Angeles when the Jewish community there took responsibility for the project's funding, along with the financing of a project in an Arab neighborhood, Ajami, in Jaffa. The Los Angeles community had taken on the Arab neighborhood renovation project after I helped free it from doubt and equivocation, assuring it that assistance to Israel's Arab population did not run counter to the ethos of a neighborhood renovation project in the context of the Jewish-Zionist enterprise.

David Levy had immigrated to Israel from Morocco as a youngster and was one of the first Israelis of that background to make it to the top of the country's political establishment. I met him for the first time during this Los Angeles visit and was impressed with the shrewdness of his analysis of conditions in Israel. He showed great sensitivity about social-economic issues and also genuine commitment toward working for solutions to the conflicts with the Arab world. I garnered the impression that here was a man with values, one who blended wisdom about life with an activist track record, a politician who had his feet on the ground and was not interested in simply snatching glory with which to impress followers in a contrived media setting.

During dinner at an expensive restaurant in Los Angeles, I said a few words of greeting to city and Jewish community leaders and spoke about my great hope that Israel would find its way to the high political road leading to peace. Minister Levy responded with some enigmatic words. Later, as we ate around the table, his assistant Uri Oren whispered to me, "Take note that the minister was hinting that he would like to work with you, and the ministry you belong to."

I was slated to return to Israel to serve as deputy director general of the Foreign Ministry, responsible for U.S. affairs and arms control, but before going back I visited Washington and the Israeli embassy's political officer, Shimon Stein. We met with the officials at the State Department and the National Security Council who were in charge of crafting Middle East policy. From there, I continued up to Ottawa, as the guest of Israel's ambassador to Canada, Israel Gur-Arieh, one of the pillars of Israel's diplomatic corps. We talked with officials in the top echelon of Canada's foreign ministry. Both in Washington and Ottawa I encountered mounting worry concerning the lack of progress in the political process, and also ever-increasing sympathy for the Palestinian cause and for Palestinian suffering. U.S. and Canadian officials were aware of the pain and loss of human life stemming from clashes between the IDF and the Palestinian population. The effort made by Israel's army to quell the intifada uprising was bringing a high cost. None of the officials with whom I met in Washington and Ottawa had in hand any proven prescription or well-formulated plan for making progress. Worry, confusion, and a sense of helplessness and futility pervaded the atmosphere in the two cities, threatening to vanquish an earnest will to help and a readiness to allocate time and material to stir political change in the Middle East. The attitude of the American government could be characterized as good will as well as an inclination to help move the political process forward that went beyond even what U.S. interests as a superpower dictated. As it turned out, this good will proved to be an indispensable asset. Without it the Middle East could not have eventually gotten on course, that of negotiations for a peaceful settlement.

On my return home in November 1988, the task of putting together the blocs in a national unity government was in full swing. I watched in the foreign ministry as officials made pilgrimages to Shimon Peres, the outgoing foreign minister, who was about to take up new reins as finance minister. Peres was beseeched not to leave the Foreign Ministry. One of the foreign minister's senior aides implored me to join this parade of supplication; I did not see fit to join this lobbying, as it had traces of the sort of political intervention that does not become a state official. Moreover, I knew that in any case Peres would reach a decision that served exclusively his own, clear-cut personal interests.

I had a farewell meeting with Peres, and we brought up memories of his visits to Los Angeles. During one public event, Jane Fonda had turned up, bewitching those around her with her beauty and charm, and adding to the success of the occasion by underscoring the message of peace that had been the theme of the speech delivered by Peres. Alas, all of Peres's concrete efforts to promote peace—the London agreement, for instance—had failed. Not peace but the angry rasp of the intifada could be heard in the background, and the uprising imposed on Israel's government both a political conundrum and constant security stress.

Cognizant of this, I resolved to work to my utmost in my capacity as deputy director general in charge of U.S. and arms control affairs to promote the political process. It was evident that repairing breeches in Israel's relations with the United States would be a precondition to the attainment of peace. The information in my possession at the time indicated that Washington was not really examining ways to move the political process forward.

---------------------- **2** ----------------------

Efforts

U.S. foreign policy, guided generally by strategic-global calculations and by economic-trade considerations, is shaped in the Middle East with a view to energy resources and on the basis of humanitarian sympathy and other factors. America's motivations for becoming involved in the region and its efforts to advance agreements and understandings between Israel and the Arab states must be seen in light of these broad foreign-policy parameters. Its policy is fashioned and implemented by each president and secretary of state in accordance with the styles, personalities, determination, talents, and wider visions of these high officials; ultimately, the policy is a function of, on the one hand the extent of the latitude these men allow to forces that exert pressure on the United States, and on the other hand of the alignment of forces within the United States and their particular orientations toward Israel. The manner in which American policy is implemented depends upon the resolve of its makers and on the circumstances in the region. An adroit secretary of state, Professor Henry Kissinger, managed to advance his political efforts by capitalizing on the tragic circumstances of the Yom Kippur War— and it is doubtful that the errors leading to those events belonged to Israel alone.

In any event, Washington has always been sympathetic toward Israel's foreign policy. Prior to Menachem Begin's election in 1977, the American leadership took pains to explain how Israeli policy brought political benefits for the United States, and it coordinated its own foreign policy with that of Israel. By so doing, the Americans shared some tumultuous political triumphs and worked to attain optimal support and understanding for Israel's needs. Begin's 1977 triumph added a twist in the historic relationship between the countries. Long an opposition figure in Israeli politics, Begin decided as Israel's sixth prime minister that good relations with the United States could be maintained even if the coordination of policy between the two states was halted.

Increasingly, American policy in the Middle East centered on the Palestinian issue. I will long remember an incident that occurred in 1975, while I was a political officer in Israel's embassy in Washington. Walter Smith, who headed the Israeli desk at the State Department, informed me that Harold Saunders, deputy secretary of state for Middle East matters, was poised to announce to Congress that the "Palestinian issue is the heart of the Israeli-Arab dispute."

As behooved me, I responded in a forthright way to Smith, arguing that the dispute was rooted in the refusal of the Arab states to recognize Israel's right to exist. I had no doubt that Saunders's statements had the approval of Secretary of State Kissinger. The Americans insisted that the declaration was made in an impromptu, nondeliberate fashion, but it was nevertheless the start of an acknowledgment in U.S. foreign policy that the Palestinian issue was a component of the Middle East crisis and that it too had to be dealt with. Pres. Jimmy Carter was destined to be the great popularizer of the Palestinian issue, becoming the first president to recognize the Palestinian right to a homeland.

George Shultz, the secretary of state in Ronald Reagan's administration, constantly sought intricate byways that might lead toward the PLO, aiming to deflect the PLO away from terror, to convert its core from violence to politics, and thus to render it suitable for negotiations with Israel. It bears mentioning that President Reagan himself detested the PLO. During a conversation with him after terrorists took control of the cruise liner *Achille Lauro* in 1985, Reagan declared, "I spit at the PLO"— and he was just one step away from turning this exclamation into actual policy, had the physical opportunity arisen.

The president's feeling notwithstanding, in the Reagan era Israel's government was forced to assent to Secretary Shultz's initiative to convene an international conference under American patronage leading to a comprehensive peace in the region. The secretary of state brought up the question of the legitimate rights of the Palestinians in a letter sent to Prime Minister Shamir on March 4, 1988. Shultz recommended that a joint Palestinian-Jordanian delegation be established, for the purpose of discussing with a counterpart Israeli delegation the Palestinian issue and possible ways of resolving it.

The increasing awareness among American foreign policy makers of the distinctiveness of the Palestinian issue, combined with recurrent American initiatives to promote an agreement in the Middle East and the escalation of the intifada, compelled Israel's government under Shamir to present a three-pronged political initiative. Shamir presented the U.S. government with this plan to resolve the Middle East dispute during a visit to Washington on April 9, 1989. Continuing the 1978 Camp David accords, the initiative would highlight Israel's willingness and need to normalize relations with the Arab states; it emphasized the Palestinian dimension, proposing that elections be held in Judea, Samaria, and Gaza in which delegates to the Mideast conference from the Palestinian population would be elected. In parallel, the proposal recognized the imperative of working on behalf of the Arab refugees.

From its contacts in Israel, the United States had known that this plan was being formulated, and it looked upon the initiative favorably. The American government's positive response was expressed lucidly in a note sent by James Baker (secretary of state in the new George Bush administration) on the 27th of April, 1989, to Israel's foreign minister, Moshe Arens. The secretary of state applauded Israel's willingness to agree to the election of Palestinian delegates. Baker, however, called on Israel to take additional steps, ones that he perceived as conducive to an improved atmosphere and the allaying of tensions. Secretary Baker recalled that the subject of elections had been discussed extensively during the 1979–82 autonomy talks; it seemed to him that recommendations, clarifications, and proposals connected to the elections proposal had been diluted since then. In order to ensure that the elections would be acceptable to both sides, Baker contended, it would be necessary to prevent the imposition of terms at the start that might discourage a constructive appraisal of the whole elections concept. To this end, it would be necessary to allow the Palestinians the right of free speech and assembly, the right to adopt organizational measures during the election campaign, and the right to invite international experts and observers to confirm the election results. The U.S. government's support would come in the form of supervision and the provision of free access to the media and experts during the elections—the Palestinians demanded this.

Another Palestinian demand was that East Jerusalemites take part in the elections as full-fledged members of the Palestinian people. The status of residents who live on the Arab eastern side of Jerusalem was a contentious issue, laden with conflicting sets of expectations and demands; there might be attempts to seize possession of areas in the city and thus "create facts" on the ground prior to any permanent solution. Israel refuted the Palestinian claim, fearing that the Palestinians were attempting to undermine its policy by which Jerusalem is upheld as Israel's undivided capital. For its part, the U.S. government held that conferring franchise rights to Palestinians in East Jerusalem would expand the democratic basis of any future election.

Yet another Palestinian demand: the Palestinians proposed that they be granted sovereign status in the final negotiation stage. In other words, the elections were not to be perceived as an end in themselves but rather as an inseparable part of a process that would pass through an interim stage and lead to negotiations for a permanent settlement. All such talks were to be wrapped up in the issue of Palestinian sovereignty. Secretary of State Baker, for his part, expected Israel to refrain from any public utterances that would rule out future opportunities. He did not want the Palestinians to be provoked into adopting extreme counter-responses that might stifle the process altogether.

Israel's national unity government authorized a four-pronged political initiative on May 14, 1989. In its final, official version, the initiative drew a sharp distinction between an Israeli-Arab peace arrangement and resolution of the Israeli-Palestinian issue. Hoping strongly to calm the militant Palestinian public and put an end to the dangerous, exasperating intifada, Israel's government assessed at this stage that a far-reaching proposal for the Palestinian problem would constitute a precondition for direct negotiations between Israel and the Arab states. Baker and his assistants marshaled their efforts on the Palestinian dimension of the dispute exclusively. The new initiative reflected Israel's fundamental principles, meaning direct negotiations, opposition to a Palestinian state, and rejection of negotiations with the PLO; also, it expressed Israel's interest in forging a comprehensive peace with the Arab countries. This multiplicity of declared objectives notwithstanding, Israel's negotiators hunkered down, anticipating tough negotiations focused specifically on the issue of the election of Palestinian delegates, and subsidiary problems attendant to it. The truth is that Israeli officials regarded the prospect of a general peace as remote. Mainly because of that feeling, very little thought was given to the question of how Israel might pursue the parts of its new initiative that called for negotiations with Arab countries.

The Israeli decision of May 14, 1989, called for a two-stage Palestinian election process. The first would be free elections in which Palestinians in the territories would choose delegates for negotiations with Israel. The elected Palestinians would represent the wishes of the local population; the delegation would be authorized to conduct talks with Israel, initially on government arrangements suitable for an interim period of Palestinian self-rule, and subsequently for a permanent, final-status solution. The transitional period of Palestinian self-rule would last five years. This phase would be designed as a crucial test of cooperation and peaceful coexistence between Israel and the Palestinians. The test would have to prove beyond a shadow of a doubt that after more than forty years of hostility, violence, and nonrecognition, the Palestinians were indeed prepared to change their attitude toward Israel and undertake a new framework of relations. Inspired by the spirit of the Camp David accords with Egypt, Israel favored a direct-dialogue approach: in talks about the status of the territories, each side would be free to bring up any subject it wanted to discuss, and all political options would receive sustained examination, in order to forge an ultimate solution suitable to both sides. This logic showed that Israel did not perceive the Palestinian election as an end in itself. Israel could assure Baker that the elections were to serve as part of a four-point initiative, the goal of which was to achieve a mutually acceptable solution.

In this connection on June 5, 1989, Foreign Minister Arens wrote in reply to Secretary of State Baker's April letter that the U.S. government's assent to Israel's initiative bore great significance. Israel valued Mr. Baker's advice and assistance, wrote Arens, and intended to discuss with him the details enveloped in the election issue.

The Israeli initiative was relayed officially to the U.S. government, and officials in Washington spent a few weeks studying it. On the last day of June, 1989, President Bush sent a letter to Israel's prime minister, Shamir. Implicit in this communiqué and in the reply sent by Shamir were differences of opinion that were destined to lead to a crisis in relations between the United States and Israel.

In his note, Bush sent condolences to families that had been harmed by a recent wave of terror. He emphasized that the United States would not support the establishment of a Palestinian state. The president attested to the important role that America had played in repulsing the PLO's endeavors to attain the status of a bona fide state in various international organizations and institutions. Bush cited his support for Israel's elections proposal and bore solemn witness to the inseparable bonds linking Israel and the United States. He praised Israel's government, calling its initiative an honest one, one that showed broad vision and provided a basis for progress. For its part, the United States was attempting to persuade the Palestinians and the Arab states to respond to Israel's initiative with an open mind and a constructive spirit; the United States, the president promised, would persist in such efforts. Bush also declared that points agreed upon by Israel and the United States far outweighed the issues over which the two countries were divided.

In his communiqué, Bush ventured some bold words, looking far down the road to a permanent solution. Israel's final borders had to be safe and secure, and the extent of Israel's withdrawal had to be determined by the extent of security provided thereby and the scope of the proposed peaceful solution. By this formula the depth of Israel's withdrawal from the territories would be proportional to the depth of security and peace offered by any future arrangement. President Bush referred to Jerusalem as well. The United States would never allow the repartitioning of the city. An agreement that provided access to Jerusalem's holy sites should be reached. Finally, negotiations should be direct, face to face, between Israel and the Arabs, and Israel and the Palestinians. The United States, President Bush promised, was already prodding the Palestinians into a dialogue with Israel about the way to bring the election concept into being.

Shamir's reply to Bush came on July 7, 1989. The prime minister declared that the government of Israel was making efforts to persuade the Palestinian leaders that its May initiative was genuine and designed to afford them the opportunity of taking their fate into their own hands, so as to fashion a better future. However, Shamir protested the American dialogue with the PLO, which had started toward the end of the Reagan-Shultz era. This dialogue, Shamir contended, was an obstacle to the realization of Israel's peace initiative. The dialogue's effect was to upgrade the PLO, conferring legitimacy upon it and its demands. The very essence of Israel's proposal was to bring about an arrangement with Arabs in the West Bank (Judea and Samaria) and the Gaza Strip, with the terrorist PLO excluded. Israel and the populations of the territories had common interests, whereas the PLO was devoted to the perpetuation of terror and violence, to upholding a "right of return" for Palestinians living outside the country, and to the establishment of an independent Palestinian state.

These PLO demands were utterly unacceptable to Israel. Dropping another hint critical of the U.S.-PLO contacts, Shamir wrote that it was clear to the government of Israel that the terror organization was seeking a vantage point from which it might carry out more violent schemes against Israel. Only if the Arabs and Palestinians who lived alongside Israel were free from PLO threats, and only when these people displayed an understanding that their hopes depended upon cooperation with Israel devoid of PLO involvement, could progress toward negotiations for peace be made. This was the central message delivered by the prime minister of Israel to the president of the United States.

The letter now went on to the question of Israeli settlements, which had spawned controversies of various proportions between Israel and U.S. presidents. It had been discussed in detail at Camp David in September 1978. Shamir recalled that despite differences of opinion on the subject, it had been agreed at the time that the issue would not be broached in the accords.

The prime minister went on to assert that Israel's position on the question of the "conquered territories" derived from three principles:

- Israel could not consent to any prohibition banning Jews from living in any part of Israel.
- The government of Israel would not allow land and property acquisition from Arabs for the purpose of establishing settlements.
- Israel remained loyal to the commitment it had undertaken in the Camp David framework, according to which the final status of the territories was to be determined in negotiations.

Shamir pointed out that Israel had taken no unilateral steps to decide the future of the territories and that it believed that Jewish presence in the territories, like Arab presence in the state of Israel, would not thwart the reaching of a peace agreement.

The Israeli government's May 14, 1989, political initiative gave a boost to discussions with the United States about ways to move the political process forward, but also spurred talks in European capitals and in Cairo. Special attention was lavished on the elections issue. In the summer of 1989, Egypt arranged for an Israeli-Palestinian conference to be held in Cairo. The question of the composition of the Palestinian delegation proved to be thorny and contentious—indeed, it was destined to produce a conundrum sidetracking the process until the Madrid conference, in October 1991. On September 15, 1989, via its ambassador to Israel, Mohamed Bassiouny, Egypt submitted to Israel's foreign ministry an official, ten-part proposal. Echoes of this plan could be heard in the political arena for the next few weeks.

The Egyptian proposal reflected the views of President Hosni Mubarak. It recommended

- Allowing residents of East Jerusalem, along with persons held in administrative detention by Israeli authorities, to take part in the elections.

- A right of political expression for the Palestinians, to be supervised by the international community, prior to and in the course of the elections.

- An advance agreement from Israel's government to accept the election results.

- An advance agreement from Israel's government to regard the elections as part of a comprehensive effort leading to a final-status arrangement—a final arrangement based, among other things, on the formula of land for peace and on the conferral of political rights to the Palestinians.

- A prohibition against settlement in the conquered territories.

Earlier, on September 1, 1989, two weeks prior to the official presentation of the Egyptian plan, Defense Minister Yitzhak Rabin had received, during a stay in Washington, a summary of it that Mubarak had passed in advance to Bush. Condensed, the plan stipulated:

- That the PLO agree to talks between an Israeli delegation and a Palestinian panel composed of residents of the conquered territories and deported persons, along with a Palestinian American known for moderate views.

- That the PLO authorize the Palestinian delegation to conduct the negotiations about Israel's election proposal, with the Egyptian ten-point plan being considered in parallel.

- That Egypt facilitate talks between a Palestinian delegation and an Israeli one.

- That the PLO refrain from demanding that the UN be given a role in the first stage. Should the UN decide to take part in the process as an observer, the PLO would consider inviting additional countries.

It was made clear to Defense Minister Rabin that the U.S. government, meaning the president and the secretary of state, had a keen interest in President Mubarak's message and viewed it as offering potential for progress. At the same time, U.S. officials accepted the legitimacy of Rabin's position—the defense minister pointed out that innumerable issues remained to be resolved, such as who would nominate the Palestinian delegates. Israel's government demanded to vet the names in advance; it did not want its delegation to face a Palestinian delegation selected without Israeli influence.

In any case, Mubarak's message to the American president and the ten-point plan became the fundamentals of Egypt's initiative. The Egyptians invited the Israeli and Palestinian delegations to Cairo to discuss the election issue. This proposal was submitted by Ambassador Bassiouny to Israel's foreign ministry on October 4, 1989. It received the attention it merited—there was indeed a show of interest on the part of the Israeli government. Israel, however, required that the next phase in the process adhere to its own peace initiative, particularly to its demand that the invitations be sent by Egypt's president and that the PLO declare that it accepted the plan prior to actual negotiations.

Submitting his proposal, Bassiouny elucidated Egypt's point of view regarding the meeting between Israeli and Palestinian delegations. As far as he was concerned, Egypt would be a facilitator, to encourage an Israeli-Palestinian dialogue. The Palestinian delegation should include Palestinians from the territories and from abroad, so that it would reflect adequately the whole array of Palestinian positions and interests. Egypt asked for a role in the Palestinian delegation-composition issue; the problem would be resolved on the basis of sustained trilateral consultations involving it, Israel, and the United States. The dialogue was to take place in Cairo, invitations to be issued by the Egyptians.

Egypt's stance regarding the composition of the Palestinian delegation clashed with the position adopted by Israel's government. Israel held that the Palestinian delegation had to be composed almost entirely of Palestinians from the territories, adding perhaps one or two returned deportees, with Israel's specific approval. Thus, the composition of the Palestinian delegation was debated, with the terms of disagreement drawn. Meanwhile, Egypt prepared to send invitations.

Secretary of State Baker ordered the American ambassador in Israel, William Brown—a constructive, effective diplomat of unimpeachable integrity—to relay a message to Israel's government on October 19, 1989. The United States declared that "Israel could not dictate which Palestinians are to be selected. However, nobody can compel Israel to sit with Palestinians with whom it has no inclination to conduct a dialogue." Baker was hoping to convene a three-way meeting with Israel, Egypt, and the United States, for the purpose of resolving the disagreement concerning the Palestinian delegation.

Moshe Arens addressed the election issue in a letter he sent to the secretary of state on October 23, 1989. First, Israel's public believed that residents of the territories should have the opportunity of selecting legitimate delegates, in an environment devoid of fear and violence by the PLO. Second, in free elections, Palestinian delegates could be selected whom Israel's public viewed as appropriate dialogue partners. They could be empowered to respect and enforce any agreements reached. Arens added that since declaring its political initiative, the Israeli government had responded positively to a series of American proposals relating to procedural matters connected to elections, and to a process by which the composition of a Palestinian delegation would be determined through consultations involving Egypt, Israel, and the United States, paving the way for an Israeli-Palestinian encounter.

Israel's foreign minister added two more points. First, Israel refused to conduct any negotiations with the PLO. Any proposal for Israel to meet with Palestinians selected directly or indirectly by the PLO would violate the content and spirit of its proposal, an offer that had been endorsed by the American government. Secondly, essential matters would be discussed exclusively with Palestinian delegates elected by residents of the territories. The meeting then being arranged for Cairo would therefore be held for the sole purpose of advancing the elections idea; the agenda would be reduced to issues related to election procedures.

Some of the contacts with the United States were done over the telephone, this being a medium of communication favored by Foreign Minister Arens. He was given to expressing himself in a lucid, terse, and focused manner, even though such discussions could not be noted down precisely in minutes. In one instance, an important political discussion took place between Arens in his office in Tel Aviv and Baker on a public phone between a kitchen and a rest room. During this particular discussion, on October 29, Baker made clear to Arens that the United States would not be able to guarantee in advance that there would not be someone on the Palestinian delegation with a PLO background, dating back five or eight years.

Meantime in Washington officials polished formulations, trying to bring the sides closer together. On November 1, the United States submitted simultaneously to Israel and Egypt a five-point framework proposal that had been worked out by Secretary of State Baker. It held that:

- The United States acknowledged the hard work done by Israel and Egypt to advance the peace process. It agreed that an Israeli delegation was to conduct a dialogue with a Palestinian delegation in Cairo.
- The United States understood that Egypt could not serve as a substitute for the Palestinians and that Egypt would consult with the Palestinians, along with the United States and Israel, concerning all aspects of the dialogue.
- The United States understood that Israel would take part in the dialogue only after a list of Palestinians satisfactory to it was supplied.
- The United States understood that Israel would inaugurate a dialogue on the basis of the initiative its government had proposed on May 14. The United States understood that for their part, the Palestinians would come to the dialogue prepared to discuss the elections and the negotiations process in terms of the initiative sponsored by the Israeli government. The United States therefore held that the Palestinians were free to express their position regarding the question of how the success of the elections and the negotiation process could be secured.
- To facilitate this process, the United States proposed that foreign ministers from Israel and Egypt meet together with the American secretary of state two weeks later, in Washington.

Washington added an appendix to this five-point framework proposal. It detailed steps that would bring about the Israeli-Palestinian dialogue in Cairo:

- The United States urged each side to accept the five-point framework, in order to provide for consultations with each regarding the structure of the Palestinian-Israeli dialogue that would precede the elections.
- The framework proposal guaranteed that Israel would not be caught by surprise regarding either the identities of the Palestinian delegates taking part in the dialogue or the subjects to be discussed. Similarly, Egypt's concerns regarding Palestinian needs would be respected.

• When the framework proposal was accepted by the two governments, the United States would be able to attend to the needs and concerns of each of the sides, on the basis of appropriate "auxiliary promises" extended to each.

On November 5, 1989, Israel accepted the American five-point framework proposal. In its statement the government stressed its understanding that the framework proposal, together with the accompanying side-promises, would adhere to its own initiative and that the dialogue would start only after a list of Arab Palestinians—residents of Judea, Samaria, and Gaza—were designated and approved by Israel. Israel's government reiterated that no negotiations with the PLO could be conducted and that election procedures on the West Bank and in Gaza had to be consistent with its own initiative. Israel's decision centered around a demand that the United States and Egypt side publicly with its positions, and even stand by it should one of the other sides deviate from what had been accepted. Israel called on the United States and Egypt to affirm their support of the Camp David principles, which formed the basis of the Israeli peace initiative.

Relaying this government decision to the American ambassador on November 6, 1989, Arens also delivered to him a letter meant for Brown's superior, Secretary Baker. Israel's foreign minister stressed the following points in his letter:

• Israel's decision to endorse the American five-point framework had come after hard soul-searching, since the matter pertained to Israel's security and survival. The framework had been accepted on account of Baker's guarantee that American promises regarding Israel's needs and concerns were to be fulfilled.

• Any discussion of the five-point framework had to start with Israel's May 14, 1989, initiative. The plans were intertwined, and each one had to be moved forward with the same vigor.

• The aim was to move ahead toward elections as soon as possible, so as to launch the process embodied in Israel's initiative regarding Palestinian self-rule for an interim period, preceding a permanent arrangement. With this objective as the baseline, the dialogue in Cairo conducted on the basis of the American five-point framework had to focus solely on the elections.

• Palestinian participants had to be residents of the territories, because the dialogue was designed to produce an agreement relating to election procedures in the territories.

• Israel's opposition to negotiation with the PLO was unqualified and rested on national consensus. Any dialogue with the PLO, be it direct or circuitous, would undermine the possibility of free elections and thereby delay progress toward peace.

Baker congratulated Israel's government on November 9, 1989, for its decision to embrace the American five-point plan. He inserted the "auxiliary promises" that had been referred to formally, for the first time, in his November 1 letter. Underscoring his country's support for the four components of Israel's initiative, the secretary of state noted that up to then the United States had not been able to coax any Arab country out of its policy of nonrecognition of Israel. Baker expressed his hope that the Israeli-Palestinian dialogue in Cairo would lead to such recognition and also advance efforts to improve conditions in the refugee camps. (Prime Minister Shamir had referred to this matter in a special note to President Bush but had not received a substantive response.)

Baker's side promises were essentially guarantees offered by the United States to Israel. First, and although Israel would take part in the Cairo meeting only after a list of Palestinian delegates acceptable to it was completed and no surprises from Israel's point of view on this matter could be condoned, Baker wrote that the United States would not be able to guarantee that each participant on a Palestinian list would have a past entirely bereft of any PLO connection, nor could it furnish guarantees about the position to be taken by any delegate. Second, while the Israeli-Palestinian dialogue would focus on the election issue, the United States held that each side should be entitled to deliver opening speeches and address matters broader than the election issue. Third, and despite the differences of opinion between Israel and the United Sates in relation to their approaches to forging peace in the Middle East, Washington would continue to back the "general principles" of Israel's peace initiative, along with the Camp David accords, and regard these as foundations of U.S. policy in the peace process. The secretary of state added that the United States remained committed to principles and policies designed to bring about peace that also guaranteed Israel's security and promoted recognition of Israel and its regional "acceptance."

The promises had been designed to allay Israel's apprehensions and provide backing for its government as it took a concrete step on a political path that would require courageous decision making, ingenuity, and daring. Soon enough, however, President Bush and Secretary of State Baker learned that they had miscalculated when they figured that the auxiliary guarantees would reduce anxieties harbored by Israel's government. A number of doubts and reservations floated to the surface in Jerusalem regarding the value and validity of the American guarantees. Hints that the American position did not rule out indirect contacts with the PLO, facilitated mainly by Egypt, elicited some questioning. Israeli officials working with Arens were inclined to sophistic quibbling concerning precise formulations, and they were deeply skeptical when it came to dialogue with the United States. The Arens circle brought up the following issues and objections:

- The American promises did not relate clearly to Israel's demand that the list of Palestinian delegates be comprised entirely of residents of Judea, Samaria, and the Gaza Strip.
- The American promises did not refer categorically to the intervening role the United States would have to play should it become clear that the process was headed toward an Israel-PLO dialogue.
- The American guarantees did not supply a clear indication that election modalities, which were the substantive issue on the agenda, had to be consistent with Israel's peace initiative.
- The reference in Baker's November 9 letter to the existence of fundamental differences between the Israeli and the American approaches to peace in the Middle East ought to be omitted, as such differences most likely pertained to the final-status issue and not to the interim stage.
- The United States had to be asked to guarantee that Egypt would reiterate its support for the Camp David principles and for the two-stage structure of Israel's peace initiative.
- The United States should obligate itself to stand with Israel should the other side violate its part of an agreement.

Arens sent a letter to his counterpart on November 20 with remarks concerning the American guarantees. Israel, Arens wrote, had assented to a series of American requests in the past, yet it now had in hand reports of American intentions to allow the PLO to have a part in the Palestinian delegation. Arens expressed a concern that had been widespread in Jerusalem since Egyptian president Mubarak had commented that his country's part in the process was to consult with the PLO. Israel demanded that results of such consultations be provided to it and to the United States.

Arens added that since the United States was committed to bringing about free and open elections, in accord with the Israeli peace initiative, Israel had agreed to the following U.S. proposals favoring (1) an Israeli-Palestinian meeting in Cairo; (2) the formation of the Palestinian delegation via consultation with the United States, Egypt, and Israel; (3) the five-point American framework; (4) the limiting of the dialogue to the election issue; (5) an agreement about side guarantees—promises leading to a trilateral, U.S.-Israeli-Egyptian meeting. The foreign minister also remarked that the United States had in the past shown understanding regarding Israel's opposition to negotiations with the PLO. Arens even furnished an example of this understanding—Ambassador Brown had produced a revised version of the five-point proposal when the first draft created an impression that the United States was envisioning some kind of role for the PLO in the Cairo meeting. Now, again, fears were being revived that the United States would condone a place for the PLO; in fact, any form of PLO participation was impossible, as far as Israel was concerned.

The issue of Palestinian representation became ever more contentious in these diplomatic exchanges. It looked different from the vantage points of the populations in the territories, Israel, the United States, Egypt, and the PLO. While Israel demanded that the delegation be filled entirely with representatives from the territories, the United States was not definitely ruling out in advance the participation of Arab East Jerusalemites. Arens's letter reflected a growing Israeli apprehension that Baker's communiqué could be construed to allow the inclusion of deported Palestinians. Officials in Jerusalem noticed that the secretary of state did not state emphatically that the PLO could not play a future role in the political process.

The United States declared officially on December 6, 1989, that Egypt had consented to the five-point framework. Egypt and Israel exchanged thoughts and opinions relating to invitations for the Cairo meeting and to the U.S. intention to convene forthwith a three-way discussion in Washington, involving Israel, Egypt, and America, as part of bringing about the Cairo dialogue.

On the day Washington released its formal announcement, Ambassador Brown advised the prime minister's and foreign minister's offices in Jerusalem that the Egyptian response (which had for some reason been formulated as a private dispatch) did not impose any preconditions to acceptance of the U.S. five-point framework, apart from the assumption that Egyptian and Palestinian needs and opinions would be articulated during the talks. Egypt, Brown disclosed, was holding consultations with the Palestinian leadership to which the PLO had agreed in writing. According to Brown, Baker had proposed that Israeli officials confer in Washington with State Department members to resolve remaining differences of opinion. Such consultations would accelerate movement toward a trilateral meeting on the election issue, which in turn would lead straight to the Cairo dialogue.

Officials from the two countries duly met in Washington, between the 17th and the 20th of December. The discussion occurred against a backdrop of worsening disagreement both between Israel and the United States and within the Israeli government. Israel's delegation was not impervious to this domestic debate, yet it managed to represent what was perceived by its members as the consensus of the components of the national unity government: opposition to negotiations with the PLO, and the demand that the Palestinian delegations be formed of representatives from the territories alone. The United States did not readily assent to the demand that deportees and East Jerusalemites be excluded; the disputes about the composition of the delegation, therefore, did not abate but grew more nettlesome. Nor did the next round of diplomatic contacts narrow the gaps.

Arens met on January 17, 1990, with General Brent Scowcroft, Bush's national security adviser. The two agreed that propelling the process forward depended on the resolution of four outstanding issues:

- How would the Palestinian delegation be composed?
- Who was to announce the composition of the delegation?
- What would be the agenda for the dialogue? (Here, it was agreed that the dialogue would concentrate exclusively on the elections.)
- Who, apart from Israel and the Palestinians, was to take part in the Cairo dialogue?

Scowcroft, a seasoned official and an expert on Middle East affairs, was not enthusiastic on the prospects for overcoming these difficulties.

Arens spoke with Baker on the phone on February 3, 1990, and their talk provided more evidence that the prospects of the four problems' being resolved were dim. The divisive issue of deportees and East Jerusalemites taking part on the Palestinian delegation raged in full force. In essence, the demand for inclusion was a camouflaged PLO ploy, submitted as an Egyptian position with tacit American consent. Baker was adamant throughout the phone conversation; he railed against what he perceived as Israeli intransigence. He threatened, dropping hints that he was prepared to reconsider America's commitment to remain involved and mediate should Israel not ease its positions.

Baker wanted in this terse phone conversation to clarify whether Israel would consider a softer formula, by which it would allow deported Palestinians to return to the territories prior to inclusion in the delegation. Baker sought as well to assess Israel's determination with respect to Arab East Jerusalemite participation. He proposed that delegates from East Jerusalem be allowed to furnish two addresses, one from the city and the other from the territories. Israel's opposition to the inclusion of deportees was based on an estimate of the PLO's intentions. Deportee participation, as the PLO saw it, would provide legitimacy generally to Palestinians who lived abroad. Israeli officials feared that the deportees could be perceived as elite symbols of the Palestinian dispersion; concerned about precedents that might be set should it relent on this issue, the government of Israel conditioned the whole political initiative upon the rule that only residents of the territories would serve on the delegation.

Baker asked Arens to urge the Israeli government to accept the compromise proposals he forwarded. Arens replied that this was a subject fraught with implications and that as such it warranted more consultation, as well as clarification. Arens himself could not confirm Baker's compromise formulas, which were nothing but the Egyptian proposal in American dress. Baker surmised that Arens was expressing his own opinion on the deportee and East Jerusalemite issues. His anger scarcely concealed, the secretary of state warned that should Arens and the government of Israel persist with this position, the current process would reach an impasse. Specifically, he declared that should the participation of two particular deportees be ruled out, there would be no chance of an agreement, and no dialogue would take place. Should Israel's response be negative, Baker added, he doubted that there would be any point to his own continuing mediation efforts. Baker asserted that he was being put in an intolerable position (as though it was his part to drag Israel, "kicking and screaming," into affirming and applying its own political initiative). Baker mentioned at the end of the conversation that the deportee and East Jerusalemite issues had to be addressed, as the convening of the Cairo meeting was contingent upon their resolution.

Denying that he was issuing an ultimatum, he proposed that Israel adopt a new position. The government of Israel, Arens promised, would discuss the issues in a constructive fashion.

Baker persisted in attempting to make it easier for Israel to embrace a more "constructive" position. On the East Jerusalemite issue, he insisted that the persons in question have two addresses, so their involvement could not be seen as setting a precedent. Baker implored Arens in another telephone talk, held on February 5, to stop quibbling about insubstantial principles. Instead, actual names of Palestinians should be discussed, with a verdict being reached about each one. In this piecemeal, pragmatic fashion it might be possible to circumvent the sources of controversy.

Baker sent Shamir a dispatch on February 18, 1990, informing him that he had discerned during recent talks in Moscow extraordinary changes transpiring in Europe and in East-West relations. He declared that the Soviets had indicated a desire to renew diplomatic relations with Israel, should the Israelis prove genuinely interested in the peace process. Baker had urged the Soviets to discuss this directly with Israel's government. In this same placating letter, Baker cited his desire to resume his efforts and to convene the previously planned triangular meeting between himself and the foreign ministers of Israel and Egypt, as a preliminary to an Israeli-Palestinian dialogue.

Arens met with Baker in Washington on February 23. In the course of their talk, Baker reiterated his proposal that the Palestinian delegation be formed on a specific name basis, not on the basis of predetermined principles. His intention was to defer discussions about the deportees and candidates with dual addresses until talks were held between Israel, Egypt, and the United States concerning the final composition of the Palestinian delegation. The purpose of this delay would be to cultivate an atmosphere of consent among the relevant parties.

Baker reported how he had told the Soviets that if the USSR desired to take part in the Cairo dialogue as a full-fledged observer, it first had to reestablish diplomatic relations with Israel. The Soviet foreign minister, Eduard Shevardnadze, had rejected this linkage, claiming that his country was entitled by its international position to play a role; the Soviet Union had no intention of offering renewed diplomatic relations in exchange for participation in the Cairo dialogue. Baker noted that the idea of Soviet participation in the dialogue in an observer capacity belonged not to him but rather to the Egyptians. In any event, Egypt was not imposing the idea as a precondition.

During the meeting, Baker explained that his proposal to discuss the Palestinian delegation's composition on a name basis would allow Israel to avoid accepting the Egyptian position formally. Baker posed the question in formal terms; their simplicity masked the sophistication of his diplomacy. Would the government of Israel, he asked, consider the candidacy of Palestinians on an individual, name by name basis, with each person a resident of the territories? Arens declined to respond, proposing that Baker direct the question to Shamir.

Later in the discussion Arens expressed his disappointment about the absence of an Arab response to the Israeli government's proposal. Nonetheless, he declared, Israel was not making the dialogue with the Palestinians conditional upon a positive Arab answer. Naturally, Arens stressed the importance of the dialogue's focusing on the election issue, arguing that the inclusion of other issues would impede positive results. Baker agreed that the election issue should serve as the focus, though he insisted that there be an opportunity to broach other issues in opening addresses. Israel, Arens replied, grudgingly accepted this view.

Arens spoke harshly about PLO manipulations. The PLO, he asserted, was trying to drag Israel toward direct talks with it; this was the reason for Israel's opposition to the elections concept. Israel's foreign minister also warned about a PLO effort to present the delegates from the territories as though they had been appointed with its approval and direction, as though they were subservient to the PLO's will. Should the delegates indeed introduce themselves as PLO delegates, Israel would pull out of the dialogue, expecting America to do likewise. The United States, Baker promised, would not condone any such ploys, and it would communicate to Egypt its forthright position in this respect. Should there be maneuvers and "tricks" of the PLO variety, there would be no dialogue, declared the secretary of state.

On the other hand, Baker added, the United States would find it difficult to make commitments about preempting scenarios that could not be anticipated. In the event that any such event occurred through a manipulative ploy, Israel would be entitled to say the following to the Palestinians: "If you really want to discuss with us the election of representatives from the territories, we'll talk with you. But we won't talk if you mislead us and come as the delegates of the PLO." Should the Palestinians not accept these terms, Baker advised, Israel would have every right to withdraw from the dialogue; and the United States, the secretary of state added, would be likely to do the same.

Contacts with the United States and Egypt prior to the proposed Cairo meeting were marked by domestic tensions in Israel's government. The two main components of Israel's unity government, Labor and Likud, tugged in opposite directions, each representing a different degree of flexibility in foreign affairs. Mixed signals were sent, on formal and informal levels, to the United States and Egypt, and probably also to the Palestinians. Internal shuffling in the government proceeded at a heady pace, and there was no lack of partisan attempts to seize opportunities to make changes in the composition of the government and in its policies.

The official, public reason for the instability derived from the Palestinian delegation issue: could Palestinian deportees whose possession of dual addresses included East Jerusalem be included on the delegation? The Labor Party tended to be accommodating on this subject; it did not view the American compromise formula as an obstacle. In contrast, the Likud Party adopted a stridently negative view on the participation of delegates from East Jerusalem. Likud believed that the participation of such delegates in the dialogue and in the elections would give color to the perception of Jerusalem as a conquered territory. Strife between Likud and Labor over this subject knew no limits. On March 7, 1990, Labor ministers proposed a resolution, calling for positive Israeli replies to Secretary of State Baker's proposals regarding the composition of the Palestinian delegation—meaning its designation on a name-by-name basis, with two deportees and another resident or two from the territories who had an address or office in East Jerusalem also being included. This proposal was antithetical to a position taken by Likud ministers on March 5, 1990, opposing the involvement of East Jerusalem representatives in the political process.

The wrangling and quarreling culminated in the collapse of Israel's national unity government, on March 15, 1990. The Labor Party sponsored a no-confidence motion, but it failed in an effort to form a government under its own leadership. The new government that arose (on June 11, 1990) following this Labor debacle was headed by Shamir. It embraced the fundamental principles of the Likud Party. The new government escalated its opposition to a Palestinian state and to negotiations with the PLO, and it emphasized its support of Israeli sovereignty in united Jerusalem, of continued settlement activity, and of the continuation of the peace process on the basis of Israel's May 14, 1989, peace initiative.

Assessing the Israeli initiative from my standpoint as deputy director general in charge of North American affairs at the foreign ministry, I found it insufficient and flawed. I feared that it lacked the creative inspiration and thrust needed to secure genuine results. Not a forward-looking proposal, the initiative was essentially a response to pressures imposed on Israel, particularly the stress of the intifada. The intifada had generated domestic turmoil in social and security spheres, along with international pressure in the form of public opinion and foreign government declarations demanding changes in Israel's policies. Israel also confronted an assertive American policy, whose character derived from, among other things, public opinion in the States—the American public was skeptical about the policies of Israel's government, especially with respect to settlements. In short, Israel's government was heading for a showdown with the United States, at a time when the Americans were not hesitating to show in their Middle East policy their weight as a superpower.

In my judgment, the Shamir government's initiative was tempered by a lack of trust. I had the impression that those at the helm were only paying lip service to the goal of peace between Israel and the Arab states, not really believing that there was a prospect of attaining it. Perhaps the reason that the peace negotiations between Israel and the Arab states had not gotten the enthusiasm and emphasis they deserved was that they were bound up in a trilateral model, a paradigm that the Shamir government opposed. It preferred to keep the Palestinian issue wed to the congenial Camp David parameters, which boiled down to a Fabian-gradualist conception of the future and a desire to keep all options open.

In fact, the efforts of the national unity government prior to its collapse had served only to bog down the negotiations bandwagon. The government had one wing that favored flexibility and openness; it sent messages along these lines to various parties, including the United States, Egypt, and perhaps the PLO. Some members of the government went so far as to operate in the United States, with the aim of compromising Israel's government, arranging for it to be pressured from the outside. On the other hand, the Likud branch of the government, which itself encompassed a range of political attitudes and degrees of negotiation flexibility, was on the whole captive to the image and personality of its leader, Prime Minister Shamir, whose travails and achievements had produced an unyielding, rigid orientation as well as an ability to wait with endless patience, as adversaries eventually wilted. My guess is that Shamir himself would not deny his lack of trust in the other side in any proposed negotiation process. This quality of Shamir's temperament was paramount so long as an opposing element did not prove its merit.

Shamir's personality had been shaped by his experience in the Holocaust, as an underground leader in the partisan Lehi force at the time of Israel's independence struggle, and in a number of other spheres. His negotiation trait emerged out of this personality: until the other side had proved its authenticity, any proposals and initiatives from Shamir himself were laden with doubt and suspicion. His character, I believe, came to the fore during his term as prime minister. He was dragged by necessity toward a number of political steps. He took them with utmost caution.

In fairness, it bears mention that this lack of confidence regarding a constructive peace process with the Arab states was not monopolized by Shamir. It was reflected as well in the deeds and initiatives of members of the Labor Party who tackled the Palestinian issue, however much openness and flexibility they tried to show to the world.

Similarly, as the official in charge of Israel's foreign ministry, American native Moshe Arens did not exude much optimism regarding the chances that the peace process could move forward. He convened the ministry's senior officials for a meeting on the subject once only—and on this occasion he projected to those around a sense of skepticism, along with a reliance on his own staff at the expense of foreign ministry professionals. Arens chose to trust his own assistants, and this influenced the character of his diplomacy.

My substantive acquaintance with Arens dated from the time when he was appointed to serve as Israel's ambassador to the United States. I was at this stage the director of the North America Department in the foreign ministry. I was asked to help him get ready for his new post. I noticed that Arens projected considerable personal charm, that he was a man of culture, a scientist who persistently inquired into the causes of phenomena and their meanings, and a man committed to a high-tech vision. The latter was proven by his unflagging efforts on behalf of the production of the Israeli Lavi, a state-of-the-art combat plane whose first test models had gotten off the ground. In the end, the Lavi project collapsed, due to possibly myopic financing and feasibility calculations; indeed, in terms of Israel's long-term interests, in retrospect it seems very likely that Arens was justified in his enthusiasm for the Lavi. He was motivated by a desire to hone Israel's technological edge, to transform the fighter-plane project into a large-scale program that would employ the finest scientific brains in Israel and fine tune their professional skills. In any event, at this early stage I had good working relations with Arens. I did my best to equip him with the resources he would need to succeed as ambassador in Washington.

Later on, while serving as consul general at Los Angeles, I hosted Arens, and we shared a meal together. Abruptly, he unleashed a remark that caught me entirely by surprise: "I'd like to see you, Eytan, alongside Bibi [Binyamin Netanyahu], in a leadership position in the state of Israel. It's important that both of you contribute your talents, for the benefit of the country."

That was then. By the time Arens arrived atop the Foreign Ministry, he had been coached to be wary of a government worker who had, heaven forbid, "leftist" views. The innuendo mill had ground at full tilt, spinning round a conception that a state official must not have his own worldview. The mill's keepers apparently reasoned that a government worker must be a faceless "Zelig," like the chameleon hero of the Woody Allen film who adjusts his appearance to all new circumstances, subordinating his own features to blend with a succession of superiors, devoid of any personal sense of professional challenge. Zelig-men are expected to carry out orders blindly. For my part, I always believed that a civil servant is obliged to implement the directives of those above him and yet need not conceal his own worldview or the intellectual heritage precious to him. I regretted deeply that I did not always find my colleagues committed to this position. Looking back, I feel that many of them rode along the crest of each period and work routine, worried exclusively about their own professional advancement and therefore refrained from any personal confrontation with policy and from trying to leave their own mark on the work. Career advancement is indeed important, but it is no less imperative to contribute, to fashion and influence realities, especially when one's country is as riddled with turmoil as Israel. When each new day comes, the final measure is your own sense of worth; and here, in my field, at my place in time, you had to ask searching questions about the scope of your contribution toward the peace process, and about how you had stood up to those who had designs against it. Between personal views and orders from on high there is room for maneuver— indeed, the space between must stretch as wide as Israel's national consensus itself. If a civil servant cannot countenance this consensus, then the time has come for him to tender his resignation.

So it was that when Arens entered the foreign ministry, he called me for a meeting. He opened by recalling the friendship that had characterized our relations since he had started out in Israel's foreign policy sphere. The three of us, Arens said, "myself, you, and Netanyahu have experience with American issues, and we will conduct the Foreign Ministry's relations between Israel and the U.S., while the director general I choose will blaze a trail for Israel in the Far East." He indicated his interest as foreign minister in building a place for Israel in Asia. The future belonged to Asia, he contended, whose economic potential was vast; he had asked the Israeli embassy in Tokyo to appoint forthwith a sixty-man staff, hoping that the embassy's expanded activities would warrant such a hefty crew. I understood from this that Arens was going to appoint somebody else to be director general; I wished Arens well in his new post.

After a short spell, I became curious about what had happened to this vision of Israeli penetration in Asia. As it turned out, after a year of his term as foreign minister, there had been exactly one small change in the Israeli embassy in Tokyo. What had happened? The sole secretary there who worked with Hebrew correspondence, whose desk would have been flooded according to the Arens's expansion plan, had returned to Israel without being replaced. Her loss was the only change in a diplomatic post that was supposed to have been transformed.

Arens's aides, who were skilled, sharp-edged types and veteran diplomats in the Foreign Ministry, surmised that Arens's staff was calling his shots. Above Arens loomed a strong-willed prime minister, and Arens was regarded as belonging to Shamir's ideological camp. Arens had to stand up to a tough-minded American administration, and coping with the Americans required the premier talents of Israel's diplomatic pool.

As time passed, Arens and his associates adopted increasingly extreme formulations on the Palestinian issue, embroiling Israel in a crisis with the United States and precipitating a sharp crisis within Israel's own government. Had he been able to display bold ingenuity in his policy, commensurate with his genuine humanitarian commitment toward the unbearable human rights damage wrought by the intifada, Arens could have left a compelling, strong imprint on Israel's foreign policy. As it was, Israel dragged its feet, fostering futility, on the Palestinian issue. I attempted at one point to coax Arens and his people to attempt to transform the Palestinian issue into a lever for progress vis-à-vis the Arab states. I put down in written form, for the record, a formula to keep policy from floundering in small details. I described an interlocking nexus of relations, by which the anticipated steps with the Palestinians would be bound tightly with simultaneous moves to be undertaken toward the Arab states, via the United States. Unfortunately, no response to my plan was forthcoming.

Informally, one of Arens's aides informed me that the foreign minister had taken my proposal to Shamir. After some discussion, the foreign minister had resolved not to deviate from what had been finalized regarding Israel's position on the dialogue with the Palestinians. This particular proposal of mine for a political initiative—which was destined to be defined as a two-track (Israeli-Palestinian) route with a third lane (Israel–Arab world)—was rejected and left pending. It waited for a foreign minister who had the skill, determination, and daring it took to advance the peace process.

Until such a new day dawned, the dogmatism of Arens and his associates ruled. It left an especially conspicuous mark on the PLO issue. Arens's office released a directive banning foreign ministry officials from keeping tabs, or yet more heinous, reporting, on third-party contacts with the PLO. Woe be it to one who listened, spoke, or reported as though the PLO were a fact and part of the prevailing regional reality. It was a ridiculous order, foolhardy even from the standpoint of "knowing your enemy," the same enemy whose incorporation in the political process Arens had acted so vigorously to forestall.

Lest we forget: in this period, Yasser Arafat and the PLO disseminated unmistakable messages about a desire to talk and to compromise. I myself bore witness to this Palestinian sea change. It happened when I worked as political adviser to President Chaim Herzog, a post to which I was appointed along with my other foreign ministry duties, upon my return to Israel after my stint in Los Angeles. President Herzog asked his personal friend Dan Abrams, the manufacturer of Slim Fast diet foods, to report to him from Tunisia about a meeting he had had there with Arafat. The meeting between Abrams and Arafat had been held in the beginning of 1990, and Abrams thereafter informed Israel's leadership about Arafat's newfound inclination to negotiate, to put an end to campaigns of violence, and to search for political solutions to the conflict with Israel. Also, I accompanied President Herzog in May 1990 on a trip to Stockholm as the guest of the king of Sweden. The visit opened with a lunch hosted by Sweden's foreign minister, Sten Anderson, in honor of Israel's president and his entourage. Anderson remarked at the start of the conversation that he had received from Arafat a message to be relayed to Herzog; in it the Palestinian leader expressed his desire to halt the violent dispute and to launch a dialogue between Israel and the PLO.

Arens never responded to these messages from Arafat. Choosing to ignore them altogether, he never asked President Herzog or myself to detail them. The directive not to heed what third parties had to say about contacts with the PLO grew still stricter, verging toward sheer absurdity, even irresponsibility. Arens commanded all the tools needed to examine the PLO's will and intentions with sophistication and acuity, and to allow the organization to blow off steam, while neutralizing to some extent the difficulties posed by it en route to negotiations. In any event, it is an indubitable fact that the PLO indicated systematically an inclination to negotiate with Israel at this early date. This fact was evident long before its confirmation in the signing of the Oslo accords in September 1993.

The political effort continued to tangle itself in the thorns of the Palestinian-delegation issue. Tensions gripped Israel's major political parties, causing a futile gridlock, bringing to ruin the political process before it had even started. I had come to the conclusion that it was not within my purview to propose bridging formulas to Arens. He himself found cause to apologize for not involving me in the modeling of the process, explaining that he was constrained by the prime minister's order that only a very small cadre take part in steering the policy. I watched with chagrin a chain, whose links were lack of inspiration, skill, or volition, hobble Israel in muddy ground; the political process was stuck in the mire, with no chance to start.

This held true until Shimon Peres attempted, unsuccessfully, as I have mentioned, to parlay a perceived opportunity thrown up by Israel's restive coalition politics and topple the shaky national unity government. On June 11, 1990, his failed maneuver brought about the formation of a new, unadulterated, Likud-led, government, with Yitzhak Shamir at its helm. Defying expectations, it was precisely this Likud government that set Israel on the peace path, headed toward negotiations both with the Palestinians and the Arab world, and toward the tackling of issues in economics and development, arms control, and other subjects of consequence for the future of the Middle East. Likud-bred foreign minister David Levy played a big part in this twist of fate.

As it will be recalled, I had become acquainted with David Levy during his visit to Los Angeles when I was consul general there. We spent a couple of days together; a good relationship of mutual trust developed, and this evolved subsequently into a working relationship and then friendship. In my view, David Levy emerged as a first-rate foreign minister. A reliable, candid figure with an acute grasp of affairs and also a warm, friendly demeanor, Levy was totally committed to attaining peace in a responsible fashion, to making agreements without haste. Working in a cautious manner, Levy was now able to deploy the assets that Israel, an embattled country surrounded by enemies, maintained. He worked indefatigably to make his way to the discussion table to talk about peace, something that only a few of us really believed in and sought to attain. However idealistic, Levy's policy outlook was realistic. He was never deluded by false forecasts and entreaties.

On his first day in the Foreign Ministry, Levy recalled our acquaintance and seemed to indicate his intention to work together in the future. Indeed, within hours I was informed that the minister wanted to see me for an important discussion. Our meeting was held at the Sheraton Plaza Hotel; attending as well were Aliza Goren and Levy's aide Uri Oren, a journalist and writer who had for years compiled a track record in politics and diplomacy.

We sat together in the hotel lobby for three hours. I stressed the imperative of repairing relations with the United States, noting that they had dropped to a low ebb, particularly due to a credibility crisis engendered by misleading messages and abandoned promises. I referred to the importance of maintaining sound connections with the American ambassador, Brown, a gifted and reliable diplomat who had demonstrated a keen interest in helping to improve relations, and of moving the political process ahead. We had to focus our efforts on extricating Israel from the political thicket in which it was enmeshed, I said. Political ingenuity would be needed to chart new paths toward progress and to ensure that Israel would not be derailed by old mistakes. With these ends in mind, I proposed a series of recommendations, hoping that the foreign minister would consider adopting them as his political policy.

It is necessary to note, however, that the image of Prime Minister Shamir and his associates hovered over us. From day one, Shamir and his group had evinced a lack of confidence in Foreign Minister Levy, insinuating that he lacked competence to serve in such an important ministerial role, particularly in such a trying period. For my part, I had no doubts about Levy's abilities. I was resolved wholeheartedly to help him succeed in a bid to play a leadership role in advancing the peace process.

A short time after taking up his post, the foreign minister suffered a minor heart attack and was hospitalized in a facility in the Jezreel Valley. He recuperated swiftly, and within a few days he was back at the Laromme Hotel in Jerusalem, where he stayed for a short spell before administering affairs at the foreign ministry. Even before he left the Afula Ha'Emek Hospital, Levy asked via Uri Oren that I relay to him some recommendations on a number of topics.

From the outset, I focused on ways to unlock the political process. In several memoranda I proposed integrated steps for progress with respect both to the Palestinian issue and to negotiations with the Arab states. Any concession made on the Palestinian issue should be used as leverage for progress on the other track, in relations between Israel and its Arab neighbors, and for creating a nexus of mutual links. To illustrate the point I etched a hypothetical (and unfortunate) scenario in which we accomplished significant results, such as a bona fide self-rule apparatus, while still confronting Arab states committed to a closed-minded policy of belligerence with the state of Israel.

I recommended to David Levy that elements of the standing political process that could blend with a peace program of his own be kept, while the remainder of the May 1989 peace initiative (whose fate had been sealed by flawed handling, lack of resolve, and mutual antagonism) be scrapped. I held that we had to prove that Israel was genuinely committed to pushing peace forward, while renewing our dialogue with the American leadership, whose trust we had to reobtain. Unlike Arens, who had gone on to serve as defense minister, Levy was showing a large measure of openness, realism, and inclination to advance the process. This process now incorporated my recommendations for a new policy— one that adopted a two-track (Israeli-Palestinian, Israel–Arab states) route, with yet a third road parallel, a multilateral path framed around issues such as arms control, development, and economics. Posing such variations and multiple-track courses to the foreign minister, I heeded advice about thinking "creatively" in terms of the "big picture" that Secretary of State Baker had offered.

That said, echoes of the still-unresolved dispute in the U.S.-Israeli dialogue reverberated in the main policy principles of Israel's new government. By those principles, Jerusalem was not to be included in the autonomy to be conferred on residents of the West Bank and the Gaza Strip. It was stipulated that residents of Jerusalem would not participate either as voters or candidates, in elections to provide representation for residents of Judea, Samaria, and Gaza. Moreover, Israel's government declared that settlement in all parts of the land of Israel constituted an integral component of national security; this being so, the government would promote the strengthening, development, and expansion of the settlements.

Baker, it will be recalled, had forcefully communicated his disenchantment with the positions of the previous unity government. To his mind, that government had indulged in evasive ploys and barren maneuvers, dodging the challenge of a peace process that Baker himself had been doing his utmost to implement. In an appearance before the House Foreign Relations Committee on June 13, 1990, Baker professed befuddlement as to why Israel had chosen not to adopt his proposals; they were, he said, devoid of any provocations from the Israeli perspective. The secretary of state closed his remarks with a barb: should the government of Israel display interest in the renewal of the peace process, he challenged, it could telephone one of the White House's numbers.

President Bush too did not keep his criticism a secret. In a dispatch to Shamir dated June 15, the president noted that his country could not remain involved in a process designed merely to conjure illusions of progress. Bush called on the prime minister to help move the process forward by relenting on the Palestinian-delegation issue, agreeing to a compromise formula following lines sketched by Baker. Any deviation from this approach, be it hedging the Palestinian delegation to exclude important Palestinian groups or deflecting America's attention toward Israel's relations with Arab neighbors so as to obfuscate the Palestinian issue, would lead to an impasse, the U.S. president warned.

Bush and Baker's comments implied that even after the establishment of the new, right-wing, Likud government, the American administration remained determined to advance the political process, without brooking any revisions. It was, in other words, committed to prodding Israel to accept the formula for the Palestinian delegation that had been raised in talks between Baker, Shamir, and Arens for many months. Also manifest was the U.S. government's proclivity to concentrate on the Palestinian issue and not to cloud it by dealing extensively with any other track.

A few days after the new government took the reins, I sent a message to Ambassador Brown asking him to arrange quickly a channel for straightforward, substantive discussion between Foreign Minister Levy and Secretary of State Baker. I shared with Brown the impression I had gotten concerning Levy's ardent desire to move ahead with the peace process, avoid the blunders of the past, and mold relations with the American government on a foundation of trust and good will. Baker digested immediately the message that his diplomat in Israel forwarded. In a congratulatory note sent to Levy upon his appointment as foreign minister, the secretary of state referred optimistically to future cooperation.

There soon followed a first official communiqué from Baker, featuring an invitation to meet with Levy at the end of July (as it turned out, due to his cardiac complication, Levy was forced to defer the meeting with

Baker until September 1990). Baker reminded Levy that as early as April 1989 he had told his predecessor, Arens, that local Palestinians would consent to Shamir's peace process only on the condition that their delegation include deportees and East Jerusalemites. Baker had stressed that his country desired to include as delegation members Palestinians from the territories, not PLO personnel, and without infringing upon the principal components of the Shamir initiative. Like Bush, Baker was prone to emphasizing the Palestinian issue. Baker acknowledged that the United States upheld as a goal the "improvement" of Israel's relations with neighboring countries, yet America nevertheless regarded progress on the Palestinian issue, with the Israel-Palestinian dialogue, as taking precedence.

Ambassador Brown informed me on June 29 that the prime minister's reply to the Bush letter, sent two days earlier, had stirred excitement in Washington, where officials were eagerly searching for signs of flexibility in the Israeli position. The Shamir message was being interpreted as an indication of willingness to condone the inclusion of deportee Palestinians who were not in the PLO and whose inclusion had not been championed by the PLO.

Soon enough, this flutter of "excitement" went still. The summer of 1990 proceeded amidst the feeling that the Palestinian delegation issue had petrified and become a hard stumbling block. However, some colleagues in the Foreign Ministry, who in the Arens days had kept mum their own views in favor of advancing the peace process and had chosen not to support my practical proposals for stimulating it, suddenly found fortitude and resolve. They sent the new foreign minister a memorandum recommending conditioned endorsement of former deportees in the Palestinian delegation. Such willingness on Israel's part, they argued, would have a favorable effect on other aspects of bilateral relations between Israel and the United States, especially those with strategic import. These Foreign Ministry officials contended that (more) pessimistic thinking would aggravate the negative dynamic between the two countries.

The memorandum argued that the deportee issue could be handled in a fashion that would avoid tacit recognition of a Palestinian-refugee "right of return" comparable to the latitude given in Israel to immigrant Jews. The problem could be neutralized through a prior agreement between Israel and the U.S. government expressly negating any presumed connection between the deportees and a "right of return." Also, the Foreign Ministry staff doubted that the Palestinian delegation could be kept hermetically sealed from any connection to the PLO, even should the U.S. letter of assurances be adopted.

I sent a memorandum to the foreign minister on July 30, 1990, describing relations between the two countries up to that point. I proceeded on the assumption that the United States had embraced as a working assumption, or adopted as a strategic position, that Israel and the PLO were destined to meet and negotiate. I noted that the political process had been slowed, and the Israeli government's peace initiative had gradually ground to a halt, over a matter that reduced to two issues: questions posed by Secretary of State Baker with respect to deportees and East Jerusalem delegates, and America's assumption that a positive Israeli response would spark the Israeli-Palestinian dialogue into motion. I stressed that an inauspicious crisis of confidence existed between Israel and the United States. The U.S. government believed resolutely that it had acted faithfully, making a fair effort to advance the peace process. The Americans felt that they had been led astray by Israel's government, or at least by parts of its leadership. The secretary of state had acknowledged that the correspondence between Shamir and Bush, and Levy and himself, had cleared the atmosphere somewhat, encouraging the United States to remarshal its energy for cooperation with Israel. There could be no doubt, however, that the issue of the delegation's composition impeded renewed efforts.

Baker aspired to set the political process in motion, while patching up relations between the two states. To a large extent, his goal was served by conciliatory messages I sent in Levy's name to Ambassador Brown; they were greeted favorably in Washington. Restored hopes produced another letter from Baker to Levy, on August 8, 1990. The secretary of state noted that Washington had held from the start that peace would require reconciliation and accommodation between Israel and the Arab states, and the resolution of differences with the Palestinians. The United States hoped to act in these two domains, and it viewed the Israel-Palestinian dialogue as a first step that would beget negotiations and elections. Washington believed, Baker wrote, that such a move would enable the other crucial objective to be secured, namely, inclusion of additional Arab partners in the peace process with Israel.

The Levy-Baker meeting on August 5, 1990, was held in Washington under the shadow of the incipient Persian Gulf crisis, whose international repercussions were just starting to be felt. Iraq's army had invaded and conquered Kuwait three days before. The PLO, whose leader Yasser

Arafat was an ally of Sadam Hussein, cheered on the Iraqi ruler, standing beside him in a confrontation with an unprecedented international alliance that had been forged under U.S. leadership and was committed to uprooting Iraq from Kuwait. While the Soviets plotted to exploit developments, the United States, its secretary of state promised, would work to head off any possible connection between the Persian Gulf crisis and the peace process in the Middle East. On the other hand, Baker reasoned, the process ought to be renewed from the point at which it had been suspended. It was important, he explained, for Israel to come across as supporting the dialogue with the Palestinians, especially in light of the damage wrought to the PLO's image caused by its siding with the Iraqi dictator. Therefore, Baker concluded, prudence and realism dictated that the misunderstandings concerning the composition of the Palestinian delegation be overcome.

With polished tact, Baker posed the main question to Levy: Was Israel indeed favorably disposed toward America's continuing efforts to advance a process designed to create a dialogue with Palestinians from the territories? Baker dropped a hint that without at least tacit, silent approval on the PLO's part, it would be well-nigh impossible to find candidates from the territories for membership on the Palestinian delegation. The foreign minister listened attentively to his counterpart's remarks and then exclaimed candidly, "Wasn't it enough for you, Mr. Secretary of State, that the last Israeli government collapsed? Are you trying to topple this one as well? If we go back to plod with these two issues—the deportees and East Jerusalemites—Israel's government is liable to fall, and so the process will in any case grind to a halt." Baker reflected for a moment before replying to Levy's sincere and persuasive objection. "If that's the case, it has to be possible to find a way to advance the peace process without needing to regurgitate the old issues, thereby pushing Israel into a corner."

Toward the end of the talk, Baker slipped into a side room, reemerging after a few moments to announce that President Bush would receive Levy later on for a meeting. The secretary of state, it appeared, had phoned Bush and advised him to hold the meeting with Israel's foreign minister that had been heretofore left pending. Evident were Baker's good impression of his counterpart's candor and his judgment that Levy was a promising discussion partner in the process, and the president ought to meet with him.

Israel's ambassador to Washington, Moshe Arad, along with Levy's assistants, Uri Oren, Aliza Goren, and myself, attended the Levy-Bush meeting. Comments were exchanged regarding the situation in the region, Saddam Hussein's threats, the prospects for the peace process, and commitments with respect to the process by both countries that could be converted into action, given propitious timing and circumstances. When we returned to Israel after the meetings with the president and the secretary of state, I judged that the moment was approaching when the peace process would revive. That being the case, I reasoned, Israel should offer some gestures to the Palestinians, consenting to this or that form of representation involving deportees and East Jerusalem residents. The leadership chosen in the elections would hold talks with Israel about self-rule in an interim period, prior to the start of final-status talks.

It bears recalling that the Palestinian problem was only one part of the conflict; its "flip side" was the refusal of the Arab states to recognize Israel and establish peace. I held that the solution to the Palestinian problem could and should serve as a lever for the step-by-step integration of the Arab states in the process. I decided, therefore, to propose a series of ways and means by which progress on the Palestinian subject could be connected to developments in the Israel–Arab states sphere. The election of Palestinian delegates would be linked, according to my plan, to simultaneous consent on the part of Arab states to some act of recognition of Israel. At this stage, we continued to speak in such pared-down terms as making the cessation of the formal state of belligerency the goal to be attained concomitant to progress on the Palestinian track. Slowly, a concept was crystallizing that envisioned simultaneous negotiations on the two tracks, the Palestinian and the pan-Arab, while also looking yet beyond this dual course toward comprehensive agreements whose fruits could be reaped in the economic and development spheres.

The two-track idea was analyzed in various forms in internal Israeli discussions, and then subsequently in talks with the Americans. In fact, it was thanks largely to the prudence and skill of Baker and his assistants that a route toward an integrated, promising concept was discerned to begin with. On the other hand, it was Israel's foreign minister David Levy who eventually "refined" my recommendation of a two-track path. One channel would attend to the transitional period of Palestinian self-rule, and the second would deal with negotiations between countries, to reach a pinnacle in peace agreements between Israel and neighboring Syria, Lebanon, and Jordan.

In the context of talks about the $400 million loan guarantee issue that I conducted in New York during the second half of September 1990, during Levy's second trip to the States, I had occasion to discuss the political process with Under Secretary of State Dennis Ross. The talks supplemented the conversations Levy held with Baker. These talks about guarantees had their own value; $400 million was "small change," but it was meant to set the stage for the confirmation of major loan guarantees, on the order of ten billion dollars. The guarantees were needed to raise capital and resources crucial for the accommodation of the burgeoning immigration of Jews from the Soviet Union to Israel and for the continued development of Israel. Negotiations were held between myself and the American trio of Ross, Daniel Kurtzer, and Aaron Miller, at the Waldorf Astoria. I shuttled between Secretary of State Baker's hotel and the one where the Israeli delegation was quartered. Progress in these discussions was aided by the friendship, experience, and connections of the Jewish American leader Max Fisher, with whom I kept close contact. I briefed him and consulted with him. As was his wont, Fischer acted from a sense of mission and duty, and a genuine desire to help. He was respected greatly by Baker and Bush, and his judgments and advice carried real weight. Fisher too reckoned that agreement about the $400 million was crucial, as a precedent for subsequent comprehensive guarantees that would enable Israel to cope with the historic challenge of absorbing the mass immigration from the Soviet Union. Negotiations about the guarantees were taxing and punctuated by several moments of tension, with the Americans maintaining a tough, stubborn stance.

In the end, a draft letter from Levy to Baker was formulated, this being considered preferable to the reverse, a letter from Baker to Levy. In this way we would be able to highlight our satisfaction with a dual achievement—the U.S. government's agreement to the $400 million loan guarantees, and the removal of most of the qualifications that the United States had linked to the guarantees as preconditions for the use of the money. In the end, concurrent to the talks between Baker and Levy, I had the opportunity in my negotiations with Ross and Kurtzer to work out a formula consistent with the obligations Israel had assumed since 1967 in connection with foreign assistance.

On October 3, 1990, a day after Levy's letter to Baker, Deputy Foreign Minister Binyamin Netanyahu was to inform us that the letter had stirred a political-public tempest in Israel. Levy was being denounced as a concession-monger, as the first Israeli leader to consent to America's position on the settlements, including a demand to curb their budgets. The tempest rose. Heavy-handed comments, hints, and innuendo were expressed confidentially and also in public; I was branded as the one who had led Foreign Minister Levy astray. Criticism was leveled also against

Levy for keeping a senior, central aide who was a "leftist." Levy showed public fortitude, rebuffing these attacks. He ran the foreign ministry as though he were a representative of the whole Israeli public, demonstrating respect for the ministry's workers, for their abilities and professional skills. Prime Minister Shamir asked the foreign minister to furnish an explanation of his letter to Secretary of State Baker. At the end of a serious talk between the two, Shamir informed Levy that he "definitely [could] live with the letter," implying that he rejected the criticism and the attendant hearsay and distortions directed against Levy and myself.

On September 25, during the negotiations about the guarantees, I had hosted Ross and Kurtzer to a meal at a New York restaurant, to talk about ways of moving the peace process forward. The Carnegie Deli, a delicatessen adored by Ross, was chosen. This famous site is almost always packed; given cover by the multitude, we were able to share opinions about the future of the process for hours. I shared my thoughts with Ross and Kurtzer in great detail, stressing that the only way to make progress was on the two tracks, with each stimulating the other. I reviewed the early stages of the Palestinian track—agreement about the composition of the delegation, the venue for the dialogue, the holding of elections, and more—and suggested that these phases must counterbalance progress in negotiations between Israel and the Arab states. Specifically, and concurrent to the establishment of Palestinian self-rule, an end to the state of belligerency should be agreed upon between Israel and its Arab neighbors. The Palestinian channel alone was stalled; a two-track framework must be set up from the very start. Ross and Kurtzer listened, argued, and presented several questions; yet basically they accepted the idea, regarding it as plausible and its feasibility worth studying—depending, of course, on its acceptability to Secretary of State Baker. I added that it would also be worthwhile to think about how the Middle East ought to appear from the standpoint of economics and development in a new era of peace.

I insisted that there was a need to apply considerable thought to the creation of confidence-building measures and to their application in our region. I knew that Ross specialized in this area, having heard about his discussions with Soviet diplomat Genadi Trasov, who had developed some interesting ideas in this general connection and had alluded to their specific application in the Middle East. (About a year later, I was appointed to serve, together with other Israeli officials, such as David Aphek and Yosef Govrin, on the first foreign ministry delegation to Moscow for talks with the Soviet foreign ministry. In these talks Trasov presented directly his edifying ideas on this subject.) Ross said that he backed my evaluations. There indeed was room to change directions, disengaging from the road we had taken thus far, which had led nowhere. He concurred that a framework for two-track activity ought to be created and that preparation of a third circuit, to deal with arms control and economic development, should ensue. Progress should be accompanied by confidence-building measures. Ross said that he would report to Baker about our meeting and disclose to him my thoughts and ideas in order to secure his feedback, and directives.

The following day, September 26, Levy and Baker discussed primarily the situation in the Gulf, where war preparations were in full swing. The secretary of state interjected, "I was briefed by Ross last night about his discussion with Bentsur. The ideas which Bentsur raises are interesting. It's important that Ross and Bentsur continue to talk, in this creative mode." Baker added, "We have talked, and will continue to talk, with the Arab states about the establishment of confidence-building measures. We'll talk with Arab countries in phases parallel to the Israeli-Palestinian dialogue. We'll come back and discuss a list of additional ideas." With this remark the secretary of state validated an idea and policy path I had proposed and charted. Foundations for a new political process in the Middle East had been laid. This was the process that would beget the Madrid Conference and the Madrid formula, a system of dual talks—Israel-Palestinian, Arab states–Israel—coterminous with discussions of comprehensive issues pertaining to the Middle East as a whole.

I briefed the foreign minister about my discussions with Ross and Kurtzer, and about my recommendation to operate from this point onward on a two-track path. Needless to say, I added that should this proposal not be to his liking, or should it be likely to compromise him politically, I would assume responsibility as having exceeded my authority. "I believe that this is the way to go," I said; "however, I don't want to cause you difficulties at home, in Israel." Foreign Minister Levy listened understandingly to my comments. He was destined to give the process his complete backing, driving it forward with the full weight of his authority and with considerable craft and ingenuity.

On the basis of a schedule worked out between Levy and Baker, I met on September 27 with Under Secretary of State Ross, with Kurtzer and Miller also in attendance. The meeting was meant to develop the concept of the two-track approach, which was still in a rough, formative phase. Ross arrived with Baker's responses. Baker had asked for Ross to meet with me, so that I could pass along to Levy his evolving views. Baker was trying to put relations with Levy on a firm, productive, and credible footing. Should the foreign minister display creativity in the political sphere—it was understood—Baker would regard him as a partner with whom he could cooperate closely to advance the peace process. Ross summarized the secretary of state's approach as follows:

- Progress should be made on two tracks, not necessarily with mutual dependence between them.
- To attain progress, a process of conceptual revision in the Arab world had to start, to accustom the countries to think in terms of peace, dialogue, and reconciliation. That is how the United States had proceeded with the Soviet Union, and the approach had reaped dividends.

Ross said that in the secretary of state's last meetings in Egypt, Syria, and Saudia Arabia (in the interval between Levy's two September visits to the United States), Baker had informed his Arab hosts about his discussions with his Israeli counterpart. Baker had frequently used such phrases as "Foreign Minister Levy tells me." Baker's diplomacy on that occasion in the Arab world had pivoted around the following points: the impression he had gotten from Levy that Israel was taking into account U.S. concerns about developments in the Gulf; that the United States valued the responsible position expressed by Levy, thinking it well worth the consideration of the Arab states, as members of the developing Persian Gulf "coalition." Baker had cited also his country's observation that Israel's policy in the territories had been characterized of late by initiative and a positive approach. Finally, Ross recorded, Baker had told the Arabs that he intended to work with Israel's foreign minister on behalf of a future of peace and that he anticipated that Levy would demonstrate flexibility.

Ross's comments made clear that Secretary of State Baker viewed the two-track path, with the diverse possibilities it entailed, as a catalyst that might lift the peace process out of its rut, liberating it from the small details and undue formalism, and providing a measure of the creativity to which he himself aspired, after months of exasperating, barren negotiations.

Ross expressed Baker's urge to extrapolate on the basis of the Persian Gulf crisis and to contemplate a lofty postwar scenario, one marked by arms control, transparency of troop movements and weapons procurement, observers, and a whole slew of confidence-building measures. He also recommended drawing up a list of active responses to various contingencies—such policy statements would be a test of the other sides' intentions. Ross emphasized that after the crisis in the Persian Gulf, his country would act on the dual track, while shoring up confidence-building measures. That is, the United States would seek to develop the Israel-Palestinian dialogue, and in parallel it would try to persuade the Arab states to talk with Israel; the United States understood that Israel would be able to take longer strides on the Palestinian track should it sense that the Arabs were genuinely reconciliatory. Echoing an idea that had been articulated at the "Carnegie Deli meeting," Ross reported that with regard to the Palestinian track, Baker believed it would be possible to move ahead in a circumspect, careful manner, reviewing progress attained with Palestinians from the territories who would at one stage or another be engaged in discussion with Israel. Yet, speaking on Baker's behalf, Ross "warned" that ideas stated thus far were still raw and required further polishing and deliberation. Baker's aspiration was to be able to tell discussion partners that both the United States and Israel were thinking "creatively" about the process and that the United States could vouch for Israel's intentions and credibility. In my reports to Levy, I noted that Ross had, for better or worse, refrained from bringing up the PLO in the political context.

Baker sent Levy a message on October 14, 1990. Its main subject was UN Security Council Resolution 672, which two days before had castigated Israel for the Temple Mount incident (in which nineteen Palestinians had been killed by Israeli security forces) on October 8 and had called for a commission to investigate. However, in it Baker also asked to be updated with respect to "creative ideas in the context of the peace process which Eytan Bentsur articulated. I find his ideas encouraging, and want to develop them forthwith."

A day earlier, October 13, an official in Israel's Washington embassy, Oded Eran, reported on a memorandum received through Ross declaring a U.S. intention to support the Temple Mount censure resolution, which declared that Israel should have been prepared for such an incident. On the other hand, the Americans would not sit idly were Security Council resolutions to play into the hands of Saddam Hussein, who should have been the focus of any UN censure resolutions. The secretary of state held that after a review commission had gone to Israel as dictated by the UN resolution, it would be possible to focus anew on the Iraqi ruler. Ross recalled that Israel had hosted such commissions in the past, and so this one would not set a precedent. Baker concluded with hope that he would hear soon from Levy about the peace process, pursuant to the promising ideas communicated by Bentsur.

This message arrived on the day of a stormy cabinet session devoted to the Temple Mount events and their aftermath in the Security Council. Against the background of agitated feelings wrought by the events, the secretary of state's comments about my encouraging, creative words to U.S. officials stirred wonderment. Shamir summoned Levy to a meeting immediately after the cabinet meeting and asked him to decipher the message, unpacking the meaning of the phrase "creative ideas." Levy allayed the prime minister's suspicions, assuring him that in our contacts with Baker and his associates we had not ventured beyond the parameters of Israeli government policy; we had simply acted to advance the peace process.

The two-track formula was discussed again at an October 21 New York meeting between Ross and the director general of the prime minister's office, Yossi Ben-Aharon. The discussion centered on Israel–United States relations, the settlements issue, the American dialogue with the PLO, and more; naturally, it did not overlook the peace process. Ross stressed that opportunities for progress on two tracks—in terms of relations with Arab states and also negotiations with the Palestinians—had arisen. Baker, he said, had noted sympathetically Levy's message about the need to accomplish something in relations with the Arab states, specifically a conclusion to the state of declared belligerency. Ross told Ben-Aharon that he had been able to persuade the secretary of state to try to convince interlocutors from the Arab world that they should take as an example the political processes that had evolved in Europe, where the East and West had begun with dialogues over technical matters, such as measures to prevent incidents between militaries; later these technical discussions had been transformed into full-blown political negotiations and historic agreements.

Ross reported that following the talks with Levy and myself in Washington, Baker had embraced the double-track idea and had conveyed it during talks with Arab foreign ministers. In these discussions, the secretary of state had told his Arab counterparts that he regarded as reasonable Israel's contention that relations between it and its neighbors had to be congruent with the state of the Palestinian issue. Baker had struck this chord in a meeting with Syria's president Hafez Assad in Damascus. Assad had listened attentively, only to reply that Israel had to decide what it preferred—the Golan Heights or the peace process. Committed personally to Baker's message and excited by its implications, Ross insisted that there was room for creative thinking and that more discussions would be needed to assess ways of moving ahead.

In the final months of 1990, U.S. government policy was fixated by developments in the Persian Gulf and the effort to compel Saddam Hussein to leave Kuwait. Baker, however, was not the type to be distracted for too long. He was not going to allow the peace process to fall by the wayside.

Baker sent Levy a report on November 15, 1990, summarizing his activities since their previous meeting. He observed that the international community remained loyal to the objective of resolving the Persian Gulf crisis. Baker wrote that he had "come across leaders who believe that actions should be taken to prevent Saddam Hussein from receiving a prize for his exploits." All believed, the secretary of state added, that Saddam would withdraw from Kuwait only when he became convinced that the United States and the coalition were serious about their intention to use force. Baker informed Levy that the elements were in place for military action—Saddam Hussein could have no illusions regarding what the United States was planning to do. Baker himself had been helping to organize military action and keeping up with logistics, including details pertaining to the deployment of military forces in Saudia Arabia. In parallel, Baker had set up foundations for political support of military action once economic sanctions lost their efficacy. This work had necessitated a Security Council resolution endorsing a military operation founded on relevant portions of the UN charter. Baker stated how important he thought it was that any military operation have the authentication of the Security Council. Such international endorsement would send a dramatic, harsh, and unmistakable message to the Iraqi ruler. At the end of this part of the report, Baker described the positive responses he had obtained both in the political and military spheres. The United States preferred solving such a crisis through peaceful means; however, it now had in its possession the infrastructure for a military operation, should the need arise.

Baker added that all partners in this mobilization concurred that no linkage should be created between the crisis in the Persian Gulf and the Israeli-Arab dispute. It would be a mistake to interlock these two issues. Also, most members of the allied coalition had evinced appreciation for the low profile Israel had kept regarding the Gulf crisis. Baker's prime objective for weeks to come would be to thwart Saddam Hussein's aggression; nonetheless, he believed, thought should continue to be given to moving the Arab-Israeli peace process forward. We agreed that there could be no long-term stability in the region, even after the bellicose Iraqi behavior was stifled, should there be no breakthrough in the Israeli-Arab sphere.

Ideas that might be sufficiently creative to overcome obstacles impeding the peace process emerged during meetings held in September 1990, in Washington and New York. Ross was scheduled to arrive in the region early in December 1990 for talks with Levy and Shamir about these ideas. Baker emphasized the need to work together on the peace process, in an era characterized by dynamic transformations in Israel and the region as a whole. He affirmed anew his intention to cooperate closely with Levy and Israel's government once he was convinced that Israel's attitude toward the process was serious and credible.

On December 9, I sent a memorandum to Foreign Minister Levy, recommending consideration of a number of components of a new peace plan that might set the process in motion, under his auspices. As cornerstones, I incorporated fundamental elements from the Shamir initiative. Some of these axioms were

- Israel desired peace and wanted to continue with the political process, engaging in direct negotiations.
- Israel opposed the establishment of a Palestinian state in the Gaza Strip or in the region between Israel and Jordan.
- Israel would not negotiate with the PLO.
- No changes could transpire in the status of Judea, Samaria, or the Gaza Strip, apart from those consistent with the government's policy guidelines.

I pointed out that to apply the Israeli government's initiative would meet with friction and difficulty. Past experience, along with the dramatic contemporary developments in the Persian Gulf, provided justification for Israel's belief that it could shape circumstances in such a way as to transform the peace process from theory and discussion to reality. The fulcrum would be the two-track concept. On the Palestinian track, a solution would be advanced for the residents of the West Bank and the Gaza Strip; on the other track, the dispute between Israel and the Arab states would be eased. Progress on one track would facilitate advances on the other track, and vice versa. A process based on this dual approach would enjoy increased support from residents of the region and have a higher probability of success. Retracing the analysis I had unfolded for Baker and Ross, I reviewed in detail the stages of progress on the two tracks, stressing their interlocking features.

As mentioned, Baker had informed Levy that his emissary, Ross, would be coming to Israel in December. Anticipating that visit, I predicted in my memorandum to Levy that Ross would share thoughts about "creative" possibilities for the political process, as the secretary of state had indicated to Levy on September 26, 1990, and then repeated in a special review message to Levy on October 18, 1990. Ross's visit, I argued, had a complementary objective: to demonstrate to America's Arab allies in the anti-Iraq alliance that the United States was not downplaying the significance of the Palestinian issue and the Israel-Arab dispute. On the other hand, as the crisis in the Gulf flared, the United States was stressing in public and in diplomatic exchanges that there was no linkage, no reciprocal relationship, between the Gulf situation and a process designed to resolve the Israel-Arab dispute. Saddam Hussein would have been the first to try to create such linkage, with the aim of disrupting the coalition. In this sense, a conjunction of the peace process with the Gulf preparations could have been exploited by the Iraqi dictator, and it could have been interpreted as a reward for his aggression.

Despite these Gulf-related calculations, I cited to Levy some advantages that might actually accrue from holding peace-process discussion at that time. It was known that Israel's consent to an exchange of ideas concerning the political process had preceded the developing situation in the Gulf; the agreement to engage in talks with Ross was a signal of our preparedness to commit ourselves to this discussion program, as promised. Such a discussion would enhance prospects for cohesion and compatibility between positions taken by the United States and Israel when the process was renewed. More than anything else, the discussions would revive the momentum built up during our last talks with the secretary of state concerning the idea of pursuing Israel's May 14, 1989, initiative along two parallel tracks that would converge at the end of the process negotiations with properly authorized Palestinian representatives, and discussions with Arab states toward cessation of the state of belligerency, in preparation for the establishment of a full peace.

I noted that the preparatory discussion with Ross was likely to take place at a time when the Americans were honoring the low profile and "responsible" behavior of Israel during the Gulf events. The communications breakdown between President Bush and Prime Minister Shamir had been repaired by this newly gained U.S. esteem. The Arab world, meantime, was fragmenting as a consequence of the formation of the anti-Iraq coalition. By siding with Saddam Hussein, Arafat and his organization had managed to stir up virtually universal contempt; as a result, the question of whether the PLO could be perceived as a worthy negotiation partner was being seen in a new, doubtful light in many places. Coinciding with the PLO's loss of prestige, chances were growing that Arab states that had joined the Western coalition against Iraq would in the foreseeable future assent to America's urging that they heed the voice of prudence and moderation, and climb aboard the negotiation bandwagon, putting an end to the state of belligerency with Israel.

In my memorandum I cited a view, which was also Levy's, regarding Bush's possible inclinations: sooner or later, Bush's desire to resort to the United Nations, which perhaps stemmed from his stint as a UN ambassador, would bring the notion of an "international conference" to the fore. I referred to the Soviet dimension, wondering what might occur should the Gulf crisis be resolved by political means. Would not that rehabilitate Arafat? He could come across as the one who had prodded Saddam Hussein to relent, withdraw, and assent to a political solution. I brought out these arguments to support immediate discussions with the United States relating to renewal of the political process, subsequent to the end of the crisis in the Gulf. Such a discussion would improve Israel's relations with the United States and Egypt, and perhaps also help allay tensions on the West Bank and in the Gaza Strip.

Of course, I also cited the disadvantages that might result from discussions with the United States at this particular moment. Though there was no declared connection between the Gulf crisis and the political negotiations, any discussion with the United States could be interpreted as evidence of such linkage or as a precedent for one. It could also encourage a renewal of relations between the United States and the PLO. Acquainted as I was with pressures faced by Israeli governments and their distaste for "hard" decisions, I saw fit to mention the obvious: success in these discussions would be likely to accelerate the pace of a discussion process, thereby bringing nearer the hour when Israel would face tough decisions.

I recommended that the foreign minister center any future talks on the Palestinian question and on ending the status of belligerency between Israel and the Arab states. That is, I stressed, the political process ought to be renewed on two tracks at once, with links between them. I proposed as well other discussions concerning confidence-building measures, Ross having explored the idea with me during our New York conversations. Confidence-building measures would be designed to buttress the political process at its early stages, should it temporarily run off the rails; they would provide a basis for its resumption, after some delay. I cited arms control as another topic that warranted consideration, in a way that would supplement the two-track peace process; I stressed that Israel should discuss the Egypt-UN initiative for controlling weapons of mass destruction in the Middle East. Another recommendation related to preparation for cooperation in economics, ecology, and other matters of regional import.

I recommended that we launch discussions with the Americans about joint U.S.-Israeli activity to reduce Iraq's ability to pose a threat following the resolution of the Gulf crisis, partly by foreclosing any possibility of a future attempt to purchase nuclear capability. I believed it important that on the eve of a renewed political effort on behalf of a complex peace process, a broad memorandum on cooperation between Israel and the United States be prepared. With help from Avi Gil of the foreign ministry's North American Department, I had started to draft such a document; it would cover peace-process issues and other aspects in the Israel–United States relationship.

I urged the foreign minister to accept these proposals and bring them to the appropriate government channels, so as to guarantee their adoption of the Israeli plan for a fresh political initiative, and thereafter their programmatic, public submission when the right time and opportunity came along. I knew that the foreign minister would have to bring the proposals to the government for formal approval and that this would be a tall order; many ministers would hesitate to accept them, and the number of opponents could exceed that of their supporters.

Levy adopted the recommendations straight away and thus became the prime mover of Israel's new peace initiative. Slowly, colleagues in the foreign ministry started to join my cause, and this marked a change. In the past, none of them had seen any flaw in keeping the focus exclusively on the Palestinian issue rather than advancing the peace process as well. With my memorandum, the two-track approach became the main building block upon which the developing political initiative would be based.

Foreign Minister Levy chose to announce his new political initiative in an appearance before leaders of Jewish communities in Britain on the first day of 1991. This was a "five-point plan," designed to highlight the new aspects of Israel's policy orientation and reinvigorate Israel's May 14, 1989, initiative. The foreign minister's initiative was entitled "Principles for the Advancement of the Peace Process," and it incorporated the essence of the new two-track approach. The foreign minister's plan featured the following five points:

- Cessation of the state of belligerency between Israel and the Arab states
- Discussions between Israel and the Arab states on regional arms control
- Direct negotiations between Israel and the Arab states
- In parallel, negotiations between Israel and residents of Judea, Samaria, and the Gaza Strip (such discussions could be conducted with a joint, Palestinian-Jordanian delegation)
- Formulation of an economic development plan for the region, featuring international assistance and concentrating on such spheres as water, electricity, infrastructure, agriculture, and health.

The foreign minister reinforced the plan in an appearance before the World Jewish Congress in Jerusalem on February 11, 1991. Levy alluded to a Soviet–American declaration issued jointly on January 29, 1991, which emphasized that it would be impossible to establish stability and security in the Middle East in the absence of peaceful relations between Israel and the Arab states on the one hand, and between Israel and the Palestinians on the other. Levy called on the two superpowers to contribute to the peace process by persuading the Arab countries to end their wars against Israel and by leading those countries to direct talks with Israel, without preconditions, as such negotiation was the only way to resolve the dispute. A solution to the Palestinian question would arise in the context of resolution of the general regional dispute.

Levy's willingness to accept my proposals and fashion them into a five-point political plan gave me great satisfaction. The plan put us on a new political track; we were no longer bogged down by preoccupation with the Palestinian issue. From this point onward, Israel was committed to advancing the peace process on two tracks, with parallel elements and internal links; a third lane was also on the policy horizon, a commitment to discuss regional development in diverse spheres and to search for solutions to such vexing issues as arms control and refugee settlement. Much depended now on the determination of Israel's government, and the country's political system, which had selected the cabinet; similarly crucial would be the maintenance of an intensive dialogue with the United States, and American faithfulness to agreed-upon political principles. Secretary of State Baker had played a consummate role, as catalyst and creative participant in a process aimed toward substantive negotiations.

And so the stage was set for a bilateral and multilateral political process.

3

Shuttle Diplomacy

Secretary of State Baker conducted nine visits to the Middle East. Foreign Minister Levy and I received Baker on his visits. The two of us would climb into a car with Baker for the one-hour journey from Ben-Gurion Airport to Jerusalem; we would be the first to speak with him, hear his impressions, and exchange views and ideas. These informal discussions made a significant mark on each visit and on the advancement of the process. Relying on the privacy of an automobile, we would explore for the guest realms of the possible and the impossible, enlightening him as to policy courses that would be entirely untenable from Israel's point of view and as to ways to circumvent traps laid by various elements that were not committed to the political process. Slowly, a relationship of trust evolved with the secretary of state. Baker became convinced beyond a shadow of a doubt that Levy and I supported the peace process whole-heartedly and that we would do our utmost to advance it, while guarding unrelentingly Israel's interests.

Baker thought that a real opportunity had arisen. More than once his enthusiasm made it possible for us to allay doubts created by one provocation or another perpetrated intentionally prior to his visit. His trust in us was complete, and he felt uninhibited in our company; he made off-the-cuff comments about various personalities and events, knowing that we would never make them public. On one such visit we showed Baker the site where a terrorist had in 1989 forced a bus to swerve into a gorge, killing sixteen passengers and injuring another twenty-five. Such demonstration made palpable to the secretary of state the tragic dimensions of the security issue and the poignant costs exacted by terrorism.

During these car journeys, Baker would share with us his main impressions deriving from talks with Arab leaders, and he would unhesitatingly disclose his intentions for the particular visit to Israel. True, his seeming openness might have been a deliberate ploy; whether it was or not, his candor allowed us to brief Baker's upcoming discussion partners and increase the chances that the visit would succeed. Frequently he would ask informally for our advice concerning the course he should take and ways to promote one idea or another. He related to us in general as partners and allies, even when he suspected that other Israelis involved in the talks were strewing the road with obstacles to gain time and defer the implementation of the peace process. Time has passed, but I still have before my eyes an image of a fleeting incident during one visit: we were getting out of the car at the Foreign Ministry, and Baker, who was about to head off for a private meeting with Prime Minister Shamir, called out to me, "Eytan, do something"—imploring that we not allow the process to flounder and cease. The foreign minister did his best to keep the momentum going, while unflinchingly adhering to ironclad principles. Levy confronted a cadre of officials, particularly some affiliated with the prime minister's office, who took pride in, and tried to "score points" by, deploying delay tactics, devising pretexts and excuses so that the process would never get off the ground.

The first official talk between Baker and Levy, held during his initial trip to Israel, on March 11–13, 1991, produced an agreement. The sides concurred that concurrent progress must be guaranteed on the two tracks so as to advance Israel's May 14, 1989, initiative. Baker declared that any arrangement would have to be based on the formula of "territory for peace," and he warned about the damage liable to be caused to the process should a vigorous Israeli settlement policy continue. Baker asked Levy to deliver his message entreating Israel's government not to allow settlement activity to destroy the most promising opportunity that had ever arisen to attain regional peace.

The secretary of state stressed that the United States remained committed both to Security Council Resolution 242, passed in 1967, requiring an Israeli withdrawal from conquered territories, and to the 1973 Resolution 338, which underscored Resolution 242. Baker related that in the aftermath of the recently ended Persian Gulf War, the United States had discerned some softening in the stances of a few Arab states. At the very least, these states would not be hostile and disruptive to the political process. The Gulf War had furnished several heretofore unknown opportunities, and it behooved Israel and the United States to capitalize on them. Baker inquired once again as to the Israeli willingness to participate in a "regional conference"—as opposed to an international conference—saying that this was an idea worth exploring and expanding. Baker explained to Levy that the United States did not want to exert pressure on Israel to coerce it into approving any particular plan; the Americans were asking only to revive the political process and to move it ahead. Baker defined American intentions in the same way during his March 14, 1991, talks in Moscow with leaders of the Soviet Union.

On March 26, 1991, after returning to Washington from the Middle East, Baker met with Israeli ambassador Zalman Shoval. Baker shared his impression that a number of Arab countries were showing a certain degree of flexibility and latitude that they were beginning to think in terms of advancing the political process. Discussion partners in these Arab capitals seemed less perturbed and less concerned to dictate preconditions when the idea of an international conference as the sole available fulcrum for promoting the political process was presented; also, they showed enhanced willingness to cooperate in terms of resolving the issue of Palestinian representation. In light of these impressions, Baker continued, he believed that if Israel were to take appropriate steps, such as ceasing to deport Palestinians and reopening universities, the Americans' ability to coax these Arab governments to be still more accommodating would be redoubled.

The same day, Shoval had a meeting with Richard Haas, the National Security Council official entrusted with responsibility for Middle East affairs. Haas told him that Washington's opposition to the concept of a "Palestinian state" notwithstanding, he believed that a future settlement would be based on the establishment of a demilitarized political entity, defined taxonomically as "somewhere between an independent state, and autonomy." It can be assumed that such a formulation for a Palestinian entity was broached in this period by U.S. officials in talks with Arab leaders and diplomats and helped soften the general Arab position. In his talk with the Israeli ambassador Haas added that the help of Jordan and other Arab states would help make it possible to find Palestinian delegates who were not de jure PLO members or de facto PLO representatives for future talks with Israel.

Baker's second visit to Israel occurred April 8–10, 1991. Three days prior to his departure, the State Department's spokesman announced that Baker would probe America's ability to resolve differences in positions adopted by sides in the dispute, and forge a consensus around the two-track approach. In the Foreign Ministry we guessed that Baker would try to ascertain whether the names of seven Palestinians who did not represent East Jerusalem or compatriots abroad were still acceptable and relevant.

Baker reviewed America's basic positions during a meeting at the foreign minister's office with Levy and myself on April 8. The United States was calling for the alignment of the peace process with Israel's political initiative and featuring the two-track approach to negotiations with the Palestinians. The U.S. position, Baker emphasized, was that the peace process was not to beget a Palestinian state. As to the delegation issue, Baker declared that from this point onward his government would unreservedly accept the position of the Israeli government, which had been presented to him in a consistent, forthright manner by Levy since 1990—the Palestinian delegation would comprise purely representatives from the territories. The United States therefore divorced itself entirely from the PLO demand that delegates chosen from East Jerusalem and from among deportees be included on the Palestinian panel. Baker's pledges confirmed to Levy that his efforts to prevent the reemergence of factors that had stalled the process during the days of the unity government had borne fruit.

The Secretary of State stated that he envisioned the Palestinian delegation's composition as being dependent on acceptance of the two-track approach and commitment to peaceful coexistence with Israel. Baker affirmed his intention to promote the idea of an international conference. In this connection, he even hinted for the first time that it might be needed merely for procedural purposes, shorn of powers and authorities, with its primary objective being to put in motion the peace negotiation on the two tracks. Also, reports circulated in this period about Israeli plans to establish new settlements; indeed, a number of militant declarations on the settlements issue were being articulated by members of Shamir's government. Some reports alluded to the establishment of new settlements camouflaged as the expansion of old ones. Baker demonstrated considerable concern, repeating to Levy his request that Israel refrain from a disruptive settlement policy at such a crucial juncture in the peace process.

At a meeting held on April 9 with the secretary of state, Ross, Levy's assistants Aliza Goren and Uri Oren, and myself, the foreign minister acknowledged Baker's myriad efforts to advance the two-track approach.

Levy believed that Baker's recent efforts might overcome the stumbling blocks that had frustrated previous efforts to get the negotiations going. It was now unmistakably clear to Israel that Baker intended to work simultaneously on the two circuits, the Palestinian track and the Arab-states track.

For his part, and repeating earlier affirmations that he had seen encouraging signs in Arab capitals, Baker characterized at length positions that he regarded as indications of a desire to advance in the process. Baker had also gathered some positive responses in Israel, in his prior discussions with Foreign Minister Levy and Prime Minister Shamir. He declared that he discerned Israeli preparedness to take steps on behalf of peace. He summarized that agreement was crystallizing on the following points:

- The two-track approach—even though the canvassing to secure Arab states' consent in this connection was still going on.
- The need for steps to build confidence and foster an atmosphere conductive to negotiations.
- The need to identify Palestinians from the territories who were committed to a peace process, so as to consider them as candidates for a representative Palestinian delegation.

Baker stated that Israel's negotiating counterparts would be Palestinians from the territories and that these Palestinian delegates would conduct the talks for self-government. Baker had from the early stage of his efforts used the term "self-government," apparently believing it to be a more substantive and attractive definition than "autonomy." The evolving formulation for the composition of the Palestinian delegation would, Baker contended, bypass the jagged edges that had heretofore torn the political process apart. A multiple-stage approach, Baker continued, should be adopted, as it would accord with Israel's peace initiative and with the Camp David agreements. Summarizing further his talks with Shamir and Levy, the secretary of state remarked that no Palestinian state would result from negotiations about the political process, no negotiations with the PLO would be conducted, and that the United States would not be confronted with new Israeli settlement activity. Levy replied that the term "self-government," which Baker had used frequently in the Palestinian context, must not in any circumstance be regarded as referring to a preparatory phase of a "state in the making."

A concluding meeting between Baker and Levy was held on April 10, with Ross, myself, Yosef Lamdan, (director of the North American Department at the Foreign Ministry), and Levy aides Goren and Oren also taking part. In his farewell remarks, Baker concluded that of the array of topics about which he wanted to forge understandings, agreement had been obtained concerning at least two. It had been agreed that Security Council Resolutions 242 and 338 would be the foundations of negotiations, it being clearly understood that each side adhered to its particular interpretation of the meanings of these UN decisions. Following extensive discussions with Levy, Baker assented to the foreign minister's position, agreeing to the demand that the United States not state publicly its position on UN Resolution 242, thereby keeping to itself its view that the resolution upheld the principle of territory for peace. The two also agreed anew to revive the idea of a regional conference, a notion originally conceived of by Prime Minister Shamir during the Reagan-Shultz era. It will be recalled that the idea of a regional conference was meant to supplant plans for an international conference; Israel was wary that the latter sort of conference would accentuate its isolation and subject it to international criticism and pressure. For his part, Baker called for the involvement of leaders of countries in the European Community at a regional conference. Israel rejected this idea outright, for tactical reasons, if nothing else.

While some measure of progress had been made regarding a number of subjects and elements that Baker had skillfully managed to bind together, bringing to bear the authority of one of the world's superpowers, a number of pressing difficulties remained. These were sources of internal division in Israel's government, particularly in relations between the foreign minister and the prime minister. One unresolved issue was the composition of the Palestinian delegation. Responding to demands forwarded by Shamir and Levy, the secretary of state guaranteed that the Palestinian representatives would not issue declarations either at the start or in the course of the talk that they were PLO delegates. Should any Palestinian delegate make an announcement of this sort, Israel would have the right to withdraw from the negotiations, with the United States following close behind.

The United States, Baker argued, had gone a great distance, accommodating Israel's demand that only Palestinian delegates from the territories be included. On the other hand, speaking as a practical realist, Baker said that it had to be assumed that no Palestinian would join the delegation without arranging some sort of modus vivendi with the PLO.

Therefore, Baker argued, such delegates could be allowed to declare that the PLO did not object to their participation. An arrangement tacitly supported by the PLO would emerge. Baker himself articulated reservations about the PLO, showing that he had been influenced by the repeated entreaties of Shamir and Levy expressing their vehement opposition to PLO involvement in the peace process. Baker held, however, that it would be possible to keep the PLO out of it, so long as the delegates indeed came from the territories, they agreed to peaceful coexistence with Israel, and they accepted and endorsed the two-track approach.

Israel did not conceal its concerns that the Palestinian delegates might craftily evade these obligations. Such a scenario was discussed frequently with Baker. The secretary of state was unable to provide guarantees concerning the behavior of any particular member of the Palestinian delegation. It was therefore fitting to propose additional principles that could make it easier for Israel to take the risk of negotiating with even a non-PLO delegation that might show bad faith and infringe commitments. First, Israel would not be compelled to negotiate with anyone not acceptable to it; second, should a Palestinian delegate violate the understandings, Israel would have the right to leave the talks, and in certain situations America would follow suit. A clear-cut example of such an infringement would be a declaration on the part of the Palestinian delegates that they were full-fledged PLO representatives.

Meantime, Baker worked to acclimate his discussion partners to the possibility of an enlarged version of the regional conference scheme, with Israel figuring as a prime participant. His foreign policy strategy was now beginning to take shape. Piece by piece, brick atop brick, components were being aligned for a peace-talk framework. He was capitalizing shrewdly on the new global circumstances, especially the large anti-Iraq coalition that had been forged and the new winds blowing in the Middle East; his policy had been adjusted to rectify errors that had arisen during the ill-fated talks with Arens and Shamir, and to incorporate Levy's five-point plan.

Levy submitted a memorandum to Israel's cabinet on April 14, declaring that his talks with Baker had restored relations of trust between the two countries. Obstacles that had in 1990 impeded an Israel–United States agreement and forestalled the peace process had now been overcome. Baker left Israel on April 10 believing that 90 percent of the agreements necessary between Israel and the United States had been obtained. The secretary of state indicated that he was ready to advance a peace initiative based on Israel's political plan; Levy could discern in Baker's stance the imprint of the following Israeli government principles:

- The peace process was not to lead to the establishment of a Palestinian state.
- Palestinian delegates would come from the territories only. (This point laid to rest the prolonged argument concerning the proposal to include East Jerusalemites with second addresses and representatives of Palestinians who lived outside of the country.)
- There would not be an international conference (of a type that had been considered problematic in the past).
- There would be no public squabbling about the interpretations of Security Council Resolutions 242 and 338.

Levy's report to the cabinet left unresolved, however, the connection between the Palestinian delegation and the PLO. The subject was to be discussed at length in Baker's upcoming shuttle visits to Israel. In addition, Levy added, a few other issues remained to be discussed, clarified, and formulated in understandings between ourselves and the Americans.

Baker wrote to Shamir outlining the progress that had been achieved thanks to intensive work during his visit to the region in early April. The secretary of state, however, also noted some outstanding difficulties. He assessed, first, that the Arab side had assented to the two-track approach and had recognized the need to convene some sort of conference involving states from the region, so as to break taboos and launch direct negotiations. Second, the question of Palestinian representation remained a salient one for the Israelis. The United States aimed to form a delegation composed of Palestinians from the territories. Third, the United States could not give assurances as to what a Palestinian from the territories might say about the PLO. In any event, worry about this issue must not impede the renewal of the process. In any case, based on his talks in Arab and European capitals, Baker's feeling was that should Israel refrain from denouncing the PLO, the chances would be higher that the Palestinian delegates would not express themselves about the organization. Finally, public pronouncements on the part of Israeli leaders about the noninclusion of delegates from East Jerusalem lacked utility. The United States understood Israel's position in this respect yet was not committed to the principle of excluding East Jerusalemites. America, in Baker's words, would act to forestall the East Jerusalem issue, but it could not promise categorically that no East Jerusalemite would join a delegation at any point. Defying expectations, however, Baker did not reconfirm the U.S.-Israeli understanding according to which a Palestinian state would not be the outcome of the process. The omission went against the grain of verbal assurances the secretary of state had made during his second visit to Israel, in April.

Baker maneuvered, smoothed rough edges, moved closer and then pulled back, acting all the time as he saw fit to revive the political process and bring about historic negotiations for peace between Israel and neighboring Arab states, and between Israel and the Palestinians.

Few in Israel's leadership and political arena wagered at this stage that his endeavors would reap dividends. Memories lingered of his failures throughout 1990, which had culminated in a crisis and government collapse. From Baker's point of view, the past failure could be attributed to the rigid positions taken by the Shamir government, to the recalcitrant settlers, to the provocations perpetrated against him, and to lingering suspicions and fears. Past experience gave little reason to hope for a political effort that might blossom. Few could foresee direct negotiations between Israel and the Palestinians, and the Arab states—peace talks between sides that had been embittered enemies since the founding of Israel. If plausible at all, such a prospect appeared to loom far off in the distance.

Such a vision could indeed be seen against odds, yet I saw things differently. Viewing the political efforts to attain peace as participant and witness, relying on my knowledge of the momentum picked up by the two-track idea, and knowing that Levy's endeavors with foreign contacts and on the domestic scene to get the process rolling were indefatigable, I believed that the process had a chance. I took measure as well of the struggles Levy was waging in his own political party, Likud. He knew well that his identification with the process—his visible, persistent, and systematic efforts to advance peace negotiations—would cost him dearly, politically. That was because there were few among the Likud rank and file who sided with peace if it meant serious Israeli concessions. The peace process was, for Levy, an ax that could turn in his hand. To his detriment, innuendo also circulated in the Likud that his aide in the peace process, none other than myself, was not a party regular and was deflecting the foreign minister from the established line. Levy ignored these detractors. He displayed regard for government workers generally and for Foreign Ministry officials in particular, including those who stood up for their views and acted on them to the best of their conscience and judgment.

Wariness about the process infiltrated media coverage as well. Between Baker's shuttle visits, I asked to speak with Yoel Marcus, a journalist I knew well from the influential *HaAretz* newspaper. I wanted to show him that peace had a chance and to obtain his support, for the purpose of rallying hearts and minds to the process. I reminded him of the vision we had all dreamed about since the inception of Israel—a country that had faced Arab attacks and hostility from day one and that on more than one occasion had gasped in exhaustion confronting the threats and the violence. At long last, I told Marcus, direct negotiations for peace would be conducted between Israel and the Palestinians, and with the Arab states as well. Marcus gave me an utterly incredulous look, as though I were deluded and simply did not know what I was talking about, as though I were a naive Pollyanna with an ingenuous and flawed political outlook. I was astonished. This veteran newsman, whose Cassandra-like columns brimmed with warnings about political errors and the costs of inaction, was obdurately refusing to write a single word about what I was saying.

Baker's third visit to Israel came between April 18 and 20, 1991. Prior to his arrival, I suggested to Levy that we ask the secretary of state for clarifications on a number of issues. The two-track approach was one of them. What content would the Arab states provide to this process? Prior to the actual negotiation, would they agree to declare an end to the state of warfare with Israel? The precise U.S. position with regard to the nonparticipation of East Jerusalemites in the process, along with the stance of the Arab states on this issue, was another matter awaiting clarification.

As it turned out, during Baker's visit the question of Palestinian representation arose in full force. Trying to add an item to the understandings that had been worked out with Israel, the secretary of state asked that certain Palestinians who had in the past met and talked with the prime minister be included in the delegation. Baker proposed that the Jerusalem question be muted during the first phase, which would address the interim period; the topic would come up only during final-status talks. The secretary of state was implying that should this formula be accepted, it would be impossible to view the inclusion of East Jerusalemites as confirmation that the Jerusalem issue itself was on the agenda of the anticipated peace conference. Moreover, the United States expressed its willingness to provide Israel with a written guarantee stipulating that the Jerusalem issue could be tackled only at the final stage of the peace process. Such "spin," ingenuity, and reaffirmation was needed, Baker believed. He disclosed his view that should Israel insist that Jerusalem not be brought up for discussion at any stage of the peace negotiations, or demand as a precondition to a conference that the Arab states promise not to raise the Jerusalem issue at any phase, there would never be a peace process. The Secretary of State proposed a new formula relating to the participation of Palestinian delegates: "The Palestinian delegation, and the participation of Palestinians at a regional conference, will be without prejudice to questions which will be raised subsequently with respect to transitional phases or the final status. A Palestinian resident who agrees to the three main principles can be appointed to the Palestinian delegation, without this inclusion being considered an adopted position or precedent with regard to any topic to be discussed in the negotiations."

Responding to Baker, Foreign Minister Levy stressed how imperative it was that Israel and the United States not get entangled in a dispute about so fundamental an issue as Palestinian delegation composition. Israel was prepared to take part in a regional conference on the basis of an understanding with the United States for the purpose of launching negotiations with the Arab states; in parallel, it was prepared to conduct a dialogue on the basis of clearly accepted parameters with a Palestinian delegation comprising delegates from the territories. Levy alluded to a previous suggestion that Baker had offered and that Israel had assented to the official submission of a list of possible delegate names, from which Israel would choose acceptable candidates, it being understood that such a list must include no PLO or East Jerusalem representatives.

On April 20, Baker met with a Palestinian delegation at the American consulate in East Jerusalem. The secretary of state prodded his discussion partners, trying to ascertain whether Palestinians could be found in the territories who were not PLO affiliated supporters and who would be able to take part in the planned regional conference. Perhaps he was also examining the possibility of the delegation including Palestinians with whom he regularly met during his visits to East Jerusalem.

Baker informed the Palestinians that the PLO would not be able to play a direct role in the evolving peace process. However, he hinted that the organization would be able to act behind the scenes, give orders secretly, and authorize steps to be taken by the delegation representatives. The Palestinians insisted instead that the PLO play a central, clear role in the negotiation process proposed by the secretary of state. (Parenthetically, it bears mention that Dr. Haidar Abd el-Shafi, who was later to be selected the chairman of the Palestinian delegation, took part in only one of Baker's meetings with Palestinian representatives. Baker would recall that during this lone discussion, he accepted Shafi's view that the settlements were an obstacle to peace; Shafi inferred from Baker that when negotiations began, U.S. involvement would be active and persistent.)

During his talk with the Palestinians, Baker presented for the first time the idea that the problem of representation of Palestinians who lived outside the country or in East Jerusalem could be defused by a joint Jordanian-Palestinian delegation. Israel could not presume to define the character and composition of a Jordanian delegation. Baker stated further that he would support the inclusion of nonresident Palestinians on the Palestinian delegation proper in final-status talks. The Palestinians noted this assurance with satisfaction. The United States was maintaining that recognition of Palestinians who lived outside Israel would come in due course; it would happen at the stage of final-status talks. Moreover, the United States would not hesitate to criticize Israel's settlement activities. The secretary of state emphasized especially the two-track negotiation approach, that would stem from the regional conference.

Indeed, during a third visit between Baker and Levy, discussion ensued concerning substantive points important for the preparation of a regional-international conference. While it would serve as a spur to negotiations, the peace conference, it was agreed, would not be empowered as an authoritative mediator in the event of an impasse in bilateral talks. In its formal capacity, the conference would address regional issues that pertained to the multilateral talks. It was also agreed that the Soviet Union could play a role as a joint sponsor only if it put its relations with Israel on a footing of full diplomatic recognition, and only after it accepted the principles underlying the objectives and procedures of the peace process as had been worked out between Israel and the United States.

Baker believed that a representative of the European Community should have a role at the conference, as an observer rather than a full-fledged backer and sponsor. This status would serve Israel's interests, and it could contribute to regional development. Israeli agreement in this connection would help deflate European lobbying for a UN sponsorship role in the peace conference. The secretary of state informed Levy that the United States favored a delegate of the UN Secretary General at the peace conference, even if such a delegate received observer status only;

in exchange, the United States would oppose the UN's having a sponsorship role, or intervening, in the negotiation process. Baker stressed that UN participation as an observer should not be seen as having any substantive connection to the Security Council or its various resolutions concerning the Middle East. Finally, the Palestinian delegation would not represent the PLO and would not act in its name or on its behalf. This delegation would not be regarded as a representative of a state-in-the-making. As mentioned, the possibility of a joint Jordanian-Palestinian delegation would be examined, one way to get around potholes on the road to peace.

As it turned out, the participation of UN delegates as observers proved to be a dual source of contention, prompting debate between Israel and the United States, and between the foreign ministry and the prime minister. Foreign Minister Levy insisted that things be kept in proportion. That is, UN-European involvement bereft of any substantive authority, on a purely observer basis, could not influence the flow of discussions and would obviate unnecessary conflicts in Israel's relations with Europe and the Secretary General. The negotiations therefore ought to be handled in a pragmatic fashion—Israeli consent to European and UN delegates would come only after limitations on their roles had been promised, and only after the terms and subjects of prime importance for the peace conference had been worked out. But there were officials working for the prime minister who seized upon the UN-Europe issues, to extract from them as much political capital as they could. They generated opposition to European and UN delegates, so as to defer as long as possible the convening of the conference. The director general of the prime minister's office, Yossi Ben-Aharon, used this ploy, painting the UN-Europe issue in as stark and ominous tones as possible. Baker managed at one stage to pry out of Shamir quasi-acceptance of a Secretary General's delegate as an observer; yet, when he returned to Washington the secretary of state found waiting for him a message from the prime minister reasserting his opposition. As though that were not enough, Ben-Aharon, who was an authoritative Shamir spokesman, published an article in the *New York Times* opposing the UN's involvement in the conference, detailing the risks that, he believed, Israel would incur.

Shamir's reversal on the UN issue was one of many messages that the prime minister dispatched directly to the U.S. secretary of state, willfully ignoring and bypassing his foreign minister. Nevertheless, in most instances somebody would within a short time bring the latest Shamir missive to my attention; of course, I would immediately brief Levy. This created a cumbersome situation, one detrimental to the negotiations. Shamir concealed the letters from Levy and did not know that the latter was being informed of their contents. Levy, whom Shamir strove systematically to keep in the dark, went on with negotiations with Baker, trying to mitigate creatively Shamir's positions, which he regarded as petty and designed to defer and derail the talks. Baker, for his part, did not always know whether Levy was up to date. On one of our visits to the United States, Baker was confused, not knowing if Levy was cognizant of Shamir's renewed opposition to the UN Secretary General's participation.

The extent to which Baker had managed, if at all, to wrest consent of Arab states for a regional conference as a fulcrum for direct, bilateral negotiations was cloudy at this stage. The Syrians, as was their wont, kept their position obscure. We had not forgotten, despite the passage of years, an episode of a 1973 international peace conference: after protracted preliminary negotiation, President Hafez Assad had announced to an exasperated Henry Kissinger that Syria would not participate. The enigmatic rigidity characterizing Assad's moves also made it tough this time around for anyone to decipher Syria's intentions. In one of our automobile discussions, Baker reported on lengthy talks with Assad; the secretary of state struck an optimistic chord about Syria, but his report could not be conclusive. Still, the fact that Syria had joined the large coalition that fought in the Persian Gulf War against Iraq provided some room for continued solidifying of relations. Nor, of course, could Assad have failed to notice the Soviet Union's woes in this period of its disintegration—his patron's era as a superpower was rapidly drawing to a close.

Italy's ambassador to Israel, Pierre Luigi Reschel, told me that in contacts with officials from Syria's foreign ministry, his colleague in Damascus had identified some elements articulating interest in peace negotiations. I reported on this to my superiors, evincing the skepticism warranted by the fact that this was the first signal to be emitted from Damascus in years. Subsequently I asked the Italian ambassador, a talented observer with a keen eye for internal Israeli politics and for twists in the political process, to analyze Syria's position from his own national standpoint. The ambassador's view was that Syria's position on a Middle East peace conference, in the aftermath of the Persian Gulf War, was characteristically uncompromising—that is, the Syrians opposed direct negotiations in a conference framework. Damascus's express policies were the same as ever—full implementation of UN Resolutions 242 and

338, with the full participation of the UN and the European Community. On the other hand, the Israeli embassy in Rome had picked up some indications of flexibility that had to be assessed alongside Syria's declared policies. On March 12, the Italian foreign minister, Jani de Miclis, conducted talks in Damascus with the Syrian leadership. The talks did not lead to any concrete breakthrough, but the Italians took notice when Assad declared that "Syria is not prepared to embitter the lives of other states," even if the Security Council resolutions were not fully implemented.

At the beginning of April, an Egyptian diplomatic official was asked to describe Egypt's and Syria's positions on a peace conference. He replied that there was some tactical advantage inherent in the Arab demand that an international peace conference be convened, as an opening step in a comprehensive process. In addition, as early as April 13 the Italian embassy in Damascus distinguished between, on the one hand, Syrian goals in terms of a comprehensive arrangement in a peace process, based on the full implementation of the Security Council resolutions, and, on the other hand, routes and steps to be taken to attain those goals. In the particular instance at hand, Syria viewed an international peace conference as the ideal mechanism for the obtaining of its goals; at the same time, the Syrians were keeping other options open, so long as they were conducive to attaining a comprehensive arrangement, meaning one involving other Arab states.

At this stage, the Italian embassy in Damascus believed that the Syrian position on the Palestinian issue was designed to ensure the unity of the Arab world, such unity being crucial if Syria's own distinctive goals were to be promoted with the backing of moderate Arab states. Syria, in other words, viewed the Palestinian issue in terms of its implications for Arab unity; it did not formulate the issue or its resolution as an absolute precondition for talks with Israel.

On April 25 and 26, Baker conducted his fourth trip to Israel. As always, Foreign Minister Levy and I welcomed the secretary of state and capitalized on the car journey to Jerusalem to cull his impressions, read his thoughts, and exchange with him views on how to advance the process, including our estimates as to the boundary between the possible and the impossible. In retrospect, these car journeys, which together totaled eight hours, appear to have been of paramount import for Israel in the fashioning of the process. Mutual trust was strengthened during them. We found that Baker was increasingly receptive to Levy's and my own ideas as to how to move the process ahead, while guaranteeing Israel's clear political-security interests.

During this visit, the secretary of state reiterated his position that the issues of East Jerusalem and representation of Palestinians abroad could be raised only during the final stages of negotiations. Baker's optimism had grown concerning the probability that a joint Jordanian-Palestinian delegation would circumvent obstacles that had in the past kept the process bogged down. The secretary of state noted during the talks that he was encouraged by the developing signs. He believed that it would be possible to advance the peace process on the basis of Israel's political principles, meaning, among other things, the Camp David accords and the two-track negotiations. At this stage there would be no point, he added, to quibble over interpretations of Security Council Resolutions 242 and 338. Baker adamantly refused to overlook procedural issues, fearing that if they were not tackled the present opportunity to attain peace could be squandered. His persistence derived from his estimate that an opportunity under such unique and propitious circumstances might never arise again. In addition to everything else, there was an unprecedented show of interest in the Arab world in resolution of the conflict with Israel; Baker insisted that this interest should function as the point of departure for the process.

In his mind's eye, Baker was at this stage viewing the unfolding of a process, one that would set the stage for the inception of the first comprehensive peace process in the history of the state of Israel and of the Middle East conflict. Discussing matters with Levy and Shamir, the secretary of state raised the issue of the Soviet Union's participation as a sponsor with the United States; he alluded as well to the need to involve the European Community and the UN. Baker believed that the peace process deserved as broad a base of support as possible, so that it could proceed under optimal conditions.

Levy grasped from the onset that this approach had within it a chance of coaxing the Soviet Union into establishing diplomatic relations with Israel. Indeed, relations between Israel and the Soviet Union, which were at this stage conducted on a consular level, now began to develop. Israel was represented in Moscow by Arieh Levin, a senior foreign ministry official; Levy was hoping that Baker would be able to prod the decision makers in the Soviet Union into embracing the final steps leading to formal recognition.

On the other hand, Levy found cause to limit the role and the status to be accorded to Europe and the UN, parties that Israel had not always in the past considered as displaying a sympathetic, or objective, approach. Levy's perception was strategic, not tactical, in essence. He believed that Baker was attentive to our expectations and could maneuver and act in a fashion consonant with our hopes. But Levy did not always get the necessary backing from the prime minister and his aides. Shamir and his associates tried to exploit disputed matters, to "spin" them so as to gain time and procrastinate, to thwart momentum in a peace process that might possibly become one of the most significant events in modern history.

In his talks with Baker, Levy disclosed that Israel indeed agreed to view the Soviets as cosponsors (with the United States) in a process to be started at the peace conference, on the assumption that the USSR would abide to conditions agreed to by Israel and the United States. Levy added that he was prepared to recommend that a European delegate take part as a participant or observer, though Israel would not consent to a European designation as "cosponsor"—and even Levy's partial assent here was conditioned upon Europe's consent to terms and qualifications imposed by Israel curbing its role at the peace conference. At this stage, Israel continued to oppose a UN delegate taking part at the conference, opposing Baker's assessment that it was inconceivable to prevent the UN, meaning its Secretary General, from sending a delegate as an observer.

Substantive discussions for the convening of a peace conference started. It was decided that invitations for actual participation in the conference, beyond attendance at the opening session, could be issued only with Israel's express consent. The conference invitation was to be phrased entirely in terms of broad regional issues; otherwise, the conference was likely to serve as a kind of mediation tribunal, probing specific negotiation issues that were liable to be especially divisive. Israel's approach was predicated on the assumption that a majority was likely to crystallize at the conference supportive of positions not its own.

During the discussions, Baker promised to encourage Arab states outside of Israel's immediate vicinity, such as the Gulf countries, to take part in work groups, in a multilateral framework that would accompany the peace process. Here was the first flowering of an idea that was implicit in the two-track approach: namely, that this pair of tracks be accompanied by a third, multilateral circuit, which would foster and develop the Middle East region, and in which the full dividends of peace would be reaped. At this stage, discussions were phrased in modest terms. The idea was to approach states not contiguous with Israel, to interest and involve them in the multilateral framework and to annul or at least circumscribe their hostile militancy toward Israel.

On the second day of Baker's fourth visit, April 26, Levy referred to the idea of incorporating in the direct peace negotiations Arab states that did not neighbor Israel and that had remained in a declared state of belligerence. Baker disagreed, claiming that the proposal was not realistic. His reasoning was based on the fact that Arab countries neighboring Israel refused at this stage to allow other Arab states to join the bilateral talks. Were Saudi Arabia and the Gulf states to be invited to the peace conference, matters with Libya, Iraq, and other countries would become unduly complicated. On the other hand, Baker reckoned that the states that were not in the forefront of the Israeli-Arab conflict might be incorporated in work groups organized on a broad regional, or multilateral, basis. The United States was in a position to persuade these countries to participate in such a model.

Speaking with Levy, Baker said the following: "The good thing about the two-track model is that when Israel speaks with the Palestinians, it will at the same time have face-to-face, direct, discussions about lingering, pertinent political issues with the Arab lands who persist in a state of war against her. In addition, the United States will be able to encourage the Gulf states in particular to support, and take part in, regional work groups." With such prompting, the secretary of state aligned himself with the Israeli position, as articulated by Levy, according to which of the Gulf states, particularly Saudia Arabia, were to be persuaded to issue a declaration repealing the state of war with Israel.

Striking the same chord, I sent on May 1, 1991, a telegram to Israel's ambassador in Washington, Zalman Shoval, asking him to submit three claims to the State Department. First, Israel expected the United States to exert its influence on leaders of Arab states, calling for them to annul the state of belligerence, the boycott, and anti-Israel propaganda, concomitant to the establishment of a "new order" in the Middle East. Second, it was implausible that Saudi Arabia and Gulf states, which had profited from crucial, massive, American support at the time of the Gulf war, would refrain from publicly supporting the peace process, choosing not to ride the crest of the process. It would be fitting for these countries to declare at this stage that they were prepared to join multilateral work groups. Finally, Israel expected that America would strive to prevent damage from being done to the two-track approach, which had been proposed by Israel and adopted by the United States and the Arab states.

Developments followed one after another, as in a chain reaction. The advancing process, in which the idea of a peace conference moving from a formative stage to the brink of realization, along with other accelerating factors, brought the Soviet foreign minister, Alexander Bessmertnykh, to Israel on May 10. I sat in a car in the convoy that brought the Soviet guest from Ben-Gurion Airport to Jerusalem, along with three of Bessmertnykh's top aides. They did not conceal their excitement, as the convoy approached the gates of Jerusalem. A shiver ran down their spines, and it was unmistakable that the religious sensitivities that their atheist training in the communist school system had tried to eradicate were now throbbing with ardor.

The Soviet foreign minister's convoy reached the foreign ministry, where the first meeting was to be held with Levy, the foreign minister's deputy Binyamin Netanyahu, and the top officials in the ministry. During the discussion, Levy noted that Moscow had urged Israel time and again to speak with the Palestinians and with the Arab states. Here, Levy added, Israel was proposing a two-track approach that would in fact facilitate simultaneous talks with the Palestinians and the Arab states; this proposal's cogency had to be seen in light of the fact that no other party had ever offered to the Palestinians the gestures that Israel was prepared to propose. Bessmertnykh commented that Israel's approach was correct and pragmatic, and that his government appreciated Israel's willingness to talk with the Palestinians via the two-track mechanism.

The secretary of state's fifth visit to Israel, from May 14 to 16, provided a major push to the preparation for and organization of the peace conference. Israel and the United States exchanged a diplomatic "nonpaper" that detailed the principles and understandings upon the basis of which the process would be pursued in the future. The idea was to develop and formulate a cohesive Israeli-American document that would reflect the understandings reached thus far, along with differences of opinion waiting to be resolved, inasmuch as possible.

This diplomatic effort produced on May 16 a document that accorded paramount priority to the two-track approach. The joint paper certified that agreements had already been reached about the following principles:

- The two-track approach was the foundation of the peace process.
- Security Council Resolutions 242 and 338 would be the basis of this negotiation.

- Israel would not be required to negotiate with any specific party against its will.
- The peace conference would not have the authority to impose solutions or to veto agreements reached between the sides. The conference would not be empowered to reach decisions concerning one of the sides, and it would not be authorized to set the agenda for issues to be discussed at the bilateral negotiations.
- In the Jordanian-Palestinian sphere the negotiations would be conducted in stages.
- Multilateral talks would start shortly after the inception and orderly arrangement of bilateral discussions.

A few issues left lingering after the secretary of state's previous visit to Israel awaited discussion. These were representation of the UN and the Europeans, and the issue of a future reconvening of the peace conference.

After his return to Washington, Baker testified on Capitol Hill to a foreign policy subcommittee of the two houses of Congress about his accomplishments. He said that the U.S. preference was for the UN to receive some sort of role at the peace conference, so long as this would not interfere with the principle of direct negotiations. The United States, Baker added, held that subject to the consent of the sides, a follow-up assembly of the peace conference should be convened, so that reports could be made about the progress in the negotiations. In this respect as well, he stressed, it was vital that the rule of direct negotiations not be breached. He disclosed in his testimony that the idea of a joint Jordanian-Palestinian delegation was acceptable to the sides and that Syria was no longer demanding full withdrawal from the Golan Heights as a precondition for direct talks with Israel. Replying to a pointed question, which might have been planted, Baker stridently attacked Israel's settlement policies, branding them major barriers to the continuation of the peace process.

Baker's vehement words responded to provocative acts that occurred habitually during his visits to Israel, especially in this area of "settlement activity." Frequently, developments were dismissed as though they had occurred spontaneously and the government of Israel was unable to do anything about them. Baker spoke with blunt vituperation during our three-man car journeys, wagging a finger of blame toward government officials who directed, or at least provided an inspirational stimulus for irregular settlement activity at such sensitive moments for the creation of the peace process. Foreign Minister Levy and I were compelled to split hairs and plead, trying to soften Baker's wrath and persuade him both that the government of Israel was not deliberately attempting to provoke him and that we were satisfied with his efforts to move the political process forward.

Shamir and Levy continued to work strenuously to prevent the PLO from playing any role in talks between Israel and the Palestinians. Shamir dispatched to Baker on May 17 a letter in which he reiterated Israel's position concerning the participation of Arab East Jerusalemites and Palestinians from abroad. Prime Minister Shamir insisted that the Israeli position, which was supported by the Americans, regarding the complete ban on PLO participation in the process, and also its reservations concerning the participation of East Jerusalemites and Palestinians from abroad, be relayed to future discussion partners. His rationale was that misunderstandings on these issues would be liable to cause a crisis in the negotiations. Baker replied to Shamir's letter on May 22, writing that on the PLO issue there was some difference of opinion between Israel and the United States. Nevertheless, the United States was fully cognizant of Israel's position regarding no negotiations with the PLO and of the principle that Israel need not sit at a discussion table with a party not acceptable to it; indeed, the Americans had no intention of precipitating a dialogue or negotiations between Israel and the PLO. In general, the process that he, as secretary of state, was trying to set in motion would be acceptable to Palestinians from the territories, who accepted the two-track, two-stage approach and who were prepared to live peacefully with Israel. Baker recalled that his country had suspended its dialogue with the PLO on June 20, 1990, and was not inclined to renew it.

On the other hand, Baker writing to Israel's prime minister as a diplomatic realist, argued that the process would be possible only insofar as the PLO did not block it. Since there was some doubt as to whether Palestinians from the territories would turn up for negotiations should it be known that the PLO expressly opposed the talks, the Palestinian delegates would require some measure of personal or private endorsement from the PLO. Baker concluded therefore that the PLO's tacit consent was required, lest the process stay stalled.

Baker's explanations failed to allay the Prime Minister's concerns. On the 24th of May, Shamir wrote in another letter that the issue of the PLO's involvement in the process, along with the reconvening of the peace process following an opening conference session, had become critical to matters awaiting clarification. Shamir observed that the PLO was

moving vigorously behind the scenes to position itself to play its customary, destructive, part. He judged that should Israel accept, after being
wheedled by the United States, a situation in which the PLO could influence matters from afar, providing tacit consent and direction, it was
inevitable that at a later stage the organization would demand a more
dominant role. No Palestinian delegate would dare defy an order given
by the PLO. Thus the formula of tacit PLO involvement put the fate of
Palestinians from the territories ("Palestinian Arabs," in Shamir's lexicon)
under the PLO's control. Such an arrangement grated against Israel's
policy, which categorically opposed the conferral of legitimacy upon its
most loathed enemy. Shamir phrased his conclusion in emphatic terms:
the government of Israel held that Palestinian Arabs who heeded the
PLO's directives or belonged to the organization were disqualified from
representing the Palestinian population in negotiations with Israel.
Shamir hammered this point with vigor.

While this correspondence with Shamir played out, Baker made an
appearance before a joint congressional subcommittee on foreign policy
(on May 22–23) and also spoke to the Conference of Presidents of Major
Jewish Organizations. Israel's foreign ministry also responded with consternation, expressing regret about Baker's denunciation of Israel's settlement policy, and about the fact that the secretary of state chose not to
refer to the rejectionist Arab attitudes as the real, prime, obstacles to
peace. The American Jewish leaders remonstrated; calling on the secretary of state to resume a more neutral mediation role.

Shamir also brought up the settlement issue in his May 24 letter. He
referred to Baker's formulation by which the term "settlements," phrased
as a pejorative and attached to Israeli communities in Judea, Samaria,
and the Gaza Strip, cast them as a fundamental element in the Israeli-
Arab dispute, particularly in its territorial aspect. Baker had warned that
the Palestinians would, no doubt, bring up the subject in the peace-talk
framework. Shamir responded by reminding the secretary of state that
Israel made a vast concession at Camp David when it agreed to leave
the sovereignty question open until the start of discussions about the
final status of the territories. As a result of this concession, Israel had
refrained from imposing its laws and sovereignty on these regions, despite its legitimate claims to them. It was not acceptable to Israel that
Jews be stopped from dwelling on these lands. Shamir regretted that the
settlement question had been given such a high profile.

In our view, there was no doubt that Baker's criticism (the May 22–23
testimony and speech) had been leveled mainly in reply to provocative

events that, he believed, were designed to foil his efforts to fulfil objectives during his visits to Israel. Virtually each time he landed in Israel he heard about plans, or actual activity, to set up some settlement. Yet it also could not be ignored that his position on this issue had apparently crystallized before he became committed to the political process. Baker did not budge about settlements. A helicopter tour arranged during his first visit to the country, involving Levy, myself, and Major General Yossi Ben-Hanan, a brave Israeli fighter, did nothing to influence his position—on the contrary.

Ben-Hanan had prepared thoroughly for the tour. Routes that would accentuate Israel's security needs had been carefully selected for the helicopter ride. We flew above the Golan Heights, over Jerusalem's outlying areas, and elsewhere, Major General Ben-Hanan emphasizing areas in central Israel that had been targeted by Saddam's Scud missiles during the Persian Gulf War, one such point being a veritable stone's throw from the U.S. embassy installation. Ben-Hanan spoke in lucid, knowledgeable terms, but his words were garbled by the helicopter noise and communications system, which was flooded with transmissions to some air force base. Ben-Hanan had to turn his microphone off because of the babble; once in a while, he would whisper an explanation in the secretary of state's ear, though this too was swallowed by the helicopter clamor.

We landed in the idyllic Galilee town of Karmiel, where we were received warmly, and met with a number of new immigrants who were settling there. Levy served as the secretary of state's official host, and this phase of the tour went off well and as planned. Later on, as the helicopter soared above the West Bank en route to Jerusalem, I garnered the impression that Baker was not "buying" the security arguments proffered to justify our holding the territories. My feeling was that he saw the chain of Jewish settlements looming before his eyes as raw territorial expansionism in the heart of an Arab land. So this meticulously planned helicopter excursion, an outing planned as a demonstration of the crucial security imperatives inherent in the settlement movement and as a proof of the justice of Israel's ideological-political claims, came to nought.

The director general of the prime minister's office, Yossi Ben-Aharon, along with Ambassador Shoval, met with Dennis Ross, John Clay, Dan Kurtzer, and Aaron Miller, members of the State Department's peace negotiation team and Baker's deputies, on May 28. This was a "hard" talk. Each side upheld its point of view in blunt, adamant terms. Ben-Aharon declared that Israel would not be able to assent to the U.S. approach, by which the PLO would be given a formidable, if invisible, role, in the selection of Palestinian delegates. He criticized Baker's meetings with the Palestinians, claiming that they had been undertaken with the PLO's blessing and authorization; Ben-Aharon concluded that these Baker meetings conferred upon Arafat a victor's mantle and were undermining Israel's endeavors. Should this trend continue, he concluded, it might be preferable not to persist with the effort, or not to undertake it to begin with.

The State Department officials must have been wondering whether doubts and reservations harbored by the prime minister himself were to be heard in Ben-Aharon's strident language. Was this a warning that the negotiations, as proposed by Baker, were not acceptable to Shamir? Ben-Aharon was vehement about his opposition to a UN delegate's participation in the peace process, and questioned the proposed parts to be played by Saudia Arabia and the Gulf states. The picture taking shape in Baker's mind was one of an intertwined chain of criticism linked to the various components of the evolving process. Ben-Aharon's opposition was so vociferous that Baker was hard pressed to distinguish between the parts of the position that were sheer principle and the parts that were contingent and tactical; Foreign Minister Levy was always careful in his dealings with the Americans to indicate this distinction, and for that reason he had won the secretary of state's trust.

The director general repeated a contention that was at the time gaining a growing number of adherents in Israel's government and was supported by analyses of certain experts. It held that popular support for the PLO was slipping in the territories, due to fatigue stemming from the intifada and the failure of the PLO to give the population any reason for hope. There was information concerning dissent, lack of cohesion, and misadministration in the PLO leadership, and this was thought as well to be contributing to the erosion of the PLO's base in the territories.

May 1991 went into the annals of the U.S.-Israeli relationship as a month of strife and tension, and June started on the same sour note. Relations seemed to have gone amiss. We in the foreign ministry searched for the source of the breach. The foreign minister and I believed that relations could be straightened out and that formulations consonant with Israel's basic positions could be forged, thereby bringing nearer the start of a triangular peace process between Israel, Arab states, and the Palestinians. Others, however, believed otherwise; the more the process took shape, the more the opposition of these Israeli officials increased, as did their criticisms, pretexts, and measures within which matters of principle and tactic mingled together.

President George Bush wrote to Prime Minister Shamir on June 1 that the creation of peace in the Middle East would guarantee that Israel's historic mission in the absorption of masses of new immigrants would be fulfilled. It should be recalled that since his stint as vice president, Bush had shown special sensitivity on this score, rendering important assistance toward the immigration of Jews from Ethiopia and the Soviet Union to Israel. Bush wrote that Israel had been asking for direct negotiations with Arab states and the Palestinians for forty-three years; now the yearned-for moment had arisen, one conducive to bilateral and multilateral talks.

The president was aware of the risks Israel incurred undertaking negotiations of this kind; for that reason, he stressed, his country had crafted a process tailored to Israel's needs and concerns. This was a process that included Arab states and the Palestinians; it was a process that included Palestinians from the territories but not the PLO; it was a process that prevented the creation of categories that had been objectionable to Israel since the inception of his administration's political effort; it was a two-stage process commensurate with the requirements of the Camp David accords, and it guaranteed that Israel would not be compelled to deal with final-status issues the moment negotiations started. Also, the international-conference component of the process would not be deleterious to direct negotiations.

President Bush became involved at this stage with the aim, among other reasons, of resolving the issue of the participation of a UN Secretary General delegate at the conference. This demand had been made by the UN; also, it suited the interest of the Arab states, as they believed that they stood to gain from a UN presence at the conference. Bush wrote that he could not fathom Israel's negative position in this connection. How could a sole UN observer pose any sort of problem for Israel, particularly since the conference as a whole would be devoid of any coercive authority? The United States, Bush promised, would ensure that participants at the conference understood fully that the meeting was not to be transformed into a kind of court of higher appeals. This guarantee, along with Israel's right to forestall any assembly not to its liking, should suffice to allay Israel's objections to the conference's being resummoned at a later date. The president hinted to Prime Minister Shamir that Jordan's King Hussein would be willing to assist with the integration of Palestinians on the joint Jordanian-Palestinian delegation, if he was promised that a freeze on settlements would be applied with the start of the negotiations. Indeed, Bush's commitment made it less plausible for one of the sides to choose to boycott the opening act of the negotiation process on account of such issues as delegation composition or conference procedures. Such matters were not material to the future course of negotiations.

Shamir sent a long, detailed letter to Bush on June 4 to clarify Israel's positions on outstanding issues. He started with the assumption that Arab states viewed any international forum as a mechanism to be deployed against Israel. The Arab states favored enlarging the number of participants at the conference's opening, believing that should it have an international character, their challenge to Israel's right to exist and its legitimacy as a state would be reinforced. Israel demanded that any Arab state slated for participation in the conference declare publicly that it was willing to undertake direct talks with Israel, with the aim of attaining a peace agreement. Shamir clung to his view that an international conference would undermine the prospects of Israel's undertaking direct negotiations with its neighbors. This line of thought determined Shamir's stance on the question of the future reassembling of the peace conference.

He also worried that should the peace conference "accompany" the negotiations it would serve as a vehicle for evading commitments to bilateral talks. With such calculations in mind, the Arab states sought to involve a UN delegate in the peace conference; Israel, for its part, opposed the idea. Shamir stressed that the two-track idea that Israel had opposed was designed to integrate most, and if possible all, of the Arab states in a process whose goal was to put an end once and for all to the Israel-Arab dispute. Despite this goal, Israel had evinced its willingness to start with a process that would include just one or two Arab states, at a time when the remaining countries were still refusing to rescind the state of belligerence against it.

Shamir drew the U.S. government's attention to problems that continued to trouble his own government. He stated that an understanding had been reached by which the Palestinian delegates would adopt the two-track, stage-by-stage approach for resolving the dispute and would also, of course, declare their intention to live in peace with Israel. Shamir believed, however, that at this juncture such terms and demands were insufficient to guarantee that the delegates selected would categorically not heed the PLO's authority. This was crucial and necessary, since Israel could not accept a peace process if the PLO had a role in it. Israel believed that this issue required discussion with Jordan, since (in Israel's view) a Jordanian-Palestinian delegation would be the best possible mechanism for defusing this delegation's composition controversy. The Palestinian component of such a joint delegation would have to be approved by Israel, in any case. Shamir contended that the PLO continued to hold the Palestinian-Arab population under its sway. The organization had at the time of Shamir's missive been behind the murders of seven Palestinian Arabs, and such an act bore witness to the PLO's true terroristic character, the prime minister suggested. The murders had aimed at intimidating anyone who intended to join the negotiations. This fact underscored the need for additional activity to arrange Palestinian representation devoid of any link to the PLO. The matter required persistent effort, patience, and endurance.

As far as President Bush was concerned, Shamir's letter was an act of defiance, an attempt to undermine his efforts to establish a "new world order." The president's likely reaction was analyzed in a report sent by Michael Shiloh, the political officer in Israel's Washington embassy, on June 7. The president, the report relayed, would see an impasse in the political process in the Middle East as a direct threat to his international standing. Should the trend continue in that direction, the president would cast the blame squarely on Israel, especially since he already viewed measures taken by Israel—deportations, land expropriations—as provocation aimed against him. Israel's settlement policy had always stirred the president's wrath. Now, as was customary at times of tension in Israel–United States relations, the matter of America's ample financial aid was not being neglected: the president and the secretary of state viewed Israel as a country that received huge financial benefits but that did not miss an opportunity, with cause or not, to demand more assistance from the American public.

This reminder was raised in connection to Defense Minister Arens' request at the time for $600-million to cover costs incurred by Israel as a result of the Gulf War; the aid request supplied more ammunition for Bush's and Baker's orientation. The U.S. government was keeping in mind a request that Ambassador Shoval had forwarded for more financial aid; in a newspaper interview, Shoval had couched his appeal in phrases regarded by Washington as arrogant and contemptuous. The Bush administration's response had been adamant, nearly a demand that the ambassador be recalled. Looking back, I attribute this excessive response to the ambassador's statement to pent-up anger in the Bush administration concerning the policy statements and acts of the Shamir government, and also to an irascibility that sometimes gripped the American government as it engaged in the unprecedented Gulf war effort.

These findings in hand, the Israeli diplomat, Shiloh, predicted that President Bush was looking for an opportunity to teach Israel a lesson. Up to now Bush had restrained himself, in view of signs that the political process could succeed; now, however, following Shamir's negative June 4 dispatch, it was possible that the president might throw caution to the wind and conclude that the time had come for a direct standoff with Israel. Shiloh estimated that should Israel defer the president's requests, the United States would be likely to move closer to the Arab states; this could also happen as the continuation of Israel's settlement policy pushed the United States closer to the Palestinians.

With difficulties mounting in U.S.-Israeli relations, Foreign Minister Levy traveled to Washington. He met there on June 13 with Secretary of State Baker; Dennis Ross, and John Clay; Margaret Tutweiler, the State Department spokesperson, was also in attendance. Accompanying Levy were Ambassador Shoval, the foreign minister's political aide, Uri Oren, and myself. The meeting was laced with tension. Baker expressed his disappointment, consternation, and frustration concerning positions adopted by Israel's government. The secretary of state emphasized Shamir's June 4 letter to Bush, but he also noted a number of letters he himself had received from Shamir, letters that, he asserted, had been sent behind Levy's back. (In fact, they were attempts to bypass him, but the foreign minister was actually aware of these communications, in some measure.) Baker reviewed the inflexible, extreme formulations and positions adopted by Israel and the deviations from and denials of agreements that the prime minister had reached with Baker during the latter's visits to Israel. The secretary of state alluded as well to a letter that Yossi Ben-Aharon had published in the *New York Times*, labeling it a personal affront to himself and to his policies.

As a diplomat, Baker could display measured degrees of anger and disappointment, always directing his mood toward some sought-after objective. This time, however, his fuses were blown; he seemed uncharacteristically furious, personally insulted. Among other things, Baker told the Israeli foreign minister that Shamir's letter reneged on a clear understanding that had been reached with him in prior conversations. Baker said he had been hurt personally by Shamir's judgment that he had been devoting his labors exclusively to advancing two purely procedural matters—going beyond the opening session of the international conference, and the participation of the UN Secretary General. Baker recalled that he had been intensively involved in other questions as well, including the issue of Palestinian representation. With respect to the participation of the UN observer, the secretary of state rejected outright the claim that such participation was liable to lead to the involvement of the Security Council, should Israel's partners in negotiations demand it. The secretary of state was willing to furnish guarantees in writing, saying that so long as the peace process kept on track, the United States, with its veto power, would forestall Security Council sessions relating to the political process. Finally, using Levy as his mouthpiece to deliver the message to Shamir and the Israeli government, the secretary of state reiterated that any reassembling of the conference could be only with the consent of participants in the political negotiations. Israel therefore retained the ability to veto any such intention. It was to be regretted that the prime minister's office had backtracked on an agreement he had reached with Shamir on this matter.

Baker was, he confessed, at a loss to understand why Israel's leaders would look askance at a process based on their own initiative. Was Israel, he queried, serious about its intentions to attain peace, or would it prefer no political momentum? He reflected bitterly that the United States could not aspire to peace with greater yearning than did Israel and that peace could not be imposed coercively on Israel. The absence of a peace process in the region could ultimately have devastating implications: the Arab states might eventually outfit themselves with nuclear arms. It was clear to Baker that there were within Israel recalcitrant elements that opposed peace and that these forces would always find a pretext to respond negatively to constructive proposals.

Raising his voice, the secretary of state declared that the prime minister was surrounded by aides who maneuvered to convince him to renege upon his prior commitments. The sequence of events had led Baker to conclude that these assistants (the oblique reference was mainly to the director general of the prime minister's office, Yossi Ben-Aharon) were the ones fashioning Israel's positions on the political process. Under such circumstances it was hard to maintain relations of trust, and he had to wonder "who in Israel's government was running the show." In private discussions as well, the secretary of state frequently expressed frustration and perplexity concerning the manner by which Israel conducted its diplomatic contacts. He was often astonished during discussions with Shamir to find the prime minister content to say a few sentences and then to allow the remainder of the talk to be led not by ministers who were present but by advisers, Ben-Aharon and Elyakim Rubinstein—who competed with one another to prove who could adopt the most extreme stance and "stand firm." Baker showed contempt for this spectacle, which put him in the position of conducting diplomacy with civil servants, not elected officials. (Foreign Minister Levy, for his part, also recoiled from this behavior. He would complain that with Prime Minister Shamir's endorsement, Ben-Aharon had arrogated to himself the right to articulate positions, oppose others, and reject and propose alternatives, as though the government of Israel lacked spokesmen and authorized decision makers.) Yet, only during this acidic June 13 meeting, did Baker find cause to express dismay at this continuing trait. Due to the deep trust that Baker accorded to Foreign Minister Levy and his staff, he now felt at liberty to excoriate the prime minister's officials, castigating behavior that he could not countenance. These aides were acting to undermine, the secretary of state contended, agreements that had been reached at the highest levels; they would come to Washington to clarify the prime minister's "real intentions," acting at variance with agreements reached beforehand with Shamir, basing their revisions on such flimsy pretexts as the claim that the prime minister's "fluency in English was inadequate."

This outburst was enough to make clear Baker's grave doubts about the desire of the prime minister's circle to advance the peace process. The secretary of state posited that this circle was escalating its efforts to foil the process, and that each time its chances for success rose. Simultaneously, he made a point of telling Levy that he viewed the foreign minister and his camp as possessing a genuine desire to set the peace process in motion, as possessing a perspective of history and an awareness that peace must indeed be the ultimate imperative and the supreme interest of the state of Israel. Positions we presented were, in his eyes, credible, for they took as their common point of origin the need to lay a solid foundation, for the first time in the history of the state of Israel and of the Middle East conflict, for a genuine peace between Israel, the Arab states, and the Palestinians.

In his reply to the secretary of state, Levy affirmed both that only the prime minister, the foreign minister, and the defense minister bore legal authority for the modeling of Israel's positions in the political process, and that these three leaders were indeed keenly interested in the advancement of the peace process. Baker and Levy agreed to continue to deal with the issue of Palestinian representation with the utmost discretion.

Meantime, the issue of European representation at the peace conference also remained unresolved. The Council of Europe released on June 29 a declaration on the peace process in the Middle East, affirming Europe's desire to contribute, as a participant at a peace conference, to the success of the negotiations. The council favored handling the negotiations in a way which would promote recognition of the Palestinians' right to self-rule, regional stability, cessation of the declared state of belligerence between states in the region, and peaceful resolution of disputes. The European declaration did not ignore the settlement issue. The council held that Israel's settlement policy in the conquered territories was illegal and inconsistent with a desire to advance the peace process.

Each year, Israeli foreign ministers review their policies, generally in the context of the Knesset deliberations on the annual budget. Levy's address to the Knesset on July 15, 1991, centered mostly on progress in the political process. For many years, he said, the Palestinian question had been regarded as the heart of the dispute in the Middle East. The Persian Gulf War had altered this perception. Now there was enhanced preparedness abroad to accept Israel's contention that the Palestinian matter ought not to be addressed in a vacuum, severed from a comprehensive solution tying together recognition of Israel, termination of formal belligerence and economic warfare against Israel, and transition to cooperation between Israel and the Arab states.

Levy listed in meticulous detail the principles for progress he had promulgated since the beginning of 1991. This was a peace-process platform, and its logic and details had risen anew out of the ashes of the Gulf war, at the end of February 1991. These principles, he mentioned, had paved the way also for Baker's policy; during his trips to Israel, the secretary of state had been able to forge a series of agreements between the United States and Israel, using the principles as a basis. These developments had ushered in the prospect that a regional conference might be convened with the aim of initiating direct talks between the sides, on the basis of the following assumptions:

- Concurrent progress on the two tracks, peace negotiations both with Arab states and with the residents of the territories; the latter would be represented by a joint, Jordanian-Palestinian delegation.
- Direct negotiations, without preconditions.
- A Palestinian state would not arise as a consequence of these negotiations, nor would it be a subject to be addressed by them.

- The PLO would not take part directly or indirectly in negotiations.
- The Palestinian subject would be addressed in stages.
- Palestinian delegates from the territories would commit themselves to the two-track, two-stage approach and at the same time obligate themselves to peaceful coexistence with Israel.
- The "territory for peace" formula would not be a precondition for the direct negotiation.
- The exclusive objective of the "regional peace conference" would be to promote direct negotiations between the sides; the conference would not be empowered to decide on negotiation issues, would not be a debating forum, and it would not be authorized to function as a court of appeals.
- An agreement was to be reached on the establishment of multilateral committees for regional development projects, with international financing.

With these strokes, the foreign minister painted a portrait of the crystallizing negotiation framework and the principles underlying it, which had been formulated and ironed out in the course of discussions led by secretary of state Baker between Israel and the U.S. government.

Despite the difficulties, he continued, activity in the political context had picked up steam, due both to the determination and impetus provided by the Bush administration generally, Baker in particular, and to America's emergence as the sole superpower as the Soviet Union tottered on the brink of collapse. Seven leading economic powers, assembled together in the group known (then) as the G-7, had released on June 21 a statement calling for a political process whose goal would be to attain a comprehensive, viable peace between Israel and the Palestinians, and Israel and its Arab neighbors. The process, the G-7 announcement stated, had to be based on UN Resolutions 242 and 338, and on the principle of territory for peace. Naturally, the seven states had expressed support for the convening of a peace conference that would launch a two-track political process—that is, direct, simultaneous negotiations between Israeli and Palestinian delegates on the one hand, and Israel and Arab states on the other. The G-7 had called as well for confidence-building measures and for the flexibility required to give such steps meaning. In this context, the G-7 had urged delegates from the Arab states to lift the anti-Israel boycott, whereas it asked Israel to refrain from erecting settlements on conquered lands.

Israel had been hoping that the "land for peace" formula would not crop up as a pillar in the process. It was, therefore, surprised when the G-7 developed nations deployed this phrase in its announcement, after the Council of Europe had avoided it. In his mid-July Knesset address, Foreign Minister Levy emphasized that Israel could not be expected to embrace the principle of territory for peace as a fundamental principle in direct negotiation; nor, certainly, would Israel accept the formula as a precondition for talks. Our assumption was that the G-7 language had been inspired in great measure by the Americans. Indeed, not only the territory-for-peace formula but the equating of the cessation of settlement activity and the lifting of the economic boycott reflected Baker's attitude, as evinced in public comments on May 22, in an appearance before a joint congressional subcommittee.

This convergence of the settlement and the boycott issues was fraught with complications. To many Israelis, the latest twist marked a deviation from, or at least an essential different interpretation of, agreements that had been reached between Israel and the United States on launching the political negotiations.

Baker came to the Middle East yet a sixth time during the middle of July 1991. On the 14th of July he held a joint press conference in Damascus with Syria's foreign minister, Farouk al-Shara. This event marked Syria's inclusion in the political process, establishing that from this stage onward it would be a side in negotiations. Syria displayed willingness to accept the U.S. initiative and take part in a peace process founded on Security Council Resolutions 242 and 338. Baker claimed that all of the parties with whom he had discussed the convening of the conference had assented to common principles. Syria was prepared to concede that the UN delegate to the peace conference come as an observer only; this was a departure from its previous demand that the UN be ranked as a cosponsor of the conference. Baker noted that the United States did not recognize the annexation of the Golan Heights by Israel.

The secretary of state flew to Israel on July 21. As the limousine sped to Jerusalem under heavy police escort, Baker briefed us on his meetings in Damascus. He was delighted by what he regarded as unqualified Syrian agreement to U.S. proposals with respect to a muted UN role at the conference, and to terms stipulating that the reassembling of the conference would be contingent upon the agreement of the sides.

Baker found the formula calling for a passive UN role at the conference particularly alluring. Lobbying to erase Israeli resistance to UN delegate presence at the conference, Baker was wont to emphasize humorously that any such delegate would keep his mouth clamped and merely listen to conference doings. Covering his own mouth with his hand, the secretary of state illustrated the extent to which the UN delegate was to be kept passive, as though he was to see and not be seen.

Such agreements blended tactical and essential matters. An element going beyond tactics, Baker explained, was Syria's agreement to hold direct, face-to-face negotiations with Israel, following the start of the conference. This, the secretary of state insisted, constituted a historic opportunity that had no precedent in Israel's forty-three years of existence. Baker would repeat this estimate in talks he held with Shamir, Levy, and Arens. As we parted from him at Jerusalem's King David Hotel, Baker warned that should this new opportunity be squandered, it was doubtful that it could be revived in the foreseeable future. The secretary of state also disclosed tidings of another positive development. King Hussein had launched contacts with the Palestinians, with the aim of forming a Jordanian-Palestinian delegation. Naturally, this disclosure on Baker's part elicited an Israeli request for clarification: was it clearly understood that such a joint delegation would include only Palestinian representatives from the territories who did not belong to the PLO and who did not purport to represent the organization!? Requests for clarification in this respect were still pending when Baker concluded his visit to Israel and went home.

Ambassador Shoval met with the secretary of state's assistant Dennis Ross on July 24. At the instruction of the prime minister, Shoval brought up points concerning the peace conference that awaited clarification. In particular, Shoval asked for explanations concerning the composition of the Jordanian-Palestinian delegation, insisting that its Palestinian members not be promised a second, final, stage of negotiations with them. Of course, he also wanted to know what was happening with respect to participation by Palestinians from abroad or from East Jerusalem.

Shoval delivered a draft memorandum to Ross asserting that promises provided to third parties by the United States on these issues would not bind Israel. He reiterated Israel's vehement opposition to PLO involvement in any capacity in the process. In presenting these points, Israel was expressing its sensitivity and discomfit stemming from Baker's talks in Israel with Palestinians, including Faisal Abad el-Qadre al-Husseini, a leading Fatah figure in Jerusalem. During his trips to Israel, Baker had by now institutionalized as a ritual such meetings with Palestinians. Israel's ambassador underscored the importance attributed by Israel to the policy of not offering the Palestinians promises concerning East Jerusalem representation. Ross, for his part, stated that the United States opposed the participation of East Jerusalem representatives in the first stage of the negotiations, meaning the interim phase; America, however, would agree to their involvement at the second stage, prior to talks about the final status. Shoval countered that such U.S. acquiescence would not bind Israel.

At this juncture, a need was exposed to find a way to extricate the countries from the situation in which the gap between their positions had placed them. Ross, a virtuoso in the art of compromise, proposed a formula saying that the United States did not exclude outright the future, second-stage participation of representatives of East Jerusalem or of nonresident Palestinians, and that its position did not obligate Israel. Ross also indicated that Baker was not inclined to associate Faisal Husseini with the PLO. The secretary of state, Ross elaborated, did not view Husseini as a PLO delegate; in any case, his dealings with him did not operate on this basis. It was to be understood that Baker's Palestinian discussion partners were at pains to display their links with the PLO, during their contacts with the secretary of state and otherwise, though they refrained from explicitly referring to the organization, employing such euphemisms as "the Palestinian leadership."

Baker visited Israel for a seventh time on the first two days of August 1991. The question of Palestinian representation still remained unsolved, and thus it was a primary topic in his talks with the prime minister and with the foreign and defense ministers. Baker implored them to maintain the maximum discretion in handling this topic, including King Hussein's endeavors to put together a joint delegation. Baker even promised that he would make a great effort to annul UN Resolution 3379, from November 10, 1971, which equated Zionism and racism. Such a move would have intrinsic significance, and it would remove a terrible symbolic stain on the UN's reputation, prior to the arrival of a UN delegate to the peace conference. Baker promised that his country would stifle any Security Council attempt to address a subject wedded to the peace process, or issues discussed in negotiations between the sides.

Levy's efforts to persuade the prime minister and his colleagues to stick to the main issues and fight only for what was imperative rather than squandering energy and, more importantly, credibility on subsidiary, procedural or technical, matters, reaped dividends during this seventh Baker visit. The secretary of state received a positive answer on topics raised in President Bush's June 1 letter to Prime Minister Shamir. That is, Israel agreed to the presence of a UN observer at the conference and to the reconvening of the conference under conditions that had been agreed upon thus far.

Baker held talks with Palestinian representatives at the U.S. consulate general in West Jerusalem on August 2. Presenting him with a document, the Palestinians described it as being delivered on orders from "President" Arafat. The document's contents reiterated previous demands. The first was for representation of East Jerusalem at the conference. Second, the Palestinian delegation had to represent both parts of the Palestinian people, those under the Israeli conquest and those who lived abroad; only such representation would accord with the principle of self-determination. Third, the formation of the Palestinian's own delegation was their own prerogative and should therefore be immune from outside intervention. The Palestinians themselves would elect representatives for their own delegation, and they would announce the names of the elected candidates at an appropriate time.

The secretary of state and his staff urged the Palestinians to act quickly to help with the formation of the joint delegation with Jordan. The Americans urged the Palestinians to abstain from measures and declarations that would provide Israel with a pretext to derail the process and withdraw from it. The Americans agreed that the formation of the delegation represented an exclusive Palestinian right and promised not to relay names of delegate candidates to Israel for advance confirmation; however, the secretary of state stated an obligation to respect the principle by which no side could be compelled to conduct talks with people or delegates unacceptable to it. In this connection, Baker affirmed that his country supported the red lines which had been drawn by Israel pertaining to the noninclusion of PLO or East Jerusalemite delegates. He also signaled to Palestinian delegates that there had been no erosion in the U.S. position regarding the involvement of East Jerusalem delegates throughout the first stage of the negotiations; the American opposition in this regard had prevented the Palestinians from making a positive reply to the U.S. initiative.

The officials on the U.S. peace team met with the Israeli group on August 7 and 8, to polish final details on a memorandum of understanding between Israel and the United States. This document was to include a series of points that Israel had requested as binding American commitments that would buttress the direct negotiations, which were scheduled to start immediately on the heels of what was now referred to as the "Conference for Middle East Peace."

Negotiations for the understandings memo were arduous, with controversies flaring, especially with respect to the prohibition of PLO participation under any guise throughout the process. The American side relied on a constructive evasiveness, judging that the tactic had helped ignite the political process; the Americans were thus loathe to become explicit or adamant in their commitment to the principle of no PLO participation. Special attention was also given to the form of the invitations to be sent by the conference sponsors to the Palestinian delegates, to the phrases used to describe the role to be played by Egypt in the multilateral framework, to the issue of the reassembling of the conference, and to stopping the Security Council from holding discussions in tandem with the negotiations.

On his eighth visit to Israel, on the 16th and 17th of September, 1991, Baker presented a "paper" bearing promises to Israel, as a replacement for the memorandum of understanding. The paper established that the essential purpose of the peace conference would be to generate direct negotiations on two tracks, two days after its opening. The United States emphasized that it's goal was not to compel Israel to engage a dialogue with the PLO. A storm had nonetheless swirled in Israel's government on account of Baker's formulations on this topic; some feared that the secretary of state was biding his time, waiting for a propitious moment to prod Israel into negotiating with the PLO. This fear had been aggravated when it was discovered that the drafters of the U.S. promises paper had ignored the Jordanian-Palestinian delegation and the demand that no PLO East Jerusalemite representatives be part of it. It did not help that the Jordanians and Palestinians had not yet started to consult about this delegation issue.

Three days after he returned to the United States, Baker sent a letter to Shamir. Baker expressed his hope that the good will and trust that had heretofore characterized relations between the two countries would overcome the misunderstandings and disputes that had recently arisen.

In the remainder of his letter, Baker summarized his talks with the Palestinians, President Hosni Mubarak, President Assad, and King Hussein. He had strongly urged the Palestinians to go to Oman for talks with the Jordanians about the establishment of a joint delegation. This would be the last step prior to the summoning of sides for a peace conference and the launching of direct negotiations. Baker reported that he had asked Mubarak not to nurture in the Palestinians a mistaken impression as to what could be expected "at this stage" with respect to the complex issue of Jerusalem. Baker was, in other words, settling down for the last stage before the historic goal of convening a conference to launch peace negotiations.

The last item for resolution on this agenda was the formation of the Palestinian-Jordanian delegation. This body would have to be devoid of any declared PLO members, and the Palestinians would have to be compelled not to demand representation for East Jerusalemites. A compromise "bridge" formulation appeared to be taking shape. This being the case, it was necessary to persuade the relevant parties to act swiftly and persistently to finish the bridge, so that remaining gaps could be crossed on the way to actual negotiations.

Eight days after Baker returned from the Middle East, on September 25, Foreign Minister Levy went to Washington for talks with the secretary of state. The discussion did not lack tense, angry moments; and Baker, as noted earlier, was not shy about raising his voice if the discussion took a turn not to his liking. Levy asked that the United States refrain from publicly reaffirming its commitment to the principle of territory for peace and from offering elastic interpretations of Security Council Resolution 242 by which it became applicable to all disputed areas. Should U.S. leaders articulate such positions in public, the Arab states would interpret the statements as American commitments relevant to the anticipated negotiations; this would, of course, be to Israel's detriment, right from the onset of bilateral talks. Levy hinted that such honing of positions on America's part would further aggravate relations between Israel and the United States. I recall one especially trying moment in this discussion, when a livid secretary of state declared that should the government of Israel not be prepared to come to the peace conference, then it need not. This was a transparent hint that the joint U.S.-Israel peace efforts, which had been undertaken by that time for years, had reached a critical, meltdown level, with the abyss a short distance away.

The secretary of state argued that differences of interpretation concerning UN Resolution 242 were nothing new. The United States was not going to alter its old positions. On the other hand, Baker promised Levy that the United States was not going to adopt a position that would predefine the results of the process or declare a substantive interpretation regarding UN Resolution 242. Baker reiterated yet again both that his country was promoting Israel's own peace initiative (meaning that it supported the two-stage process) and that America opposed the establishment of an independent Palestinian state, as Bush had declared since his accession to the Oval Office.

At this stage the Palestinian responses still had yet to come. Baker was waiting for Palestinians to depart for Oman for talks about the establishment of a joint delegation that would include Palestinians from the territories. Levy, cautious as ever, reminded the secretary of state that Israel expected to receive in advance the names of members of the Palestinian delegation, prior to their being issued invitations.

In this period, cloudbursts impaired relations between the two countries, on account of the U.S. linkage on the loan-guarantee issue. The view harbored by the prime minister and his advisers was that Washington was trying to use loan guarantees, which Israel so badly needed to manage the absorption of masses of immigrants from the Soviet Union, as leverage to wrest changes in Israel's policies. Talks—more precisely, the lack of quiet, practical negotiations on the guarantees matter conducted dispassionately by trained professionals—increasingly strained relations between the two countries.

The low ebb in this conflict occurred on September 13, when Bush issued some controversial pronouncements. He appeared on television, pounded his fist on the podium, and exclaimed that Israel's obstinacy on the guarantees issue constituted a threat not only to the impending conference but to peace as a whole. In responding, Prime Minister Shamir was perhaps insufficiently respectful to the president of the superpower, a country that also happened to be Israel's most committed friend in the world. Officials on the U.S. peace team, led by Dennis Ross, sensed that an ill wind was blowing; they recommended to their superiors that steps be taken to deflate tensions. They maintained that circumstances warranted new assurances to Israel regarding the American commitment to the "special relations" between the two nations. Should these renewed pledges not come, Israel's feeling of isolation and betrayal would reduce its ability to mount the dual-negotiations track after the peace conference. The perception of the United States as a just mediator had become entangled in the thicket of tensions; that perception occluded, the normal relations between the countries was impaired. Caught in a dispute with Israel, the United States could hardly call itself a fair mediator. The U.S. officials reasoned that Israel needed to hear its ally affirm that the special relations between the two countries remained.

On September 30 Ambassador Shoval met with Ross and his associates. The officials reviewed the draft of the understandings memorandum from September 26; this was the document that Israel had been hoping to sign with the United States, as such agreement was a norm prior to the undertaking of a far-reaching political initiative. Following this meeting, the U.S. government submitted on October 3, 1991, a revised version of the document. At the start of October, it could be inferred that Baker's intention was to convene the peace conference toward the end of the month; so, after the late September meeting Ambassador Shoval discussed possible venues for the conference. Israel articulated a desire to hold the conference, and certainly the direct negotiations in its aftermath, in its part of the world. The principle was satisfactory to the United States, but the Americans warned that it was unlikely that such a wish would be fulfilled during the early stages of the negotiations.

At this stage, Israel was asked to embrace the following understandings prior to their ultimate polishing and formulation:

- Israel understood that each side would be entitled to deliver opening remarks at the conference, and that this condition applied to the Palestinian component of the joint Palestinian-Jordanian delegation.

- Israel would not have a veto over the composition of the Palestinian delegation. Concurrently, Israel would not be obligated to sit at the negotiation table with any participant not acceptable to it.

- Israel would not act to prevent the Palestinian delegates on the Jordanian-Palestinian body from exercising their right of free speech and assembly throughout the negotiation period.

- Israel understood that the process was conducive to the recognition of the legitimate rights of the Palestinian people.

- Israel was aware of the U.S. intention to maintain its positions relating to the Israeli-Arab peace process and to express them when it considered appropriate.

- Israel intended to present its own interpretation of Security Council Resolution 242, and it understood that the sides, including the United States, were entitled to present their own positions.

- Israel understood that the United States could not make guarantees as to the contents of the Palestinians' positions before, during or after the peace conference and the negotiations. On the other hand, the United States would make an earnest effort to encourage all sides to act responsibly and in a manner not detrimental to the process.

In parallel, the United States proposed to Israel a set of understandings designed to allay worries troubling officials in Jerusalem:

- The United States did not support the establishment of an independent Palestinian state, though it did not favor either the annexation of the West Bank and Gaza or permanent Israeli control of these territories.
- It was not the U.S. goal to bring the PLO into the process or to goad Israel into a dialogue, or negotiations, with the PLO.
- The United States believed that the Palestinians should be represented at the conference in the framework of the joint Palestinian-Jordanian delegation. Palestinians serving on it would be residents of the West Bank and Gaza who accepted the concept of two-track, multiple-stage negotiations and were committed to living peacefully with Israel and to discussing transitional arrangements with it.

Members of the U.S. peace team believed that these understandings encapsulated fully the strenuous efforts made by Secretary of State Baker, who had done his very utmost to respect Israel's positions and to take into account Israel's concerns articulated in the various documents submitted by its representatives. Ross wondered what better served Israel's interest, a letter of promises or an understandings memo. In his view, such a memorandum would cause the Arabs to demand similar documents. Meantime, Ross relayed Baker's intention to summon the conference at the end of the month, so as not to forfeit momentum that had picked up. In order to complete preparations for the conference, swift decisions had to be reached forthwith. Ross reported that talks in Jordan between the Jordanians and the Palestinians had yet to produce an agreement. Meantime, Shoval passed along to Ross Shamir's criticisms of a few of the obligations that the United States demanded that Israel incur, for example, the denial of a veto concerning the Palestinian delegation. Shoval reported to Jerusalem that the United States government was willing to entertain only superficial revisions in this connection, arguing that time was of the essence.

The deputy chief of mission in Israel's embassy in Washington, Michael Shiloh, and another embassy official, Shimon Stein, met on October 11 with U.S. peace team officials Daniel Kurtzer and Aaron Miller. Baker was preparing for his ninth visit to the region, and the Israeli diplomats were ordered to make clear that the peace conference was contingent upon a satisfactory solution to the issue of Palestinian representation.

Levy and I instructed the embassy in Washington that the issue had to be clarified before invitations were issued, lest unresolved issues becloud the process and disrupt further steps. Kurtzer and Miller concurred that the Palestinian representation issue was indeed a vital element in the process, even if their country lacked definitive influence concerning it. Israel declared to the United States that it would prefer the letter of promises to an understandings memorandum; drafts had been polished in exchanges between the American peace team (Ross, Kurtzer, Miller, and others) and Israeli officials (Ben-Aharon, Rubinstein, myself, and others).

Israeli policy on the question of Palestinian representation was guided by several principles. Negotiation delegates must not formally represent the PLO, which Israel regarded as a terror organization whose basic article of faith was the annihilation of Israel. Formal links between the Palestinian delegation and the PLO were defined by Israel's government as utterly antithetical to the negotiations, which were to be anchored on the concept of Palestinian credibility. The lack of a formal link made it necessary to monitor public statements concerning the PLO. The chances of precluding such a PLO connection had grown; an "independent" Palestinian ethos was growing in the territories. The intifada had nurtured new Palestinian attitudes and had given rise to a leadership that viewed itself as representing the population in the territories, not as proxies of the exiled PLO heads.

Israeli policy sought to widen the gap between the population in the territories and the PLO abroad (in Tunisia). The chairman of the Palestinian delegation, Haidar Abd el-Shafi, told me much later that the Tunisian leadership indeed feared that as negotiations progressed, its status and influence in the territories would decline. Operating in the background, the PLO wanted to mitigate as much as possible this policy of forestalling links binding the Palestinian delegation to it; the organization did its utmost to leave its imprint on the delegation and its members. A kind of inverse dynamic had evolved: Israel endeavored intensively to prevent the forging of any formal link between the Palestinian delegation and the PLO; hiding behind a smoke screen, the PLO scrambled to influence, get involved in, and carve out for itself a role in future negotiations.

One thing was certain, and it was destined to accompany the negotiations in the future. The PLO transmitted innumerable signals, requests, imprecations, and appeals, but the decision as to its fate remained in Israel's hands. Any Israeli government, led by the Labor Party or the Likud, had the option of responding affirmatively to the PLO request to be involved. After talks had started, one night an anonymous mediator proposed to me in Washington that I meet with a PLO delegate so as to create an informal pipeline that could have utility with respect to the advance of the talks and to the overcoming of difficulties and obstacles farther down the road. I reported this secret request to the chairman of Israel's delegation on the Palestinian subject, Elyakim Rubinstein. An order immediately came down from Prime Minister Shamir to let this appeal go unheeded. The incident illustrates how willing and prepared at all phases the PLO was to get involved in the process.

It remained for another Israeli government to draw new conclusions on the basis of these circumstances. First and foremost, the Oslo process was to gain its historic importance due to the decision reached by Israel's government to assent to PLO entreaties and speak with the organization before it had shed the Palestinian covenant, with its clauses calling for the destruction of Israel.

The American government continued to hold talks in Washington with Palestinian leaders from the territories, Ms. Hanan Ashrawi and Faisal al-Husseini. Israel's embassy reported that the U.S. government was acting diligently to ensure that no member of the Palestinian-Jordanian delegation possessed identity documentation based in Jerusalem. Due to this principle of East Jerusalemite exclusion, one that the Likud government upheld steadfastly, Ashrawi and Husseini were subsequently disqualified from the Palestinian delegation. (Ashrawi's noninclusion did not keep her in the future from emerging as the most articulate spokesperson for the Palestinian cause, working with evident skill to cause the Palestinian positions to echo around the world.) While Palestinians with official Jerusalem residences were barred from the delegation, the Americans told Palestinian discussion partners that it condoned the inclusion of Palestinians who lived abroad. The Palestinians were happy to hear the Americans reiterate for the umpteenth time that their government did not recognize Israel's annexation of East Jerusalem or the enlargement of Jerusalem's municipal jurisdiction.

When the Madrid conference was convened, the head of the Palestinian component of the joint delegation with Jordan was Haidar Abd el-Shafi. Shafi, from the Gaza Strip, a medical doctor by profession, made from the start a strong impression; I viewed him as a man of ideological conviction, a genuine leader. Shafi kept a dignified demeanor and projected credibility. Following the Oslo agreement, we met for a friendly talk at a hotel in East Jerusalem, and he told me that the Oslo accord had caught him by surprise, and also had mildly disappointed him. He had believed during the Palestinian delegation's talks with Israel in Washington that followed the Madrid conference that we would be able to attain a still more far-reaching agreement. To a great degree, it was "the leadership" that had obstructed this—Shafi's allusion was to the top PLO echelon in Tunisia, which, he believed, had in the end been satisfied with less than it might have obtained on the "Washington" track. Shafi affirmed that he believed in the political process with all his heart; in his view, the basis for the Israeli-Palestinian discussion derived from the PLO's declaration in 1988, which called for mutual recognition and the establishment of two states alongside one another, Israel and Palestine.

Shafi spoke with this critical edge, despite his status as one of the PLO's founders—in fact, there are those who maintain before he withdrew from political activity and returned to his vocation as a doctor, Shafi was the PLO's patriarch, leading the organization when it emerged as a national Palestinian entity. Shafi related that he had taken part in only one meeting with Secretary of State Baker with whom he had upheld his principal contention that the settlements were the real obstacle to peace. Baker, he recalled, had accepted this analysis. Looking back, Shafi reflected that for as long as he had served as the head of the Palestinian delegation, he had tried to bring about much more active U.S. involvement in the negotiation process launched at Madrid.

Dr. Shafi was a figure who stirred respect; he in fact received it from me, and from the Israeli delegation as a whole. Subsequently it was claimed that he had been selected chairman of the Palestinian delegation due to his status in the territories, and because the opposition to the process there was strong; it was assumed that he could rally support more effectively than any other candidate. Shafi believed that the two-track political process indeed had a chance of leading to historic compromise, one with the potential to secure goals of dialogue, coexistence, and peaceful relations.

Shamir opened the winter session of Israel's Knesset on October 7, 1991, with a political announcement. In so doing, he tried to counteract the impression that might have been gained by Arab leaders concerning the American involvement in the process. Shamir denied that such U.S. participation would entail pressure being exerted against Israel. Any impression to the contrary was mistaken, Shamir contended. He then addressed entanglements that had complicated Israeli-American relations at the time—disputes and collisions that I myself and Foreign Minister Levy believed could have been reduced in magnitude, eased, or even prevented had a correct measure of prudence been exercised. Shamir argued that only direct negotiations could reap dividends.

The United States, the Israeli prime minister explained, was to play the part of an "honest broker," or fair mediator. This meant that the Arab states had no cause to count on America imposing pressure on Israel. After calling for the convening of the peace conference in Madrid, Secretary of State Baker would provide the sides with ample opportunity and space for action and discussion, so that the process might move forward without his intervening. Baker would be the one who laid the foundations for a two-track peace process, solidified its mechanisms, determined its procedures, helped with the logistics, and tied together loose ends; yet, as the secretary of state himself promised, he would leave the actual work to the parties themselves.

In his Knesset speech, the prime minister reviewed both the details of the negotiations conducted up to then with the United States and preparations undertaken for an international peace conference.

- It was agreed that after the formal issuing of invitations to the peace conference, direct bilateral talks would start, their aim being to attain peace agreements.
- The talks with the Jordanian-Palestinian delegation (which would include on the Palestinian side only persons from the territories) would be focused on interim agreements, this being consistent with the stipulations of the Camp David agreements. Israel would not negotiate with PLO representatives or with anyone from the territories who purported to represent the PLO.
- Israel would take part in multilateral talks designed to tackle regional issues.
- The peace conference would be concluded after the opening declarations. No powers would be given to it. Israel did not see any need for a future reconvening of the peace conference, as issues that were not resolved in the framework of bilateral talks could not be resolved in a multiparticipant conference.
- Should the Arab side place territorial issues at the focal point of the negotiations, Israel would conclude that the Arab declared interest in peace was doubtful.

- Discussion about an autonomy proposal should ensue, in accord with the Camp David agreements.
- The Golan Heights, on which Israeli law, authority, and administration had been in effect since December 14, 1981, constituted a crucial component of the defense of the state of Israel.
- United Jerusalem, the capital of Israel, would not be put on the agenda of peace negotiations.
- Israel's position negating the principle of "land for peace" had a firm basis.
- The operative clauses of the Security Council Resolutions 242 and 338 essentially called for negotiations to attain a just, viable peace. The remaining clauses were instructions, nothing more.

The secretary of state visited Israel again on October 16. As in the case of his eight previous shuttle visits, Foreign Minister Levy and I traveled with him to Jerusalem, buoyed this time by the sense that the genesis of the peace process was visible on the horizon. Baker had visited some Arab states before coming to Jerusalem. On the 14th of October he had held a joint press conference with Egypt's President Mubarak. Journalists had prodded the secretary of state, trying to ascertain whether "territory for peace" represented an apposite interpretation of Resolution 242. Banking on the peace conference being just around the corner, Baker had chosen to bypass this particular question. It had sufficed for him to review the various interpretations furnished by the various sides on this UN resolution issue. He had cited explicitly in this press conference that he, and the United States as a whole, viewed the settlements as obstacles to peace.

Two days later, just a few hours before his meeting with Levy, Baker had held a press conference with King Hussein in Amman. He had stressed the U.S. position holding that the Palestinian delegation must comprise "Palestinians from the territories" whose involvement adhered to terms worked out up to then: the gradual, two-stage approach, and willingness to live at peace with Israel. The United States, Baker added, was not conducting negotiations with the PLO, and it did not intend to compel Israel to undertake such talks.

During his official meeting with Baker and his staff, Levy expressed regret about the sequence of events that had impaired Israel–United States relations and damaged the mutual trust that had obtained, and had to exist, between the two countries. Baker emphasized again that America's commitment to Israel's security was rock solid and immutable.

The United States would never infringe this obligation or undermine Israel's security. The secretary of state accepted our plea that immediate action be taken to improve the atmosphere in relations. His country would act, Baker promised, to apply the criteria agreed upon by the United States and Israel concerning the composition of the Palestinian delegation. Baker informed us as well of Syria's refusal to take part in the multilateral negotiations. He hinted that some sort of compensation should be provided to King Hussein for his positive contribution to the peace process.

Baker and his aides conferred on October 18 with the prime minister and the foreign and defense ministers; Ben-Aharon, Rubinstein, and I also attended this talk. The discussion centered this time on Israel's request that future bilateral talks be held in the Middle East, so as to stop the Arab countries from dodging direct negotiations. Conscious of problems likely to arise in this connection, Baker replied that the first two meetings ought to be held outside of the region but that later he would act to bring the talks to the Middle East.

The secretary of state advised his hosts to let this topic rest at least for the time being, so as not create a pretext for waylaying a promising peace process. In his view, should Israel insist that the region be the venue for talks planned after the opening conference, the Arabs would abstain from attending the peace conference. While a dispute was brewing between the sides concerning the location of the negotiations, Baker said, he could not see any reason why an additional meeting outside of the region ought to be an obstacle. In such instances, Baker would hint that we should avoid getting obstinately mired in procedural matters, so as not to cast Israel in the negative role of objecting to the peace conference and to the process that would come in its wake.

The Israeli ministers replied to Baker that their request to hold the bilateral meetings in the region was based logically on an estimate that should they be held abroad, Israel's delegations would be unable to maintain daily, continuous communication with superiors in Jerusalem. Lurking behind this claim hid suspicion harbored by some of the prime minister's aides, a concern I did not share—they suspected that the Arab side favored the holding of the talks at a remote site so that the host country might exert pressure on Israel. For some reason, Israeli purveyors of this argument failed to consider that it applied in equal measure to the Arab delegations.

Baker disclosed in his meeting with the prime minister that he had received from the Palestinians the names of seven delegates who matched the agreed-upon criteria: no to the PLO, no to East Jerusalemites, no to overseas Palestinians. Shamir, suspicious as ever, expressed his hope that the Jordanians would not "thrust a surprise upon us, by appointing people from East Jerusalem to serve on the Jordanian component of the delegation." Baker replied that in his opinion Jordan had the option of appointing a Jordanian citizen who lived abroad, even if he had links with East Jerusalem.

That day, October 18, Baker affirmed in writing to Shamir that he had in his possession the names of those seven Palestinians and that he expected shortly to obtain a list of another seven names. Baker added that on the same day he and the Soviet foreign minister, Boris Pankin, were to issue invitations to the peace conference, which would in turn generate direct bilateral talks between Israel and its neighbors. The secretary of state declared emphatically in this letter that should the Palestinians not respond to his requests by the dates he had spelled out, the onus for the deferral of the process would rest upon them.

A few hours later, Baker and Pankin held a joint press conference in Jerusalem. In an opening statement, Baker stressed that for the first time in history, an American secretary of state and a Soviet foreign minister were standing together in Jerusalem. That very morning, Baker reported, the Soviet Union had restored diplomatic relations with Israel. With this achievement, a sustained diplomatic effort undertaken by the government of Israel and the Foreign Ministry, with stimulus provided by Baker, had reached a peak; the U.S. secretary of state had capitalized astutely on the unprecedented special status that his country had attained following the Persian Gulf War. Baker's second disclosure: President Bush and President Mikhail Gorbachev were inviting Israel, the Arab states, and the Palestinians to a Middle East peace conference, to be held on October 30 in Madrid. During Baker's ninth visit to the country, substantive preparations for the conference had been launched, and the United States had taken responsibility for bearing most of the costs, along with Spain.

At the conclusion of his statement, Baker declared that following the conference, direct negotiations would ensue, their aim being to effect a substantive peace. Pankin said in his own announcement that the renewal of diplomatic relations between the Soviet Union and Israel had been made possible by the significant accomplishment represented by the setting of a date for the convening of the peace conference.

The United States, said Baker in reply to questions posed by journalists, had never demanded that Israel freeze its settlement activity as a confidence-building measure in exchange for a thaw in the Arab economic boycott. Such an equation had indeed been broached, and the G-7 industrially developed nations had issued a statement along these lines, but the resolution had been unacceptable to the government of Israel. On the other hand, he remarked that the United States viewed the settlements as obstacles to peace. On another matter, Baker commented that it would have been best had the intifada been suspended for some indefinite time, as a confidence-building measure.

Invitations to the peace conference, signed by Baker and Pankin, were sent to the sides on October 18. In the invitation's preface, the two explained that their countries believed that a historic opportunity was at hand to advance the prospects of a genuine peace in the region. As sponsors, the United States and the Soviet Union were prepared to help the sides secure a just, comprehensive, and viable peace based on Security Council Resolutions 242 and 338, via direct, two-track negotiations involving Israel, the Palestinians, and the Arab states. In light of this opportunity, the presidents of the United States and the Soviet Union were inviting the sides to the peace conference. The sides were asked to inform President Bush and President Gorbachev by 6:00 P.M. of their acceptance of the invitation, so as to leave time for the conference to be adequately organized.

The invitation scheduled the opening of direct negotiations four days after the conference, and the start of multilateral talks two weeks after. Multilateral talks were to pivot around topics of regional import, such as arms control, security, water, refugees, environment, economic development. The sponsors stressed that the conference would not have authority to impose solutions or to veto any agreements reached between sides. The conference could be reconvened only with the consent of all the participants.

Negotiations with the Palestinians, who would take part as members of a joint delegation with Jordanians, were to be conducted in stages, starting with discussion about an interim stage featuring self-rule; the sponsors alluded to hopes of reaching an interim accord within a year. Interim arrangements for self-rule, to be detailed in an agreement, would be in effect for five years. At the start of the third year in this period, negotiations for a final-status accord would start. Such negotiations would be founded on Resolutions 242 and 338.

At the conclusion of the invitation, the sponsors expressed their belief that the process would bring to an end decades of dispute, conflict, and strife, ushering in a viable peace. To this end, the sponsors hoped that the sides would bring to the negotiations a spirit of good will and mutual respect. Only with such spirit could the process eradicate mutual suspicions that had been perpetuated by the dispute and enable the sides to start to resolve their differences. Only on the basis of such an ameliorating process could true peace and reconciliation between Israel, the Arab states, and the Palestinians be obtained, and the peoples of the Middle East enjoy the peace and security they so clearly deserved.

This was a hectic, event-filled day. The United States delivered to Israel the security-promises letter (by another name, the understandings memorandum) that had been formulated to remove fears. Studying it, Israel could enter on its side of the ledger several achievements.

The letter stressed that the conference's aim was to bring about bilateral and multilateral negotiations. Honing its position, the United States declared that the purpose of the process was to attain peace treaties. The fact that there was no one, unequivocal interpretation of Resolution 242 was stressed, as was Israel's right to refuse to talk with elements not acceptable to it, at any stage of the political process, not simply for the duration of the conference. The particular form of Palestinian representation, which needed Israel's confirmation, was not limited exclusively to the conference. The meaning of the term "conquered territories" was circumscribed. Final-status negotiations would start during the third year—after, not before, the establishment of interim procedures.

The security assurances letter affirmed that the United States continued to abide by the promise delivered by President Gerald Ford to Prime Minister Yitzhak Rabin concerning the Golan Heights. In a letter sent on September 1, 1975, during Rabin's first term as prime minister, the U.S. president had pledged to support a position by which a comprehensive agreement with Syria forged in the context of a peace accord had to guarantee that Israel would be secure from attacks launched from the Golan Heights. When America's final outlook on the boundaries issue eventually crystallized, Ford wrote, considerable deference would be given to Israel's position that any peace agreement had to be based on its remaining on the Golan Heights. The United States would be prepared to propose a guarantee for border security arrangements, to be worked out in an agreement between Israel and Syria, "contingent upon our constitutional processes."

Referring to Israel's northern border with Lebanon, the security-assurances letter reiterated U.S. support for the withdrawal of all non-

Lebanese troops (meaning the Syrians) from Lebanon and the disarming of the militias.

This combination of an invitation to a peace conference issued by the world's superpowers, supplemented by the security assurances letter, sufficed for Israel, providing it with an adequate basis for joining the Madrid peace conference, en route to a historic peace process.

Baker had promised in his talks in Jerusalem that any assurances letter provided by Washington would not be classified but would be available for scrutiny by the other side. Each side would be able to study any American assurances document furnished to the other side. In actual fact, this promise was not fulfilled, and each side was forced to speculate about assurances furnished to the other by the United States. It was clear, in any case, that Baker would utilize his fullest diplomatic skills and maneuvering agility in the assurances letters, attempting to bring widely divergent views and outlooks under one rooftop. Since Baker chose not to provide copies of assurances letters to outside concerned parties, Israel could learn the contents of an October 18 assurances letter given by America to the Palestinians (the same day Israel received its letter) only from a report in the English-language *Jerusalem Post*. Some clauses in the letter to the Palestinians were virtually identical to ones in the document Israel had received. Other sections, however, were in response to particular Palestinian needs, and it was doubtful whether these supplements adhered entirely to the Israeli-American understanding. Among other things, the letter to the Palestinians stated:

- The United States believed that the Israeli conquest had to be brought to an end and that this could occur solely through authentic, meaningful negotiations. Palestinians needed to gain control of political, economic, and other spheres that shaped their fates.

- The United States did not seek to determine who was to speak for the Palestinians in the peace process and who should propose ways to secure for them legitimate political rights and involvement in the forging of their own future.

- Only the Palestinians could choose members of their delegation, and these delegates could not be vulnerable to a veto leveled by any outside party. The United States understood that these delegates would be Palestinians from the territories who had assented to agreed-upon criteria.

- The United States recognized neither the annexation of East Jerusalem by Israel nor the enlargement of the Jerusalem municipality.
- The U.S. position was that a Palestinian resident in Jordan who had connection with a known Jerusalem family would be eligible for appointment on the Jordanian part of the joint delegation. Moreover, Palestinians in East Jerusalem should be allowed to vote in elections for the self-rule authority that would serve during the interim period. East Jerusalemites, along with delegates representing Palestinians from abroad, who matched the three criteria would be entitled to take part in the final-status negotiations.
- On this particular representation issue, the United States would honor any result reached during talks between the sides.
- Taking into account the established American position, the possibility of the negotiations leading to the establishment of a (Jordanian-Palestinian) confederation was not to be ruled out.
- The United States had consistently believed that neither side should take unilateral steps designed to settle in advance issues whose resolution had to be reached via negotiation.
- The United States had opposed, and would continue to oppose, settlement activity in the territories that represented an impediment to peace.

Naturally, the assurances letter to the Palestinians stirred consternation and perplexity in Israel. Studied carefully, the document could be seen as holding open the possibility of a Palestinian state as a result of final-status negotiations. Nor did it rule out PLO participation in the process. Similarly, the treatment of other issues—settlements, East Jerusalem, Palestinian identity, and more—prompted criticism and left question marks at a time when Israel had become reconciled to the process and to the conclusion that there was no way to back out of it.

Levy announced in the Knesset on October 22 that Israel had accepted the invitation to take part in the Madrid conference, the issue of Palestinian representation having been resolved to its satisfaction. The government of Israel viewed the noninclusion of PLO delegates (people committed to the Palestinian covenant) and of East Jerusalemites as tangible achievements, fostering Israel's ability to take part in the conference. Foreign Minister Levy referred to the Golan Heights issue, saying that in his September 1975 letter to then–Prime Minister Rabin, President Ford had affirmed that ample regard would be given to Israel's position, according to which a peace arrangement with Syria would be based on Israel's remaining on the Golan. Levy also noted that America's letter of assurances to Israel had not alluded to Jerusalem, settlements policy, or the formula of "territory for peace." The omission of these elements had, of course, encouraged Israel to decide in favor of participation in the Madrid peace conference.

Real preparations in Israel for the Madrid conference started in May–June 1991. Shamir and Levy agreed to establish a team to position papers, collate data and precedents, and prepare Israel's delegation for the political negotiation. The prime minister's representatives on this team were the director general of his office, Yossi Ben-Aharon, and his assistant, Nadav Anar; the cabinet secretary, Elyakim Rubinstein; and Arieh Zohar. As his delegates, the foreign minister appointed David Aphek, (the head of the Institute for Political Research) and myself. The team was in constant contact with Sali Meridor, the director general of the defense minister's office. We members of this staff were animated by a sense that the peace conference was a historic opportunity.

Intensive preparations for negotiations ensued directed by the foreign ministry. Israel's foreign ministry had served as the real partner of the true catalyst of this moment fraught with historic expectation, Secretary of State Baker. This was a chance to convert the recent geostrategic transformations into a fulcrum for historic progress in the Middle East. We were on the brink of a moment unprecedented in the annals of the Middle East. Hawkish elements had relented and heeded the historic imperative of dialogue and a genuine search for peaceful coexistence.

Nonetheless, the closer we came to the opening of the conference, and the harder it became to deny that a real regional transformation might be in the offing, the more cantankerous and divisive Israel's internal political scene became. Rumors, and then confirmation, reached the foreign ministry that at the initiative of his aides, Shamir had decided to head the delegation for talks himself, though the Arab delegations were to be headed by foreign ministers. Foreign Minister Levy received these tidings with bittersweet emotion, a medley of pain and pride. I was in the foreign minister's office when the prime minister phoned him to announce his decision and invite Levy to join him. The foreign minister wished Shamir success but, of course, rejected the invitation to accompany him to Madrid—the way to which had been paved in great measure by Levy himself.

Two days before, Shamir had appointed members of the Israeli delegation to the Madrid conference. The delegation was to comprise politicians and government workers. The prime minister invited the foreign ministry's director general Yossi Hadas and myself to serve. I asked Levy for his opinion, and he replied that it went without saying that Hadas and myself should be included. Departing for Madrid on the special plane for members of the delegation, along with assorted spokespeople and advisers, my heart was filled with pride, hope, and satisfaction, along with some regret. The sadness stemmed from the slight to Foreign Minister Levy, whose deserved place at the head of the delegation had been denied due to a complex vortex of considerations, mainly political, party calculations. Taking the initiative, I appealed to the U.S. ambassador in Israel, Brown, and to Secretary of State Baker that President Bush allude in his remarks at the conference to Levy and the important contribution he had made to the initiation of the political process. Israel's foreign minister indeed received, and well deserved, such mention.

4

Madrid

The Middle East Peace Conference was held in Madrid, in the Real Palace, the majestic residence of the Spanish royalty. The delegations positioned themselves in a rectangle, facing the conference presidency, which was embodied by the event's sponsors, the United States and the USSR. Despite the presence of Presidents Bush and Gorbachev, it was clear to everyone that the central figure was James Baker looming behind the scenes. The secretary of state was the figure primarily responsible for the realization of the conference idea. The event opened on October 30, 1991.

President Bush delivered the opening address. He raised several important points that were to serve as guidelines for future negotiation:

- The negotiations were not designed merely to transform a situation of belligerence to one of nonbelligerence, but rather to seek a genuine, comprehensive peace, including peace agreements, diplomatic, economic and cultural relations, and also investments and tourism.
- Peace would be attained only on the basis of direct negotiations, founded on give and take, and compromise. No peace was to be imposed from the outside: it had to come from among the concerned parties themselves.
- The envisioned process involved direct negotiations on two tracks.

- Following the start of bilateral talks, multilateral negotiations would ensue as well, dealing with regional issues. Progress on the multilateral track would not be intended to substitute for bilateral talks but to assist them.

- The negotiations with the Palestinians would aim to provide the Palestinian people with a significant share of control over their lives and fates. Results would, at the same time, provide for the security and recognition of Israel. It was imperative to attain compromises on interim agreements, yet these would not predetermine the terms or results of final-status negotiations; the final-status decisions were to be taken on the basis of data and terms that arose during final-status talks.

- Peace was to be founded on fairness; without justice, stability could not be achieved; Israel now had the opportunity to demonstrate its desire for a new set of relations with its Palestinian neighbors, on the basis of mutual respect and cooperation.

- The United States refrained from characterizing a stable, tenable arrangement in the Middle East; similarly, it refrained from specifying final borders. Yet it held that territorial compromise was crucial for peace. The borders had to serve as expressions of security and just political arrangements; the United States was prepared to accept any solution reached by the sides.

- The United States called on the sides to refrain from unilateral acts, in word or in deed, that could inflame tensions, cause reprisals, or still worse, harm or threaten the process itself.

Hans van den Broek, the Dutch foreign minister and acting president (in rotation) of the Council of Ministers of the European Community, took part as the European observer, a role much discussed up to then between Israel and the United States. He raised a number of points in his speech, one was that the twelve members of the European Community attributed considerable importance to the commitment made by the sides to ensure that direct, two-track negotiations, based on Security Council Resolutions 242 and 338, were to be buttressed by multilateral talks devoted to possible regional cooperation in spheres of common interest. Also, he declared the principles guiding the European community had not been altered. These were "territory for peace," a formula inherent in the desire of all states in the region, including Israel, to live in the framework of recognized, safe borders; and the right of self-determination of the Palestinian people, with Israel obligated to submit to the directives of the fourth Geneva Convention (which addresses behavior in occupied areas). A third EC principle was adoption, as soon as possible, of confidence-building measures that would significantly help create an atmosphere conducive to stability—such a climate being crucial to progress in the negotiations. Israel should cease and desist from settlement activity in the conquered territories. Also, the Arab states should end the anti-Israel boycott. Finally, he urged, a new Middle East should be created, one in which countries would live side by side in peace, their legitimate security needs attended to. In such a new Middle East, the peoples would fashion their own futures, especially the Palestinians, who were the principal victims of the Israeli-Arab conflict.

Israel's delegation stayed composed while listening to President Bush's address, but it found Van den Broek's remarks insufferable. Indeed, during an interval after the speeches, it was claimed within the hearing of Prime Minister Shamir and others that the Dutch foreign minister had exceeded his authority. His address deviated from the parameters that had been agreed upon in advance negotiation concerning European participation in the peace conference.

The conference's first day culminated with a speech by Egypt's foreign minister, Amre Moussa, who expressed the general, well-known, Arab position concerning questions fundamental to the dispute.

Special attention should be given to the position held by the Soviet Union before and during the Madrid peace conference. This was a different Soviet Union, led by President Mikhail Gorbachev; it articulated an enlightened liberalism, even as it was taxed increasingly by the endeavor to hold the reigns of power at home. I had wondered during the Soviet foreign minister's visits to Israel whether this respectable contingent leading the Soviet Union really represented the major transformations that were then transpiring in that large, federated country. Without qualification, this leadership accepted Baker's premier role in the political process, and it harnessed itself to the historic turning point represented by the Madrid Conference. Apparently, the stages of normalization endorsed by the Soviet Union in relations with Israel were facilitated and accelerated by the general circumstances, and in particular by Baker's dealings with the Soviets. Here too Baker was crucial, though in making this judgment I do not mean to belittle the direct diplomatic efforts of Israel and its able delegate in Moscow, Arieh Levin—who went to the Soviet Union without any specific post and rode the tide of circumstances in a new era, becoming Israel's consul general there and later its first ambassador.

In their speeches to the conference, President Gorbachev and his colleagues stressed that forging peace had been made possible by the end of the Cold War and by the cooperation and coordination between the two superpowers, who would continue to provide advice and sponsorship, in a noncoercive fashion, with the goal of producing peace treaties.

They held that Security Council Resolution 242 applied to all of the territories. In addition, Gorbachev and his comrades stipulated that:

- The Palestinian right to self-determination was anchored in the UN Charter. Its fulfillment was contingent upon negotiations between the sides, based on a balance of interests; in the Soviet Union's view, such conflict resolution entailed the return of territories to the Arabs, in exchange for security for Israel.
- The Soviet Union maintained that the Israeli-Arab conflict was to be resolved in stages.
- Jerusalem, an extremely sensitive and complicated issue, would be best addressed at the final stage of talks.
- The cessation of settlements would be regarded by the Arabs as a positive gesture, and it would stir a favorable response from them.
- The Soviet Union accorded great significance to the multilateral negotiations slated to deal with such topics as arms control, regional cooperation, and the termination of terror.

No doubt, the "new" Soviet position reflected claims and allegations preached by leaders of the USSR for decades. Yet these arguments had now been softened, in an evident bid to normalize relations with Israel. Foreign Minister Pankin defined the Palestinian problem as "a decades-long tragedy for four million Palestinians"; he argued that it had been the source of prolonged instability and turmoil, in the Middle East in particular but also in the world at large. In the same breath, he called for "historic compromise," one that muted the malice and conflict, mitigating their territorial, national, and psychological components.

Prime Minister Shamir was the first speaker on October 31, the second day of the Madrid Conference. He said that prior to the bilateral talks, Israel had consented to the holding of a ceremonial conference. Israel hoped that Arab agreement to take part in these talks stemmed from a recognition that there was no other route to peace. Direct negotiations were the only available method, the Middle East dispute being rooted in Arab refusal to recognize the legitimacy of the state of Israel. The goal of the bilateral talks was to forge signed peace treaties between Israel and its neighbors, and to reach an agreement for the establishment of interim self-rule for Palestinian Arabs. However, he declared, the basic issue was Israel's existence, not territories. It would be unfortunate if the talks focused primarily, or exclusively, on the territories issue. That was a tried and tested route to impasse. More than anything, it was necessary now to build security, to negate the danger of conflict, and to foster relations in most spheres. Finally, the best venue for peace talks was Israel's own region, in proximity to its decision-making, leadership echelon.

Naturally, the prime minister's speech promulgated his government's considered positions. Arguably, it downplayed the magnitude of historic moment, hesitated to characterize the occasion as an opportunity to be seized lest tragic consequences arise. In general, the Israel delegation was not inspired by a sense of uplift, as might have befitted the turning point transpiring before our very eyes. The main thrust of its endeavors was to provide credible public-relations explanations of Israel's policies. Some of the "explainers" recruited by Israel for the conference viewed their paramount chore as resistance to the Arabs; one of them even slyly infiltrated a press conference held by the Syrians, coming close to being removed in an abject, humiliating fashion. This rule, however, did not apply to then–Deputy Foreign Minister Binyamin Netanyahu, the head spokesman of Israel's delegation. With some real measure of success, Netanyahu, Israel's future prime minister, countered the policy-explanation effort of Hanan Ashrawi, the effective head spokesperson, of the Palestinian delegation. Meantime, meetings of Israel's delegation, led by Shamir, were riddled with doubt, suspicion, and even dread concerning what the future might bring. It was patently evident that the prevailing desire was nothing more than to get the Madrid Conference over and done with.

The Madrid Conference was an awesome logistical challenge, and it was handled with aplomb by Spain's government, despite the short advance warning. Also impressive was the job done by Israel's foreign ministry staff in Jerusalem. They displayed a high level of professional skill, quickly organizing matters with efficiency and without hitches.

It would be hard to deny that speeches were aggressive, contentious, corrosive, and propagandistic. Yet the very image of the Israeli and Arab delegations sitting under one roof bore witness to authentic prospects.

Nothing like this had ever happened before: a new chapter had opened in the history of the Middle East. During one intermission, Baker came over and embraced me enthusiastically. He whispered, "Here, we've done it, we've brought about the biggest transformation in the history of the Middle East conflict."

Speaking after the Israeli prime minister, Jordan's foreign minister, Dr. Kamel Abu Jaber, urged that hostility be replaced by a comprehensive, genuine, and viable peace agreement. He declared the following:

- The conference had to put an end to Israel's self-righteous approach of demanding that other parties act according to its rules alone.
- The goal was to attain a real peace based on UN Resolutions 242 and 338, whose meaning was that territories must not be gained by war, and the realization of the principle "territory for peace."
- The peace could not and needed not reflect the military balance prevailing between the states in a state of war at the time of the agreement.
- The land-for-peace formula was more prudent and true than any other principle or slogan. More land does not necessarily entail more security. The establishment of settlements and the expropriation of lands were at variance with international law: the settlements were illegal and should be removed, and certainly not expanded.
- The Palestinian refugee issue was to be solved on the basis of relevant decisions reached by the United Nations.

The next speaker was Dr. Haidar Abd el-Shafi, the chairman of the Palestinian component of the Jordanian-Palestinian delegation, the body whose establishment had meant so much labor for Baker. Shafi concentrated on the injustices done to his people by the Israeli conquest, along with the right of the Palestinian people to self-determination. He spoke of the importance of "Palestinian Jerusalem," and of the need to establish, immediately after the interim stage, a sovereign Palestinian state. To complement these demands, he declared that the Palestinians were prepared to put an end to the conflict, that they desired peaceful coexistence and good, neighborly relations. Shafi complained that Palestinians at the conference had been denied the right to declare openly their loyalty to their leadership (he was probably referring to the PLO Tunisian leaders). (On August 19, 1993, this selfsame leadership was to surprise the official Palestinian negotiation delegation in Washington by signing behind its back an agreement with another Israeli delegation, in Oslo.)

Shafi expressed skepticism about the viability of the land-for-peace formula, so long as illegal settlement activity in the territories encapsulated the official policy, and prime activity, of the state of Israel. The Palestinians, he asserted, would continue to seek sovereignty and would continue to prepare the ground for the establishment of a confederation between the two states, Palestine and Jordan.

Lebanon's foreign minister, Fares Bouez, described his country's bitter fate, its ailments, and its need to overcome its woes and rebuild. Bouez pronounced support for the traditional Arab position on Palestinian and Israel-Arab issues. He added that in accord with the position adopted by the Lebanese government, the cease-fire agreement reached between Lebanon and Israel on March 23, 1949, remained in effect and set standards for relations between the two states. Further, Lebanon demanded the fulfillment of Security Council Resolution 425 of March 19, 1978, calling for the territorial sovereignty and political independence of Lebanon within its recognized international borders. Lebanon praised the United States for having relayed to it in writing the American position, by which the implementation of UN Resolution 425 was not dependent upon, or connected to, a comprehensive solution to the dispute, though such a resolution could contribute to stability in Lebanon. In addition, the Palestinian refugees dwelling in Lebanon had to be returned to their country, and Lebanon opposed the coerced migration of Soviet citizens to Israel, with their "being uprooted from their 'natural surroundings.' "

The harshest, most critically vitriolic, speech with regard to Israel was the last one of that day, October 31; it was delivered by Syria's foreign minister Farouk al-Shara. Virtually each word in his remarks was brash and vituperative. He declared that Israel must withdraw from every inch of the Syrian Golan Heights, and from conquered Jerusalem, the West Bank, the Gaza Strip, and South Lebanon, as stipulated by UN Resolution 242. Palestinian political and national rights, particularly the right to self-determination, had to be guaranteed. Third, Israeli settlements had to be liquidated and terminated. The fact that the settlement activity persisted even after the inception of the peace process was tangible proof that Israel did not seek a genuine peace. The speech and speaker left little doubt about the nature of the negotiations. They would be tough, taxing, demanding. Yet it should be recalled that these obdurate words were being spoken by a man whose country was, for the first time, expressly indicating willingness to achieve a comprehensive peace with Israel.

During the Madrid Conference, direct, groundbreaking diplomatic conducts with the Arabs were conducted behind the scenes, thanks to the mediation of American and Soviet officials. Preliminary thoughts were broached as to the location and framework of the negotiations. During one meeting between the Israeli and the American staffs, Edward Djeregian, the secretary of state's assistant for Middle East affairs, announced that the Jordanian airline Alia was considering opening an office in Ramallah. It was the first olive branch, an offering intended to represent a new conceptual universe, a new road to be taken.

Friday, November 1, 1991, was designed as a full working day for the Madrid assembly. But members of the prime minister's entourage had announced to the conference organizers the preceding day that Shamir had to leave that day, since he could not observe the Jewish Sabbath outside of Israel's borders. This pretext was very much not to my liking, as it represented a denial of the importance of the occasion. Israel, however, did not depart entirely from the arena; Shamir decided to leave in Madrid a few delegation members who would constitute an Israeli presence.

Friday afternoon I joined the prime minister, his entourage, and most of the delegation's members for the return flight to Israel. I felt that they were treating the Madrid Conference as a trivial affair, not one that was laying a cornerstone for a peace process that, however arduous, tiresome, and risk filled, might promise Israel its yearned-for peace. Inwardly, I wondered why Shamir and his camp, who never hesitated to observe the Sabbath in the United States and in other nations around the globe, refused to do so precisely in the context of the peace conference.

In any case, on the morning of November 1, before the plane took off, Shamir was the first of the delegation leaders to respond to the allegations that Israel's detractors had leveled. His speech was trenchant and polemical. Israel, Shamir declared, could rebuff one by one the claims and distortions articulated by the Arab speakers. It would abstain, however, from doing so, as that was not a conference goal. Futile exchanges of allegations would not bring the sides a single step closer toward mutual understanding, and peace. With this aim of peace in view, Israel had persistently called for face-to-face talks. Shamir added that the attempt made by the Syrian delegate to pass off his country as a paragon of liberty and as a noble champion of human rights exceeded the confines of plausible reason. Syria had attained the dubious honor of being one of the most repressive, truculent regimes in the world. The character of the regime ruling Syria could be inferred from the persecution of Jews there and the encouragement Syria offered to terror. Though Israel did not intend to force it, Syria's removal from Lebanese territory would restore stability and security to the Israel-Lebanon border. In contrast, between Israel and Jordan, a de facto state of nonbelligerence prevailed. Israel hoped that a peace agreement with Jordan could be reached, one that would resolve pending issues. As for the Palestinian delegate, Shamir lamented, he had distorted history and twisted facts in a bid to solicit sympathy. Shamir listed a long series of violent incidents arising from Palestinian initiatives and terror. He called on the Palestinians to agree to Israel's just proposals and to take part in the negotiations.

Jordan's foreign minister, Dr. Abu Jaber, spoke after Shamir and accused Israel of bringing up, albeit in refined form, past positions, and of thereby circumventing a spirit of compromise. Calling for full Israeli withdrawal from the territories, Palestinian self-determination, and the cessation of settlement, he rejected Israel's contention that the primary issue was not the territories.

Dr. Shafi, the leader of the Palestinian part of the joint Palestinian-Jordanian delegation, joined the chorus of mutual incrimination. Characterizing the speeches delivered by Arab delegates as just, prudent, and serious in intent, Shafi argued that Israel remained enslaved to its anachronistic and antagonistic rhetoric. In his view, Israel had infringed the principle of land for peace, an internationally supported formula that was both the heart of Security Council Resolution 242 and the legal authority for the conference and the negotiations that were to come in its wake. Holding the conquered lands would perpetuate hostility toward Israel. Palestinians, as he characterized them, were not residents of territories but a united people, whether they lived as captives of conquest or in exile abroad. As a people, the Palestinians were determined to establish an independent state. It would be necessary to put the territories under the stewardship of an international authority until a final-status accord was attained.

Lebanon's foreign minister, Bouez, reiterated the main points of his previous address. He too charged that Israel remained hostage to old ideas and traditional accusations that had been obstacles to the peace process. Stressing again the familiar formulas of land for peace and Palestinian self-rule, Bouez rejected outright claims that had been aired concerning Syria's conquest of Lebanese territory. Echoing the views of his

Syrian patrons, the Lebanese foreign minister maintained that his country could consider involvement in multilateral talks only when significant progress on the bilateral track became evident.

The turn now came of Syria's foreign minister, who continued to symbolize the extreme flank of the Arab camp. Al-Shara spoke with blunt defiance, not concealing contempt for the denials and countercharges issued by Prime Minister Shamir. In a rush of rhetoric, he denied both that there was a Jewish dispersion and that there was anti-Jewish discrimination in Syria; he accused Israel of undermining the chances of peace, complained of Jewish conspiracies to destroy holy sites in Jerusalem. He leveled more charges of this ilk, speaking stridently, with spleen and malice. Al-Shara's speeches produced the heaviest obstacles in the process. His remarks provided ample ammunition for all the skeptics and detractors of the peace process; in their eyes, the Syrian foreign minister had confirmed that there was no way to bridge the yawning gap between the Syrian position and a peace process that was supposed to lead to a just, full resolution. The world media described al-Shara's comments as not constructive. Yet even at the time, those who were dedicated to the search for peace could argue that there was no reason to be deterred by unyielding, acerbic, and damaging Arab language. Before Madrid, such views had been articulated in the context of war, or preparation for war. Now they were being uttered at a peace conference, prior to direct negotiations designed to forge peace agreements, talks whose very essence and definition would compel the Arab states to accommodate compromise, reconciliation, mutual concession, and the bridging of gaps.

The final Arab speaker, Egyptian foreign minister Amre Moussa, called for the sides to halt the mutual incrimination, hinting that the contents of and approaches inherent in some of the emotion-charged speeches would in the future have to be revised. Israel's status, he declared, was not open to doubt; Israel must for its part respect Palestinian rights in the territories, and also the Palestinian right to self-determination. Such recognition on Israel's part was a precondition for peace. The sides now bore the weighty responsibility of proving that peace had a chance. In this context, Moussa added that illegal acts, such as the establishment of territories, must be frozen. He affirmed that Egypt would support the legitimate rights of all peoples in the area and would tackle regional problems, particularly the arms race and the proliferation of weapons of mass destruction, primarily nuclear weapons.

Soviet foreign minister Boris Pankin linked the peace conference to an understanding reached at the Helsinki Summit on September 9, 1990, between Presidents Bush and Gorbachev. Cooperation and close links between the two great powers had been sealed at this encounter, and the Helsinki agreement had become a decisive factor leading to the convening of the Middle East peace conference. The Soviet foreign minister called on the states and peoples of the Middle East to promote the possibility of living in peace and harmony. Recognized international borders, safe for all parties, would turn this possibility into reality. Pankin added:

- The objective of peace could not be achieved in the absence of agreements related both to the territorial aspect and also to the Palestinian problem, the crux of the dispute.
- The principle of "land for peace" must be applied on all fronts; therefore, the West Bank, the Gaza Strip, and the Golan Heights had to be returned to their former owners, so as to remove the principal obstacle impeding peace.
- Palestinians had a right to self-determination, and negotiations about this right had to take into account the interests of both the Palestinians and Israel.
- The unrestrained arms race, which had turned the Middle East into a veritable minefield, had to be reduced.
- Israel had to end its settlement activity, and the Arab countries should respond to this step in kind, with positive measures.

James Baker, the main protagonist in the Madrid drama, opened by praising regional leaders whose cooperation had brought this historic moment to fruition. That said, Baker, speaking as the most authoritative voice at the conference, quickly put things in order and perspective. Direct negotiations, he recalled, would be conducted on two tracks, and in stages. After that, multilateral talks on a wide range of topics fraught with implications for the welfare of peoples of the region would be held. The basic axiom of U.S. policy, he stressed, was that negotiations are the most effective means for resolving disputes and attaining peace. Negotiations themselves do not guarantee peace, but there is no other way to work toward this end. The American role, the secretary of state explained, was to act as a just mediator; lest there be any misunderstanding, the United States was not going to alter its consistent positions. Declarations promulgated at the conference had made it clear that fundamental issues of land, peace, and security were integral components, inseparable from a search for a full, comprehensive peace. No viable peace could be attained without both security and a resolution on the territorial issue. It was certain that a territorial solution in the absence of peace and security could not solve the dispute; security in itself could not be achieved without a territorial solution, and peace. The issue of the location of the talks had not yet been solved, the secretary of state acknowledged. He elaborated on this subject, verging toward sarcasm. From the point of view of the conference's sponsors, and in fact in the perspective of the rest of the world, it was hard to understand how a side could refuse to take part in direct negotiations due to disagreement about the venue.

Holland's foreign minister Van den Broek spoke last at the peace conference. He alluded to the European Community's traditional links with all of the states in the region. Europe did not prefer one side at the expense of the other, he explained. Instead, it sought a viable peace arrangement with security and justice for all parties, without any exceptions. Europe was prepared to help attain the conference's objectives, acting as a real partner.

By this time, all of the senior figures in Israel's delegation were gone. Their places had been taken by aides and consultants who had accompanied the delegation, like David Kimche, former director general of the foreign ministry; Yosef Govrin, foreign ministry deputy director general for East European affairs; and other staff workers. The prime minister and the rest of us, the official delegation itself, were at the time aboard an Israeli Air Force plane, flying back to Israel. During the flight, I thumbed my passport and noticed that the Spanish authorities had stamped on it "Departure—October 32, 1991." That was fitting. Indeed, October was the longest month, at least as far as the thousands of Spaniards who had done so well in the arduous logistical job of preparing and organizing the historic peace conference were concerned.

5

Washington

After the 1991 Madrid Peace Conference, an Israeli team stayed on, working with the Jordanian-Palestinian delegation to lay a foundation for the meetings to come. This complex, unglamorous task—like so much diplomatic work—of creating procedures and communication channels was nevertheless indispensable if formal talks were to succeed. Indeed, we immediately saw the types of problems that were to bedevil the Washington negotiations, right up to the signing of the Oslo agreement on the White House lawn two years later.

In the midst of this work, Foreign Minister David Levy informed me that he and Prime Minister Yitzhak Shamir had agreed to make me deputy to Elyakim Rubinstein, head of the Israeli team negotiating with the Jordanian-Palestinian delegation. Later on, when the bilateral talks were held in Washington, I became involved in them, up to the 1993 Oslo agreement. Subsequently, I was also engaged in the negotiations with Jordan leading to its peace agreement with Israel in 1994. All these efforts were as fascinating as they were difficult and complex.

From the start, in the negotiations with the Palestinians there was a wide gap between the two sides' fundamental positions, conception of internal arrangements, and in the authority of the delegations. The Palestinians inevitably wanted an interim arrangement in which self-rule powers would proliferate, leading directly to only one possible option: a Palestinian state in every sense of the word. They wanted this arrangement to embrace the territories as a whole and also their entire population, meaning whoever had lived in the areas in the past or returned to them, along with prisoners who demanded freedom—and it also meant Jerusalem. Israel's initial position was aimed at trying to work out not a territorial arrangement but rather a functional-administrative one, in which a broad scope for self-rule would be given in diverse spheres of power.

The original Israeli-Jordanian-Palestinian negotiations were conducted between 1991 and 1993, with the Palestinian group acting as part of a joint delegation with Jordan. Its members maintained a guise of not representing the PLO, and declared that they did not belong to that organization. But disagreements between the Jordanian-Palestinian delegation's two parts were evident from the start. The Jordanians, headed by Dr. Abd as-Salam al-Majali, were open, moderate, and helpful from the very first session. In contrast, the head of the Palestinian half of the delegation, Dr. Haidar Abd el-Shafi, put forth a variety of requirements and complaints. He demanded that:

- Each stage of negotiations had to be linked to further steps and a predetermined outcome.
- The building of Jewish settlements had to stop as a precondition to talks; it was "inconceivable that we would talk with a conqueror who creates facts on the ground."
- Palestinian negotiators had to be accepted as a delegation separate from the Jordanian group.
- During interim agreements, Israel had to transfer all powers of governance in the territories (including land and water) to the Palestinians and withdraw from the territory.
- A Palestinian right of self-determination had to be accepted and also the Palestinian refugees' right of return, in accord with UN Resolution 194.

Under the final agreement, Israel would have to undertake a full withdrawal, including a pullout from East Jerusalem. In the interim, the talks would adopt an interpretation of the Geneva Convention, pertaining to conquered areas, that would make Israel's activities in East Jerusalem illegal. Also, the Palestinians were prepared to accept a confederation arrangement with Jordan, but they did not forgo their demand to establish an independent state. Finally, the fact that the PLO would not take part in the talks did not mean that it did not represent the Palestinians.

In short, the underlying problem is that the Palestinian side wanted Israel to concede at the start of talks what Israel might give—if at all—at their conclusion. Moreover, these demands were presented as preconditions without any—not to say any equivalent—Palestinian concessions to Israel.

Still, the Palestinians' willingness to talk as non-PLO members—even though they had the PLO's permission to do so—had been a key breakthrough in making the negotiations possible. In my opinion, U.S. secretary of state James Baker's talent for maneuvering was, in the final analysis, the decisive factor inducing them to renounce a formal link with the PLO, a position that reversed their earlier stand.

Beyond Baker's diplomacy, several background factors also accounted for the situation enabling the first direct Israeli-Palestinian negotiations in history. Israel's navy had killed or captured a large terrorist force from a PLO group en route to attacking Israeli beaches during the Shavuot holiday in 1990. When the PLO refused, contrary to its earlier undertakings to the United States, to denounce the attack, the Americans had suspended their dialogue with the PLO.

Within a few weeks, Arafat had moved to a position of strong support for Saddam Hussein, which is to say that he moved to the other side of the political divide. When Iraq seized Kuwait in August 1990, the PLO's stance infuriated both the United States and an anti-Saddam coalition that included many Arab states. Iraq's defeat in early 1991 simultaneously very much weakened the PLO and also made possible a major step forward in Arab-Israeli negotiations.

Arafat had put himself in a difficult position. Saudi Arabia and Kuwait did not forgive him for his adventurism with Saddam and cut off funds to the PLO. At the same time, frustration with the PLO's inability to end Israel's presence on the West Bank and Gaza Strip damaged the PLO's status there. Palestinian leaders in the territories were closer than ever before to taking an independent path to negotiations, without direct PLO involvement. At least, they were ready to put all the pressure they could on the PLO to find some way to begin talks with Israel.

In the end, the solution they found was to make an agreement with the PLO: figures from the territory who were not PLO members would negotiate with Israel, but they would coordinate each step with the organization. Further, they agreed to Israel's demand that the Palestinians be part of a joint delegation with the Jordanians, but, as made clear by Shafi, they did everything possible to terminate this arrangement at the first opportunity. As early as the first bilateral meeting in Madrid, the

Jordanians and the Palestinians evinced a desire to be separated, claiming the United States had guaranteed they would be allowed to do so. Jordan would supposedly participate as one of the Arab states, and separate talks would be held between Israel and the Palestinians.

We knew that each of the sides had been given American guarantees, and that it would not always be possible—if it were possible at all—to reconcile even in a theoretical manner this grab-bag of promises. Our position was that U.S. pledges did not necessarily bind us. We stated that we knew nothing about any agreement to separate the Palestinian-Jordanian delegation into two parts and that we wanted to continue the talks within the existing framework. Eventually, this position could no longer be sustained. After several months, the talks were transferred to Washington, and the other side demanded that separation between Jordanian and Palestinian teams be symbolized by holding sessions in separate offices, an arrangement that created a number of procedural complications. The heads of the Jordanian, Palestinian, and Israeli delegations sat together for countless hours on a sofa in a corridor outside the meeting room in the U.S. State Department building trying to resolve these and other issues.

These talks were, in my view, far too protracted; as media-oriented showmanship replaced serious dialogue. Of course, the issues were fraught with difficulties, suspicions, and sensitivities beyond even the normal high pressure and stakes involved in international negotiations. Even the tiniest symbol could become a major controversy, and history had invested every phrase uttered or incorporated into documents with several layers of meaning.

In the end, after laborious and exhaustive negotiations, the rules for the talks were agreed on, and the actual substantive process could begin. The representational agreement retained the framework of a joint Jordanian-Palestinian delegation while separate talks let the Palestinians claim that they were acting as an independent group. During each round of talks, there would be a plenary session of the two delegations, with Jordanians and Palestinians on one side of the table and Israelis on the other side. This would underscore the fact that there was a joint Jordanian-Palestinian delegation. But there would also be an Israel-Jordan track and an Israel-Palestinian track. Israel would be represented by thirteen delegates, as opposed to eleven Jordanians and eight Palestinians. A total of eleven Israelis, nine Jordanians, and two Palestinians would take part in talks on the Israel-Jordan track; on the Israeli-

Palestinian track, there would be eleven Israelis, nine Palestinians, and two Jordanians. This arithmetic satisfied the Israeli demand that on both negotiation tracks there must be reciprocal representation involving Jordanians and Palestinians.

Slowly, patterns of direct dialogue took shape, along with written and oral agreements between Israel, the Palestinians, and Jordan. Even when discussing procedural matters, there were useful, direct exchanges between the delegations' leaders. All this happened under the watchful yet detached eye of an American mediation team, which generously supplied the setting for the talks and allowed time and dynamics do their work, without meddling or trying to speed things up. The process was an educational one, designed to enable the sides to create by themselves a network for mutual, continuing contacts that would allow for real progress.

From the start of the Washington negotiations, the Palestinians and Israelis placed considerable emphasis on the media, to explain their positions but also for propaganda. Both sides had a legion of "experts" for public relations and media purposes. But as the number of spokespeople grew, pressures on the delegations' leaders to meet with the media, issue declarations, and give briefings also increased. But the pursuit of media exposure impeded the substantive negotiations. The Palestinians had spokespersons who did their work effectively and forcefully, sometimes creating the impression that the negotiations were being conducted exclusively in a public realm of mutual incriminations and clashes. The work of a talented spokeswoman like Hanan Ashrawi, who was not a formal member of the Palestinian delegation, furnished the Palestinian side with rhetorical ability and reached an international audience.

This, in turn, made Israel's media advisors concerned about responding. We tried to reduce this emphasis, sometimes to no avail. The Palestinian presentations were more effective in that they were based on firsthand accounts, describing for example ordeals of interrogation by Israeli authorities. It was not easy to listen to such accounts, which were inevitable results of the high level of conflict prevailing in the West Bank and the Gaza Strip after the intifada erupted. Less excusable were lengthy Palestinian historical-ideological accounts of their ties to the land since the Biblical era, with the constant suggestion that we Israelis were unwanted trespassers who had no right to be there. In our eyes, such historical descriptions were artificial and distorted, lacking any scientific-historical foundation. To a great extent, it reminded me of the manner in which Soviet communism would mangle and reconstrue historical events, subordinating them to the political needs of the present and future.

Sitting with my delegation, I often felt this situation had reached a state of absurdity and that the relentless need to appear on the media had turned the negotiations into an insubstantial contest for scoring points and winning public approval. Naturally, the other side tried to compete and to stake its claims, harming the attempt to conduct orderly negotiations. I had a strong feeling that the flood of media coverage would, sooner or later, lead to the opening of a secret channel of talks—and this indeed occurred.

At any rate, I could not fully understand the Palestinian emphasis on public relations when there was such an important matter at hand. The political process was offering them a rare, historical opportunity to pursue their demands and aspirations within a genuine international political framework. They had a prospect for attaining self-determination and real peace. Of course, there were several factors that created both a propagandistic orientation and internal competition to demonstrate militant credentials. First, while the PLO was weaker than it had once been, it still cast a strong shadow over the delegation, pressing it toward public declarations. Second, there were internal fissures among members themselves. Finally, there was an exaggerated faith in propaganda—whether or not based on fact—as a powerful factor in the diplomatic process. The effect, though, was to deflect attention away from substantive discussion and to waste valuable time.

Members of the Palestinian delegation tried for a long time to present us with daily reports of human rights violations on the West Bank and the Gaza Strip. This reporting invariably featured complaints about the Israel Defense Forces (IDF) and the Civil Administration, and it derived largely from newspaper coverage. We dismissed efforts to exploit such reports for propaganda purposes and explained that we would be willing to discuss specific grievances, to investigate them and take care of them. The Palestinians responded to this offer very rarely; I often wondered why they failed to take advantage of a potential channel for improving the actual welfare of their people, choosing instead to focus on the declarative-propagandistic level. Yet this does not mean that important progress did not take place. There were days when the Palestinian delegation responded to our statements, letters, and papers in a practical fashion—though the polemical element was never completely lacking—and presented their positions in a clear manner. At times, I would return to my hotel room, after a long day of discussions, mired in deep despair, telling myself there was no chance in the world of bridging the vast gaps or overcoming the tremendous suspicion and malice. At other times, I would feel elation, supposing that despite everything, we would find a joint path and the common denominator for attaining understandings and an agreement, thus creating neighborly relations of peace between ourselves and the Palestinians.

After procedural agreement was attained, the discussions with the Palestinians and the Jordanians turned to setting up an agenda. This was no mere mechanical exercise but an attempt to determine priorities that would both shape the future talks and would precondition their success. In parallel, at a relatively early stage we submitted responses to a list of the powers that the Palestinians wanted devolved to the bodies that would operate under interim agreements. The list was impressive, a range of items amounting to self-government in the West Bank and Gaza Strip, relating to commerce, industry, agriculture, education, religion, health, culture, local government, police, administration, law, finance, tourism, and more. The Israelis were amenable to additional requests— apart from issues of security, foreign relations, settlements—and also territorial claims. The list of our recommendations and proposals crystallized as the Interim Self-Government Arrangements (ISGA).

For their part, the Palestinians submitted their own model, the Palestinian Interim Self-Government Authority (PISGA), which envisioned an entity that was a state in every respect other than its name. Their paradigm was not acceptable to us. The Palestinian model encompassed all institutions of government, including a quasi-parliamentary legislative council. This Palestinian model did not come as a surprise. It featured the demands and expectations that the chairman of the Palestinian delegation, Shafi, had presented from the start—that a Palestinian state be established alongside Israel. Whereas the Madrid guidelines required negotiations for an interim agreement over a five-year period, they proposed a model that would facilitate a direct transition to statehood from the very beginning. In so doing, they wanted to make a statement about their political-ideological goal. This would be the Palestinian strategy in the future, though in the Oslo agreement they would accept much less at the start and no guarantee that this endeavor to make statehood the explicit goal would be the process's outcome.

We responded to a Palestinian demand that elections be held forthwith, that we did not rule out the holding of elections for an administrative-functional body whose existence would be recognized under interim agreements. But first the arrangements themselves would have to be discussed; only then should ways of establishing self-rule bodies be considered. We proposed also that municipal elections be held, in parallel. This proposal was, of course, received with deep suspicion about whether the state of Israel was at all committed to a process that would bring about a final arrangement different in essence from the existing situation. Our explanations that municipal elections would strengthen democracy did not relieve their doubts.

In fact, the negotiations were being kept on a low burner. In view of the lack of progress, we decided to propose that self-rule in several spheres come about quickly. These areas would include health. Up to then, the local population had furnished medical crews and health service workers, whereas budgets, planning, and development were taken care of by Israel. Israel was now suggesting that the whole sphere be integrated under Palestinian control. Yet this proposal was spurned by the Palestinians, who appealed to various pretexts and excuses. Beyond hints that Israel was dodging the principal issue, they did not conceal their suspicion that the transfer of authority would be incomplete, that Israel would retain an ability to handicap matters. A suspicion grew among some members of our team that in the final analysis the Palestinian delegation feared taking responsibility for the daily life of the Palestinian population.

Meanwhile, since the conclusion of the Madrid Conference, Israel had been making efforts to move the discussions' location to the Middle East. On November 12, 1991, Foreign Minister Levy sent a note to Secretary of State Baker, praising him for his help in achieving the historic breakthrough of bringing the sides together. Levy stressed that contractual peace agreements between states were extremely important but had to be supported by mutual recognition and real reconciliation between peoples. He emphasized the importance of the two-track approach on which the process was based and called for the broadening of the exchanges in order to create a comprehensive peace for the whole region. In addition, peace would be made stronger and more durable not only by an end to warfare but also by joint efforts for regional development.

In this same letter, Levy called for rescinding the infamous November 10, 1975, UN Resolution equating Zionism with racism. As President George Bush had declared to the UN assembly in 1991, this resolution was tantamount to denying Israel's existence. One month after Levy's letter, on December 16, 1991, this goal was achieved.

Responding to Levy in a letter sent November 22, 1991, Baker expounded on the difficulties of moving the negotiations to the Middle East, although he showed sympathy for the Israeli position—concurring that it would be wrong to allow the problem of the location to detract from the breakthrough attained in Madrid, let alone halt the continued direct negotiations. Instead, Baker reissued his invitation to conduct a round of talks in Washington, starting on December 4, 1991.

In his note, Baker also shared some thoughts of the United States, as the process's sponsor, that were meant to help put negotiations on a more efficient footing. For example, the question of bilateral and border issues between Jordan and Israel might be easier to resolve than some of the other questions. The two countries could speak about the nature of the peace, daily problems in the Akaba-Eilat Gulf, purification of waste water, joint potash production, tourism, civil aviation, and other topics. The secretary of state also suggested that a simulation exercise might be conducted to show how a negotiation process with Syria could develop. It had been agreed that the first stage of the talks with the Palestinians would focus on self-rule arrangements for the interim period. The United States urged both sides to refrain from prolonged arguments about such principles as the source of authority or the nature of the mandate for self-rule. Instead, Washington suggested, the sides should work out a model for a Palestinian authority, setting out the administrative council's powers and responsibilities for the interim period.

Like the preliminary talks, the formal negotiations with the Palestinians had many ups and downs, with every step forward quickly ensnared in complexities that brought efforts to a standstill or even dragged the process backward again. Palestinian demands were sweeping, encompassing all realms of life—water, land, the removal of settlements, Jerusalem, and other vexing issues.

Our efforts to deal with these issues, however, including offers of changes, were received with great mistrust. The Palestinians interpreted each Israeli step not as a starting point for bargaining but as a plot designed to derail all progress, perpetuate the existing situation, and at best offer totally inadequate remedies. They constantly accused us of rejecting compromise and the spirit of historical reconciliation embodied in the peace process started by the Madrid Conference.

For our part, we repeatedly expressed our gratitude for the U.S. effort. On January 20, 1992, for example, Prime Minister Shamir sent Baker a letter praising the Americans for letting direct talks proceed rather than trying to mediate or intervene in the negotiations. He was sure that the two-track approach had been successfully launched. Israel was concerned, however, Shamir continued, by two problems. First, the Palestinian delegation were constantly attempting to set preconditions and demand unilateral concessions from Israel before any progress could be made. Second, there was the PLO's effort—contrary to our earlier agreements—to infiltrate the process, both on the bilateral and multilateral levels. Closing his letter, he expressed confidence that the secretary of state would be able to help us handle these problems.

Shamir had accurately described the situation. The Americans refrained from getting involved in the talks as mediators. State Department officials simply hung around the discussion rooms and received reports and papers, both during intermissions and at the end of each day of talks. Sometimes we would brief the secretary of state and his assistants. In any event, the U.S. assistance was indirect, and both sides preferred that approach.

Meanwhile, the talks with the Palestinians moved from round to round, always in the same fashion. At one point, when we were close to adopting a joint agenda, the Palestinians asked to interpolate in it clauses and demands that belonged to the final-arrangement stage. Sooner or later, in every discussion, the question of the negotiations' ultimate result would crop up, preventing formal agreements. Dr. Shafi was in the habit of concluding each round with expressions of deep disappointment and concern that the window of opportunity was already starting to close. Perhaps, he wondered aloud, it was necessary to announce mutual recognition between our two peoples—by inviting the PLO to join the process—and also mutual recognition of the rights of both peoples, the Jews and the Palestinians—by Israel's accepting an independent Palestinian state.

"We, the Palestinians, recognized the Jewish right to exist, we have recognized the state of Israel," Shafi said, "whereas you Israelis have not rewarded us with an identical recognition." He asked that his statements be sent to Israel's leadership; perhaps it would take this proposal seriously and thereby rescue the talks from the impasse they had reached. Otherwise, he suggested, the Palestinians would have to reconsider their involvement in the political process, despite their prior commitment to the negotiations.

Indeed, at the end of ten months of negotiations, the delegations' efforts had been in vain. Shafi blamed the impasse on Israel's unwillingness to give any territorial dimension to a Palestinian authority, on its strengthening of settlements, and its rejection of Palestinian claims on East Jerusalem. According to Shafi, Israel was sending out ominous signals about what could be expected in the next stage. Israel's offers did not give the Palestinians any substantive power. Perhaps, he sighed, the Madrid formula had run dry, and the two sides should move directly to final arrangements, or at least shorten the interim period.

On June 23, 1992, Likud was voted out, and the Labor Party returned to power. It was fragmentation in the right-wing camp, not an ideological turnabout among the public, that led to Likud's defeat. Shamir, Arens, and Levy were obliged to relinquish their places to Yitzhak Rabin, who became prime minister and defense minister, and Shimon Peres, who returned to serve as foreign minister.

Quickly, the new government sought new ways to encourage the negotiations and lift them from the impasse in which they were languishing. At the start, it mentioned the idea of an accelerated timetable, by which talks would end within nine months, with an agreement. This call, however, had no effect either on the Palestinian delegation's positions or on the negotiations' pace. Within the Foreign Ministry, some called for removing the chairman of the Israeli delegation, Elyakim Rubinstein, on the grounds that he was committed to the Likud government's stand. I opposed this move to replace Rubinstein and was absolutely not prepared to supply supposedly incriminating information that others might have thought was in my possession.

Reporting to the foreign minister, Shimon Peres, I analyzed the Palestinian side and its positions, making the following points:

- It was a weak, fragmented, nonrepresentative delegation, whose common core was a desire to appear militant and that took its orders from PLO headquarters in Tunisia.

- Expecting changes due to the electoral turnabout in Israel, the Palestinian delegation had probed Israel's positions, only to discover that there were no shortcuts. A mutually accepted solution to the conflict could only be the result of negotiations, not a precondition to talks.

- Members of the Palestinian delegation, however, seemed to draw the opposite conclusion. Perceiving that Israel would not deal with such issues as the source of powers for a Palestinian authority, Israeli withdrawal, and an irreversible transfer of authority in the territories, they had concluded that Rabin would continue with Shamir's policy.

- The Palestinian delegation's work was still being curbed by the PLO leadership; with a Labor government in power, the Tunis headquarters feared that the moment of truth had arrived, and it did not want the breakthrough to be achieved by the non-PLO delegates.

- The Palestinian delegation's goal was to use every discussion and agreement to build a Palestinian state. Consequently, it was in no hurry; it had no interest in making concessions regarding this point, and it considered small advances irrelevant. Members of the delegation expressed concern that there was no sense in working out an accelerated timetable if there was no guarantee that Israel would meet its demands at the end.

Dr. Shafi, the Palestinian delegation leader, found himself at a crossroads. A former communist, he tended toward deterministic thinking, specifically that historical necessity would inevitably lead to the establishment of a Palestinian state. This being the case, he apparently reflected, why make haste? Why should the Palestinians compromise and settle for less than a state, or even agree to an arrangement that would slow down the fulfillment of history's verdict?

In this context, I reviewed for the new foreign minister the key issues we should consider and some possible options for Israel. The current framework of talks in Washington was really one of negotiating about potential negotiations. Such talks might go on for some time, especially given the very real gap between the two sides' conceptions and bargaining positions.

One possibility was that forbearance, steady nerves, or attrition might gradually lead the Palestinian side to recognize that it had no alternative but to work within this framework in a constructive manner so as to make real progress. Alternatively, slow, protracted negotiations could encourage the U.S. government to act in some way to break the deadlock. At the same time, I emphasized that the new Israeli government might come up with a new concept of autonomy that could lead to narrowing the gap between the two sides' positions. One such approach would be to offer a clear transfer of powers, put the Jewish settlements on the agenda, explicitly discuss the IDF's redeployment, and explore the issue of the source of authority for a Palestinian administrative apparatus. I suggested a declaration that Israel would not rule out in advance the option of a Palestinian state in the final stage.

I further proposed that we seek a direct or indirect contact with the PLO. Based on the PLO's willingness to change its historic policy, that organization would then have to put aside or suspend ultimate goals, in order to focus on interim arrangements. At the same time, PLO approval of any agreement—whatever its content—would demonstrate to the Palestinian majority that the possibility of an independent state had not been foreclosed.

The efficacy of an indirect, secret, contact with the PLO had already been proven in the Washington talks, inasmuch as the Palestinian delegation saw itself as an intermediary. I argued that even the "most indirect of indirect" contacts with Dr. Nabil Shaath, the chairman of the Palestinian National Council's political committee, would help, while maintaining contacts with Faisal al-Husseini, Ashrawi, and their colleagues. Such links would strengthen the population in the territories and its delegation in reaching tough decisions. I added that a breakthrough with Syria would also likely have a beneficial impact on the Palestinian position. The Syrian ambassador in Washington, Muwaffaq Alluf, had already hinted as much.

Breaking with what had become the accepted routine, I recommended the intensive contacts with the United States be resumed to tighten cooperation, coordinate positions, and enable it to intervene in a discerning fashion. I referred to an early sign of increased involvement, wherein the United States had urged us to agree to a Palestinian request to include in the delegation experts to help with its work. Therefore, a need arose to maneuver between direct negotiations and reliance on American bridging efforts.

One of Foreign Minister Peres's aides, who sat in when I briefed Peres, had subsequently told me that my point of view compelled Peres to search seriously for an alternative to the protracted, floundering negotiations in Washington. In the end, this search was to lead to separate, secret negotiations and the Oslo accords.

In contrast to the Palestinian channel, negotiations with the Jordanians were from the start characterized by good will, a cordial atmosphere, and civil discussion. The Jordanian delegation comprised diplomats and officials, each well educated and impressive. The delegation's head, Dr. Majali (who subsequently became Jordan's prime minister) had been founder and commander of the Jordanian army's medical corps. His deputy, Dr. Faiz Tarawnek, formerly a minister of economic development, had completed his doctorate at UCLA. When he worked there as a research assistant, some of his pupils had been Israelis. In the course of the negotiations, Dr. Tarawnek was appointed to become his country's ambassador to Washington, and he also served for a time as chairman of the Jordanian delegation. There were also delegates of Palestinian origin on the Jordanian team.

As a first stage of the negotiations with Jordan, we prepared a draft peace treaty. The Jordanians were not yet ready to discuss this step, though at one point, Dr. Majali agreed to initial a draft agreement whose realization was conditioned on substantive progress being made on both the Syrian and the Palestinian tracks. For our part, we did not publicize the fact that a draft peace treaty had been submitted, so as not to push the Jordanians into a corner.

On establishing a joint agenda, we certainly made faster progress than in our talks with the Palestinians, though a formal agreement came only after the Israel-PLO accord was signed in October 1993. The Jordanians crafted a formula of "having and not having" a link with the Palestinians. They were careful not to speak in the Palestinians' name, and they took pains to present their distinctive identity as Jordanians. They addressed the subject of the settlements from a demographic angle, arguing that a proliferation of settlements would cause an influx of West Bank Palestinians into Jordan.

Starting at an early stage of the talks, we decided to speak with the Jordanians about specific subjects: environmental protection, water, energy, tourism, commerce, and banking. We were able to lay the basis for many specific agreements that were later incorporated into the peace treaty. For example, we overcame the historical controversy concerning the allocation of waters whose sources are the Jordan and Yarmuk Rivers. But again that and other issues were completely resolved only at the final stages of the negotiations, on the eve of signing of the peace agreement.

My responsibilities included heading the working group that dealt with the issues of refugees, tourism, and commerce. My Jordanian counterpart was Jawad al-Anani, and after him Marwan Dawdin; both were former and future ministers in the Jordanian government, and both were of Palestinian descent. Anani emerged as sharp, forceful, and professional; Dawdin was collegial, well mannered, and friendly. In the framework of the Washington talks, we also initiated discussion on Jordan Valley development, discussion that later produced an agreement in the trilateral United States–Jordan-Israel framework. We also addressed the Dead Sea–Red Sea canal plan. It is to be hoped that in the future the Jordan Valley will bloom, flourishing with projects in tourism and industry.

When I reported to Jerusalem about talks with the Jordanian delegation, I took to quoting the Fabian adage, "Make haste slowly." The will was there to reach agreement, but regional political conditions required caution so that Jordan did not seem to be acting unilaterally in making a comprehensive peace with Israel. Actually, every move Jordan made was thoroughly considered and argued for with consummate professionalism by its talented and well-informed delegates. Foremost was the legal counsel, Awn Khasawneh, who habitually embellished his statements with quotations from the best of English verse, and Dr. Montar Hadadin, the delegation's spokesman.

It is clear in retrospect that in my evaluations I foresaw neither the dramatic change that would occur in the PLO's policy nor King Hussein's determination and courage that would lead him to sign the peace agreement with Israel in November 1994. The entire process was a good example of how interests, conditions, and the courage of individual leaders combine to determine the political course of events. After all the arguments are made, a leader still must make decisions that can transcend pressures, excuses, and reasons why something cannot be done at a certain time.

I developed a special friendship with Abdallah Tukan, one of the advisors to the king and to Crown Prince Hassan. His sister Alia had been married to the king but had passed away in a helicopter accident. Tukan had a splendid educational background. He was a true man of the world, with great personal charm and impressive rhetorical ability. As a delegate on the Jordanian-Palestinian delegation in Washington, he became one of the first to dare to break the ice. In 1993, during multilateral working-group discussions devoted to regional security and disarmament, we had lunch at the Rusalka Restaurant in Moscow, with Russian balalaikas serenading us in the background. We exchanged opinions, impressions, and ideas with respect to how progress could be made, particularly toward the yearned-for goal of forging an agreement between Jordan and Israel. Tukan subsequently told me that the king had once stated to him that there were in the Israeli delegation many delegates who strongly desired peace, including myself and Hanan Bar-On, deputy director general of the Foreign ministry (and later a vice president of the Weizman Institute).

A day or two before the signing of the Palestinian-Israeli agreement at the White House, scheduled for September 13, 1993, we Israelis met for a concluding review with the Palestinian delegation. I addressed the chairman of the Palestinian delegation, Dr. Shafi, whom I greatly respected, and the other members of this delegation, telling them among other things:

> We are meeting for a review meeting, prior to the agreement signing. We have behind us many months of hard discussions, in the course of which we dealt with the examination and detailing of issues and problems; we exchanged views, and we undertook trial efforts to bridge positions and gaps.
>
> This negotiation process was in essence an extended confidence building measure. We exchanged messages to one and another, and learned about each other. You, Dr. Shafi and your colleagues, asked and also implored that we turn toward your leadership, that we strengthen direct contacts with it. This we have done.
>
> We are on the threshold of a dramatic revolution, whose import and scale cannot be underestimated by any of us. We must harness our energies and be committed to its success, this test being a mutual one. We Israelis are determined to redeem the details and requirements of the agreement to the final letter. Consistent with this commitment, we will protect the peace and well-being of the settlers, and we will retain our responsibility toward general security, and the IDF's place in the territories.
>
> And you, Palestinians, will start on a long march, undertaking the daily administration of your own affairs. From this point, supreme authority for the Palestinian population rests with you. Results of the test represented by this agreement depend upon both of us.
>
> Negotiations for the final agreement will be influenced by the extent of neighborly relations, security, mutual understanding and cooperation which takes hold under the interim stage of the agreement. It is incumbent upon us all to take the high ground, and prove ourselves worthy of the historical opportunity which has been created, to not only eradicate the dispute, but also to find solutions beneficial to the future welfare of the region. Speaking as one who was involved with the birth of the Madrid formula, this is a moment fraught with potential for redeeming its logic: an agreement with one side can stimulate other sides, and I am sure that an agreement with Jordan will come soon. Onward we might go, to that lofty edifice of comprehensive peace, which will transform the face of the entire Middle East, turning disputes into peace and cooperation.
>
> I want to personally thank you, Dr. Haidar Abd el-Shafi, and also the members of your delegation. I think that we, Israelis and Palestinians, have had the chance to cultivate understanding and a

close relationship. I believe that the talks were conducted seriously, and with mutual respect. Let us hope that this spirit will continue in the future.

We have left work of a great scope to be done, with the prospects of attaining peace in the region depending on its outcome.

Let us all wish success upon ourselves.

6

Moscow

The multilateral track was designed to reap the fruits of peace, meaning that it would capitalize on economic and social dividends arising from progress and peace in the Middle East. In parallel, talks on this track would deal with issues whose resolution would set the stage for a comprehensive peace agreement in the region.

In the Foreign Ministry, we were not tardy in the preparation of documents that addressed regional development, refugees, arms control, environmental issues, and other matters. Such subjects had become integral elements in Israel's strategic thought, as it was framed by the foreign minister. At relatively early stages of the political process, then–Foreign Minister Levy had started to contemplate and form positions on these long-term aspects.

As early as 1989, Dr. Yaakov Cohen, deputy director general for economic affairs at the Foreign Ministry, had established a unit whose job was to collate and analyze materials relevant to regional frameworks for economic cooperation. Cohen's unit benefited from outstanding research projects completed by Israeli universities and specialized institutes. The unit's work picked up steam. In 1990–91, Dr. Cohen put together an interministerial team that included representatives from the Ministry of Defense, the planning department of the IDF chiefs of staff, the IDF's coordinator of government activities in the territories, the Ministry of Tourism, the Ministry of Environment, and the municipality of Eilat. The crossdepartmental staff discussed joint projects that might be presented as confidence-building measures. Their submission, of course, would be in conjunction with hoped-for progress in the political process.

These projects were authorized by Israel's political leadership, and in due time they were presented orally and on paper to the U.S. under secretary of state for economic affairs, Richard MacCormik, at the conclusion of an Israeli-American economic development conference. At my request, in January 1991 the interministerial unit submitted a variety of project ideas to Ambassador Brown, and later to a European Community staff.

Dr. Cohen and his team developed for the Europeans and the Americans a plan reminiscent of the model applied in Europe after the Second World War, when discussions in the economic sphere between two former enemies, Germany and France, had brought about the establishment of the coal and steel union known as CELA. This conglomeration had proved to be the first step on the road to the European Common Market. In other words, it was joint economic interest that had forged trust between two historic adversaries and that had subsequently produced effective, regional cooperation.

Dr. Cohen's team also pointed to another, more local, example. For years, relative quiet had been maintained in the Jordan Valley and on the two sides of the Dead Sea thanks partly to the development of an agricultural infrastructure on the Jordanian side of the valley and the establishment of a chemical plant on the eastern shore of the Dead Sea. The Jordanians had quelled violence and terror, knowing that attacks might provoke reprisals by Israel. Hatred and incitement abated; the Jordanians had fostered a climate of stability and nonbelligerence. Extrapolating from this example, Cohen's unit predicted that economic cooperation would serve Israeli-Jordanian interests, paving the way for the normalization of relations between the two countries. The interministerial team argued that the construction of joint factories and the betterment of the standard of living for residents in the region, Palestinians included, would encourage neighboring peoples to resolve their differences through political negotiations.

There is reason to suppose that such project ideas and research reports formulated by Israel's foreign ministry were contemplated sympathetically by Secretary of State Baker in the days when he was turning his vision into the Madrid Conference framework. Baker's receptive attitude toward Israel's long-term planning conceptions was proven when he gave a positive response to our recommendation for a two-track approach, reinforced by the multilateral dimension. Israel's research-planning papers described an infrastructure for Middle East development in an era of peace, in which progress would be felt in spheres of agriculture, energy, tourism, communications, health, and transportation, and in local cooperation (in areas like the Eilat-Akaba Gulf). Progress would be achieved as the four countries—Israel, Saudia Arabia, Jordan, and Egypt—learned to work with one another.

The interministerial unit focused its proposals in the agricultural sphere on one blue-ribbon project that would be based on experience accumulated by trials in arid and semiarid areas, in particular using a paradigm known as MERC (Middle East Regional Cooperation), which had been applied in Egypt. Agricultural development ideas featured new methods for irrigation and water conservation, as well as: crop protection and prevention of agricultural diseases, genetic treatment to enhance livestock fertility, enhancement of fruit and vegetable yields, food technology, and food and seed storage.

In the energy sphere, the following proposals were discussed and studied: rebuilding the Saudi oil pipeline, and connecting it to Haifa or some other port; connection of electric grids between countries in the region; establishment of power stations, and their incorporation in regional water facilities; and stations for energy production via solar power.

In terms of tourism, proposals for free tourist movement across the region were considered. Such free flow could feature crossborder rental-car arrangements. Also proposed was the conferment of licenses to foreign airlines already operating in the region to allow flights between Israel and its neighbors. Also assessed were measures to ensure the free travel in the region of pilgrims of all creeds.

Dr. Cohen's unit proposed some path-breaking ventures in the transportation sphere, tackling areas such as civil aviation, vessels and harbors, and land travel. Some proposals dealt with establishing open ports in free-trade zones. Overall transportation goals included regional coordination and cooperation in air and water spheres; transport-safety measures, such as the pooling of meteorological data; and up-to-date aerial control facilities. Specifically, proposed transportation improvements included mutual annulment of bans and limits encumbering transportation systems in the region, and incorporation of land networks for mutual benefit, in the spheres of commerce and transportation.

In health, proposals were considered for prophylactic measures against disease, joint evaluation and treatment in cases of epidemics, information pooling, establishment of joint research and medical centers, among others.

Concerning the Gulf of Eilat (Israel)-Akaba (Jordan), ways of creating new water sources, particularly for drinking water, were considered, and also:

- Purification of sewage water
- Establishment of desalination facilities and electricity installations
- Irrigation, and storage of rain water
- Establishment of a ferry line between Eilat and Akaba, to go as far as Egypt's Taba coast and the Saudi coast
- Joint use of highways leading to Saudi Arabia, Jordan, and Israel.

Thus, Israel approached the multilateral negotiation track well prepared with a rich diversity of plans and ideas for economic cooperation in the region. This concrete preparation was a continuation of Israel's ideological re-assessment: Israel was the first country in the region to lay out a vision of crossnational cooperation. As early as the 1970s, then–Foreign Minister Abba Eban (with whom I had the privilege of working, as his political secretary) had spoken in favor of regional cooperation to enrich and enhance the welfare of the local populations, along the lines of the Benelux paradigm. The political initiative undertaken by Secretary of State Baker was also fashioned on that model.

On January 28 and 29, 1992, a conference to launch multilateral negotiations was held in Moscow, under the sponsorship of Secretary of State Baker and the new Russian foreign minister, Andrei Kozyrev. This was a new, independent Russia, which had arisen from the rubble of the Soviet Union. Syria and Lebanon were absent from the opening session. Syria suspected that any progress on the multilateral track would be premature and counterproductive—that is, it might ease tensions and lead to peace, thereby reducing its own bargaining power on the bilateral track. In other words, Damascus would consent to take part in the multilateral negotiations only after its demands were satisfied in its own direct talks with Israel, and (perhaps) only after progress had been attained in Israel's negotiations with the Palestinians and with other Arab states.

As time passed, it became clear that Syria's position was not changing. It would continue to boycott multilateral frameworks even after peace and mutual recognition agreements were signed by Israel with Jordan and the Palestinians. Needless to say, Lebanon followed Syria's lead. The Palestinians were also inhibited. Their participation had been secured on the basis of Madrid Conference understandings. The United States and Russia, Baker told them, were sympathetic to their request that delegates representing Palestinians who lived outside Israel should be included in appropriate work groups, such as ones addressing refugees and economic development. Disagreements stemming from this issue precluded Palestinian participation at the Moscow multilateral opening. Once again, by their abstention, the Palestinians missed an opportunity to promote their concerns.

Speaking at the opening of the conference, Secretary of State Baker stressed that all the attractive and promising ideas for peace would peel away like an onion skin if they were not preceded by an agreed-upon process for their application. Such a process was indeed taking shape, Baker announced. The Moscow meeting had been designed to set up a mechanism that might, as time passed, facilitate matters of joint significance for the peoples of the Middle East. Issues in dispute were counterbalanced by authentic links and common denominators between nations in the region.

The multilateral talks were not designed as surrogates for bilateral negotiations. The latter were aimed at resolving issues of territory, security, and peace—matters without whose satisfactory solution no comprehensive, viable peace could be attained. In fact, the two tracks, multilateral and bilateral, were supposed to complement and fortify one another. The secretary of state announced that five work groups had been formed, to tackle matters of economic development, environment, water, refugees, and arms control and regional security; these groups would operate in the multilateral track.

In a summary statement at the close of this founding conference, Baker reiterated that the bilateral talks remained at the heart of the peacemaking venture, with the multilateral framework serving to catalyze progress. No continuing regional cooperation could be possible, Baker explained, until solutions were furnished for the fundamental issues of the political dispute. In the multilateral talks, such complex issues included arms control and water.

Foreign Minister Levy spoke at the Moscow meeting on January 28, describing its purpose in terms of the eradication of the threat of war and the promotion of cooperation in the Middle East. Just a short time ago, he observed, the idea of such an encounter in Moscow would have been inconceivable. Conclusions drawn from the Persian Gulf War had impelled the Arab states to recognize the imperative of solving the Israeli-Arab dispute. The Israeli leader attested to the tremendous damage wrought by the large flow of arms to the Arab states; topics related to reducing this arms flow must be incorporated into the agenda of the multilateral talks. The foreign minister listed advantages to be accrued by all states in the region as a result of economic cooperation, and he called for international action to rehabilitate and raise the standard of living for Arab refugees.

Baker wrote to Shamir on February 11, 1992, characterizing the inauguration of the multilateral track as a success. He ascribed importance to the fact that eleven Arab states, the majority of which had never before sent delegates to sit face to face with Israeli counterparts, had now gotten beyond this taboo. However, as if to warn Israel not to harbor illusions, Baker repeated his assertion that the multilateral track could only supplement and accelerate progress in the bilateral arena. It was clear that genuine dialogue and treatment of such vexing, unresolved problems as water allocation, arms proliferation, and refugees were imperatives, necessary for the stability and efficacy of agreements reached on the bilateral track.

Basing our calculations on this assumption, we held that progress on the bilateral track ought to be accompanied by intensive, dynamic, and creative talks on these long-term regional issues. Israel believed that the multilateral track could bring prosperity to a region heretofore characterized by a unique set of problems and that it could also create constructive forms of mutual dependence between peoples in the Middle East. History had proven that circumstances distinctive to a particular region need not be sources of dispute, that they can be transformed into a basis for cooperation beneficial to all.

The multilateral process had its ups and downs, suffering sometimes from overactivity and lack of focus. Planning and implementation of ideas got bogged down, and the delays stirred exasperation and disappointment with this heretofore promising track. In the end, it stalled. Precious time was squandered in failed efforts to work out a set of priorities. Arab sides exploited these frameworks, trying to attain ultimate, maximal political-strategic goals and to circumvent the need to compromise; this extremist approach muddied the multilateral track.

Up to the present day, we can still see trends of politicization and maximalism when it comes to controversial security matters like arms control, or even to civilian concerns like environmental protection; these trends frustrate efforts to coordinate policy and to forge step-by-step progress. On the issue of arms control, for instance, Egypt never misses a beat in its efforts to put nuclear weapons on the agenda, to enlist international support and thereby pressure Israel into signing the international pact against the proliferation of nuclear arms.

The economic sphere was plagued by an unfortunate amalgam of political difficulties and Arab claims that Israel was scheming to dominate economically the whole Middle East. The fact is that when Israel shows willingness to undertake a supreme effort to attain peace, the Arab states maintain that it is wrong to "lighten" its burdens. Willing to seek economic development, prosperity, industrialization and modernization of the whole Middle East, Israel often finds itself facing an uncooperative, suspicious Arab response. Israel might be prepared to act wholeheartedly on behalf of a better Middle East, but it often has to deal with Arab countries that take a minimalist stance regarding economic development. The Arab position sometimes lacks creativity, inspiration, and even, perhaps, hope.

This was evident during the Casablanca Conference of 1994. Morocco played host to a meeting sponsored by Foreign Minister Peres. The conference's sole goal was to lure businessmen and international finance into investing in Middle East development. A rare moment had arisen; the financial community and holders of international capital were showing real confidence in the peace process and displaying willingness to invest in the region's future. Israel made a genuine effort, doing its part and going the extra mile, to direct capital toward Arab countries, for the sake of their welfare and their economies.

Alas, Israel's earnest activity was apprehended as through a glass, darkly. The Arab states depicted Israel's endeavor as a conspiracy to harness international capital to further its own influence and achieve economic domination in the Middle East. This conclusion was sheer delusion, but nothing could deflate the Arab fears. So it happened that a tremendous, fleeting opportunity passed by, untouched and unfulfilled; the region as a whole was the loser. In any event, the fault was not in the conference itself, even if it was flawed on some levels by the insensitivity of its Israeli promoters. In fact, Arab leaders and countries that failed to understand the magnitude of the opportunity were to blame. In fact, the Casablanca failure and its causes bring to mind a verse written by the Israeli poet Natan Alterman in response to the escape in the 1960s of a group of prisoners from the Shata jail. Eased restrictions and prison reform had precipitated the jail break, and this promoted the poet to write that "it was not the system, but rather the people, who failed once again."

Despite the lack of progress on the multilateral track, the preservation of the frameworks is important. They incorporate dozens of states that have, by dint of their very involvement, expressed faith in the peace process, willingness to take part in it, recognition of Israel, and readiness to forge a comprehensive peace with Israel. These multilateral frameworks have supplied opportunities for initial contacts between Israeli officials and counterparts from countries like Kuwait and Saudi Arabia, and for continuing relationships with delegates from other states. They reflect the major transformation in Israel's international status that has occurred thanks to the peace process and its advance.

Improbably enough, of all the work groups, it was the one dealing with arms control that yielded three regional institutions, for communications and crisis control. These new bodies could operate in a way that promotes cooperation and regional understanding. On the other hand, questions were often posed concerning the overall wisdom of the work group approach. Had these various frameworks exhausted their potential? Would supplementary, or alternative, bodies have any utility? There are those who argue today that it is only the amplification and proliferation of activities that will generate a dynamic of dialogue, breaking down walls and the hostilities that derive from them.

My own view is that in any event, we must preserve in the political process achievements reached in multilateral fora, and not risk forfeiting these attainments by establishing yet more frameworks. Possibly, a "Darwinian" process concerning these multisided frameworks will arise—a process based on trial and error, and survival of the fittest—as the participants aim to convert lofty aims into palpable institutions and projects, as they work to guarantee that the multilateral frameworks redeem their potential as boosters of the peace process.

7

Breakthrough

Western delegations met on May 30, 1992, in Lisbon, Portugal, to discuss the aid to Russia and states of the Commonwealth of Independent States, following the breakup of the Soviet Union. Levy and Baker used the opportunity to meet for a final time. Baker knew that he was about to be called to the White House to head Bush's campaign staff for the coming election and he would be forced to leave his post as secretary of state. Baker praised Levy for his work on behalf of peace. He presented me with a signed photograph, saying that he viewed me as the one who had coaxed leaders of Israel to march toward peace.

Baker was moved to the White House in August 1992. Lawrence Eagleburger, an under secretary of state who was known well to Israelis, was appointed to succeed him. Baker's parting words to State Department workers reflected the fact that the three and a half years of his term had symbolized a revolutionary change, in the course of which we had made history.

His strategy had involved dialogue with the Soviet Union about a number of topics, in order to probe whether it had indeed taken the path of peace. To this end, an attempt had been made to introduce new content into the traditional Soviet way of thinking, concerning regional disputes, human rights and democracy, the reduction of the arms race and nuclear proliferation, and economics. Indeed, the cold war had fizzled out in a quiet, democratic manner. The transformation had found expression in democratic elections held in Poland, Czechoslovakia, Hungary, and, in the end, in a united Germany. As a result, the threat of nuclear war had dissipated. As in the dismantling of the Soviet Union, the United States had acted to ensure that nuclear weapons would be registered, guarded, and supervised.

Yet just as the cold war was about to expire, a threat to the independent sovereignty of Kuwait had appeared. Iraq's president Saddam Hussein had tried to break the balance with the weapons of mass destruction in his possession. He had tried to subdue countries allied to the United States and to control unilaterally the majority of energy sources in their spheres, turning the Middle East into a nuclear powder keg. In a huge effort, the United States, with United Nations support, had forged an unprecedented international alliance in order to repulse and destroy this threat. This alliance had taken root against the odds, in the face of estimates that it could not be done.

As Baker explained it, after the Persian Gulf War the skeptics had contended that the United States might have won the war but that this success would lack meaning should it lose the peace. Thus, the United States had prepared to examine how peace might be constructed after its victory. Its efforts had worked well. For the first time in history, all of Israel's neighbors had sat with it at the negotiation table and discussed peace. Thirteen Arab states had met with Israel to discuss arms control and topics of water, the environment, and other spheres essential for the creation of a completely new reality in the Middle East.

Baker took pride in reflecting that it was the United States that had changed the agenda—from the prevention of war and nuclear catastrophe to the creation of unprecedented hopes for peace in the Middle East. America will have vanquished the prevailing "wisdom."

The determined leadership of the United States in those years was personified by Baker, who believed that "only the United States has the people, the resources, the economic power, and in particular the principles and the idealism, to confront the challenges at home and in the international arena."

The demise and eventual collapse of the Soviet Union represented the cardinal expression of the historical, global, and regional transformations that took place. The phenomenon heralded the erosion of radicalism in the region, and of recalcitrance with respect to the peace process. The war option no longer appeared to be a good one, or even feasible at all. Israel was now standing tall, in the good company of the United States, the world's sole superpower, against the Arab states, whose military and economic wherewithal had withered, due to the collapse of the Soviet Union.

The end of the cold war and the strengthening of the connection and the dialogue between the United States and the Soviet Union (subsequently Russia) begot a level of cooperation that simply could not have been imagined since World War II. The aftermath of the Persian Gulf War furnished decisive proof that this Russian-American collaboration was genuine, and operative; that the new Russia was indeed different, committed to liberalization and the reform of its government in the domestic arena; and that it would no longer stimulate extremism in the Middle East.

It was, therefore, a propitious moment for Arab moderates. Against the backdrop of a bold U.S.-Russian dialogue and of a United States, Israel's friend, stronger and more influential than ever before, they were encouraged to stand up and face extremists, who now lacked a base of support. However, these special circumstances, which came into focus after the Gulf war, required first and foremost recognition of their potential; such acknowledgment would beget leadership, statesmanship, and creative diplomacy.

The United States was the first to discern the historical opportunity. It started by inquiring how the coalition that had been so successful during the war might be turned into an alliance to promote peace. Secretary of State Baker took upon himself the task of reharnessing a war coalition as a peace coalition, devoting intensive efforts to this end and conducting aggressive, systematic negotiations, in the process confronting doubts, resistance, provocation, and disconnections that sometimes seemed entirely fatal. Through tough negotiation, the United States began, very slowly, to formulate the terms of the Madrid Conference: to help the sides forge a just, realizable, comprehensive peace via direct negotiations on two tracks—between Israel and the Arab states, and between Israel and the Palestinians—based on UN Security Council Resolutions 242 and 338, and aimed at attainment of real peace.

The Madrid Conference generated a historic breakthrough in several spheres. First of all, it put an end to the taboo that had been in effect in the Middle East since the Israeli-Egyptian negotiations, concerning direct talks between Israel and Arabs. Immediately after the conference, when the direct negotiations started, this achievement could be discerned; the talks were already helping to overcome stereotypical perceptions that had lasted generations. Indeed, the direct personal contact helped stifle doubts and remove suspicions and obstacles. This was an opportunity to absorb and impart mutual goals, concerns, hopes, and limitations, as well as avenues on which to proceed. For the first time since the Egyptian-Israeli negotiations, direct diplomacy based on contacts and dialogue began.

The Madrid Conference also overcame the issue of Palestinian representation in negotiations, a topic that had impeded the renewal of the peace process since Camp David. Following considerable effort and many crises, it was agreed that the Palestinian delegation would be comprised exclusively of residents from the territories who did not have terrorist pasts or formal links with the PLO. The format adopted at Madrid is what enabled the initial direct political dialogue between the Palestinians and Israel, which later turned into dialogue between Israel and the PLO.

The truth is that from the start, the "spirit" of the PLO hovered over the Palestinian delegation. There were extremely indirect contacts, whether declared and known or not, between delegation members and PLO representatives in Washington who guided the delegation. The contacts between the Palestinian delegation and the PLO leadership in Tunisia were visible, and were accepted by Israel. I recall how we kept close track of the seating arrangements of the Palestinian delegation. We noticed that during a surprise visit paid by Dr. Saib Erekat, whose membership on the Palestinian delegation had been prohibited by Israel on account of his being a member in the PLO, and by Dr. Nabil Qasam, one of the organization's most prominent academics, the pair sat directly to the right and left of the chairman, Shafi, as though to prove to everyone watching that they had come to represent the PLO's authority over the delegation.

Later on during the negotiations with the Palestinians, mutual accusations became rife. Israel complained about the Palestinian wavering, about the ups and downs, and about how every step forward was followed by three backward. This was characteristic of the delegation, for it lacked authority to make tough, bold, and essential decisions. On the other hand, Dr. Shafi complained that Israel was reluctant to create a direct link with the Palestinian "leadership"—that is, with the PLO.

Fusion of the nexus of Palestinian powers and interests would have been the next step, and it was supposed to have occurred in the framework of the Washington talks, but the government of Israel decided to forego it, taking the Oslo route instead.

Madrid also led to a breakthrough with respect to Syria's joining the process. Damascus had loomed as one of the antagonists to the peace process, a reservoir of Arab ultranationalism and pan-Arab agitation. Hafez al-Assad's decision to join the process and agree to the framework of direct negotiations with Israel was extremely significant. This change was, without doubt, made possible by Baker's powers of persuasion. The secretary of state found a way to impart to the Syrian leader a sense of the global and regional transformations that were taking place and of their implications for the future of the Middle East. The willingness of Syria, the symbol of Arab extremism, to negotiate sent out a softening message to other Arab countries with respect to readiness to talk with Israel.

This message helped in the attainment of another achievement in the Madrid framework: multilateral talks involving wide Arab representation. The Persian Gulf Council for Cooperation, involving Yemen, Algeria, Morocco, and Tunisia, together with Egypt and Jordan, discussed subjects crucial to the creation of a stable regional peace: arms control and regional security, economic development, refugees, water sources, and the environment. In Baker's view, the multilateral talks were to achieve two goals. First, they were to enable the sides in the region to address the sources and causes of instability and tension in the area, and to examine plans that might be implemented fully when a comprehensive peace arose. Second, they would address the transformation of the Israeli-Arab contacts into as frequent and acceptable a link as possible. In this respect as well, the frequency of the contacts and the sheer number of subjects addressed helped remove taboos, and it created dialogue and negotiations on constructive subjects of common concern, even if results from such talks remained negligible at the time.

The peace agreement with Jordan was the consequence of the negotiations, agreement, and understanding of Madrid. The agreement with the Palestinians was also born in Madrid, and it is doubtful whether it could have come into being without it, unless the government in Israel had assented to the PLO's calls for direct talks. This view is corroborated by an account given by the coordinator of the American peace team, Dennis Ross, in a detailed lecture delivered on October 29, 1993, to a conference of the Association of Americans of Arab descent.

In the Washington talks, Israel and the Palestinians conducted negotiations about a "declaration of principles." The United States furnished a draft declaration; on the basis of this document, intensive talks about all relevant issues were conducted between it and the Israelis and Palestinians, and between the latter two themselves. What was absent in these Washington talks was not an ability to conduct negotiations about each subject and to report to the leadership, but rather a main channel to the decision makers. We created in Washington a pipeline for discussion between Israelis and Palestinians. In Oslo, Israelis and Palestinians would create a channel for reaching decisions through which Israel was to bring into effect the strategy of direct contact with the principal Palestinian decision maker, the PLO. Thus, the only way for Oslo to have materialized was through Madrid and Washington. The fundamental assumption in Madrid was that the holding of face-to-face negotiations, whether formal or informal, public or secret, was essential to progress, that it would, in fact, constitute the only true basis for a solution.

The original Madrid formula was laid out in such a way as to guarantee that a peace arrangement between Israel and the Palestinians and the Arab states would be complete and comprehensive. The Madrid formula's central component was this design for a comprehensive peace. This meant that the formula would lead to a full peace, one that would not leave in its wake issues, difficulties, or barriers that could impede or nullify the peace arrangement. The Madrid formula stipulated that the peace process would reach its goal when it embraced comprehensive peace agreements and solved regional problems that exceeded mere bilateral frameworks.

Each track was expected to move ahead at its own pace. Any actual progress or any sign of momentum in other respects would be seen in a positive light; the target, however, would be a complete and comprehensive peace. Israel provided inspiration for the Madrid Conference; the moment it accepted the formula inherent in it, nobody in Israel could harbor any doubt that it would be compelled to make expansive efforts and concessions, which could lead to a comprehensive peace arrangement and to the hope that the country would remain tranquil for decades to come.

More than any other state, Syria stressed its reliance upon the comprehensive dimension of the peace process. For this reason, perhaps, it was not comfortable with the breakthroughs and progress made on other tracks. It is possible that Syria was willing to negotiate only when the issues and problems that were the sources of the Israeli-Arab conflict were resolved.

The United States viewed the Madrid Conference as the capstone of its longstanding diplomatic effort to resolve the Israeli-Arab conflict. Bush saw the Madrid Conference as a "mission of hope." Here, a page was turned in the history of the Middle East, the region moving from a yawning abyss toward a genuine, comprehensive peace, with historical reconciliation at its core.

All this is how Dennis Ross described it in his speech.

On March 6, 1991, President Bush appeared before a special session of the two houses of Congress and delivered tidings of the victory of the new allies against Saddam Hussein, the Iraqi ruler. The aggression had been stopped, the enemy had been repulsed, the whole world had instituted an embargo against him, and circumstances had ripened for a new international initiative.

Bush set forth the goals of U.S. policy in the aftermath of Saddam Hussein's fall. Among other things, he stated, it was time to create opportunities for peace and stability in the Middle East. He recalled that when he announced operation Desert Storm, he had expressed the hope that a peace initiative would emerge from the throes of war. He stressed as well that one of the lessons to be learned in the modern period was that geography alone does not guarantee security, and that security does not derive solely from military strength.

During the Persian Gulf War, Israel and the Arab states found themselves for the first time standing together against the same aggressor. All of the sides had to realize that the making of peace in the Middle East demanded compromise; the upside of this was that peace yields fruits for everyone. The United States had to do everything possible, Bush declared, to close the gap between Israel and Arab states, and between Israel and the Palestinians. The tactic of terror would not lead anywhere, and there was no replacement for diplomacy.

A comprehensive peace had to be anchored in Security Council Resolutions 242 and 338, and on the principle of territory for peace. This principle had to be developed, Bush urged, in a way that guaranteed Israel security and recognition, and at the same time guaranteed political rights for the Palestinians. Nothing less would satisfy the dual test of fairness and security. The time had come to end the Israeli-Arab conflict, the president announced. In the same breath, he announced his decision to send Secretary of State Baker to the Middle East to start with this process.

On November 20, 1991, with his appointment as under secretary of state for the Middle East, Edward Djeregian reviewed for the Foreign Affairs Committee of the House of Representatives the milestones and achievements encapsulated in the Madrid Conference:

- The sides in the negotiations had agreed that the objective was to be the attainment of a comprehensive peace agreement, via direct negotiations based on Security Council Resolutions 242 and 338.

- The sides had agreed on two tracks for the negotiations—between Israel and the Arab states, and between Israel and the Palestinians.

- It had been agreed that the negotiations between Israel and the Palestinians would be conducted in stages, with the first stage focusing on self-rule arrangements for an interim period, and the second stage devoted to a final arrangement.

- It had been agreed that the direct negotiations would open at a peace conference sponsored by the United States and the Soviet Union. Such a conference would not be empowered to impose solutions, cast a veto on agreements, or reach decisions.

- It had been agreed that the Palestinians who would take part in the joint Palestinian-Jordanian delegation, and other involved Palestinians, would be those who consented to negotiations on two tracks and in stages, and who were willing to live in peace with Israel.

- The sides had agreed to invite the European community and Egypt to take part in the conference, alongside the sponsors; also, the states of the Gulf Cooperation Council and the UN had been invited to send observers to the conference.

The United States, according to Djeregian, had decided that direct negotiations should concentrate on three central issues that were essential for the resolution of the dispute. First, the sides in the dispute had expressed their aspirations for peace, their desire to conduct neighborly relations of mutual benefit, and to accompany such relations with a peace agreement, diplomatic relations, economic relations, cultural relations, and political dialogue. Second, the sides emphasized the importance of territory and the desire of the peoples to establish authority and rule over lands they viewed as part of their homeland and their sphere of jurisdiction. Third, the sides emphasized the necessity of security, that is, freedom from fear and threat, and on the other hand, the duty of governments to do their utmost to defend their citizens.

With respect to the future part to be played by the United States, the president and the secretary of state were committed to the peace process and would put themselves at its disposal at all times in order to ensure its advance and success. The United States had long-standing views with respect to the resolution of the Middle East dispute, and these formed the basis of its policy. However, the United States understood, and had learned from experience, that a mediator is often no less effective when it refrains from forwarding its own positions, or even amends them.

When the United States was called upon to do so, it would express its views; when the need arose, the United States would work quietly behind the scenes to strengthen mutual trust. In his testimony Djeregian stressed that it would be crucial for the credibility of the political process not to undermine belief in the region that what was at hand was a process of peace and reconciliation. It is therefore necessary that the sides abstain from unilateral attempts to create irreversible facts prior to the start of the negotiations; such one-sided actions would be very detrimental to the process.

On June 10, 1992, on the eve of their departures to their places of service around the world, I briefed Israel's ambassadors, giving them an initial, detailed, description of the political process. It was an American political initiative pursued alongside an Israeli political initiative; which had come first remains controversial. In fact, mixed together here were two political initiatives; one was that of the United States, and the other had been formulated in the Israeli foreign ministry; its prime thrust was the Madrid Conference.

Levy decided that Israel should attain a state of "*bon ton*" with the Americans. It should avoid superfluous arguments and return to a setting conducive for traditional diplomacy. It was now proven yet again that no medium is more beneficial to progress than civilized dialogue between two states. Baker also signaled that he was ready to open a new page and to pave bypass routes to free the sides from the impasse. The need to think in new categories and to enhance an initiative that had yet to take off was patent.

The PLO's stock in the eyes of the world had plummeted because of its behavior during the Persian Gulf War, when it sided with the enemy of the broad coalition organized by the United States. Washington surely paid attention to the fact that by showing solidarity with Saddam Hussein, the PLO had derogated the channels of direct dialogue that had been created. The PLO's demands and ultimatums about the participation of delegates from East Jerusalem, and also of deportees, in the peace conference were not propitious.

On the one hand, Baker understood all of this; on the other hand, he was adamant in his belief that an attempt must be made to rehabilitate the surviving fragments of the May 1989 initiative. Because of the routine American way of thinking, but mainly because of a lack of other ideas, he initially wanted discussions to continue on the old patterns. On September 5, 1990, Levy made clear to Baker that this was not the route to take; one Israeli government had already fallen after taking that path, and the new government also could not cope with the old terms.

In parallel, the Foreign Ministry had an opportunity to go back and review these matters on a wide scale. An unprecedented, global coalition had crystallized in the background. The Soviet Union had lost its power and was careening toward total collapse. As a preliminary idea, I proposed to Foreign Minister Levy a complex framework composed of mutual relations in a three-way circuit—Israel, the Arab states, and the Palestinian issue. The idea was that each stage ought to serve as a platform and incentive for the ensuing stage. As a working assumption, I postulated that the Arab states would refuse to talk peace with Israel before the Palestinian question was resolved. Various committees at the Foreign Ministry were discussing and ironing out ideas for building confidence. I proposed to the foreign minister that the subject of regional economic collaboration also be addressed, with massive international support being enlisted; the idea here was to provide the states of the region with an opportunity to taste the fruits of the "tree of knowledge" prior to the forging of a peace agreement. This seemed likely to encourage their participation and involvement in the process.

Baker indeed accepted Levy's argument that a return to the old initiative would be a sure recipe for failure; thus he threw into the vacuum the magic word "creativity." He decided that the time had come to act in a nonroutine, imaginative manner with regard to the Palestinian part of the process. It was with this as background that I brought up the idea of the two-tracked process in a talk with Ross on September 25, 1990. We started as well to think about a third category, a track on which the subjects of arms control and regional economic cooperation would be taken care of. The next day, Baker told Levy that the ideas that had been broached in the talk involving Ross, Kurtzer, and myself had made an impression upon him because of their creative character. From this point onward, for Baker and his aides it was accepted wisdom that the initiative ought to be promoted on two tracks—not only on the Palestinian track—which would reinforce and stimulate one another. Baker advanced his political initiative after adopting this central idea, and thanks to it, success beyond our original assumption was achieved, culminating in the pivotal event, the Madrid Conference.

As early as the 16th of September, the secretary of state could report to Levy about his talks with Syrian, Egyptian, and Saudi leaders, in the course of which he had told them about his excellent meeting with Levy. Without any connection to Iraq, he told his hosts, Israel had taken steps in order to reduce tension in the territories. He stated that Levy had promised he would work with him to overcome the threats and obstacles that had impeded progress since February 1990. He stressed that it was absolutely crucial to establish a track that would encompass Israel and the Arab states, and initiate a preelection dialogue with the Palestinians in the territories.

Between March and October 1991, Baker conducted eight visits to the Middle East. On each trip, he visited Israel and Syria; seven times he went to Egypt, and six times to Jordan. He conducted seven meetings with Palestinian delegates. The first, on July 2, 1991, was held in Washington; four others were in Jerusalem, one was held in Amman, and the last was conducted back in Washington. In parallel, the secretary of state held a dozen meetings with his Soviet counterparts, Foreign Ministers Bessmertnykh and Pankin, who were partners in the great initiative.

The political process ensued amidst fluctuations in the character of Israeli-U.S. relations, with issues like settlements and loan guarantees to Israel taking their particular shapes because of their inherent content and also due to their impacts on the peace process and the extent of the progress that had been made. Periodically the sides conferred utterly different meanings to these issues, on the pretext or claim that their positions would facilitate the process, not hamper it. Israel stood for the protection of the settlements and the right to settle in them; it reinforced this position by the rationale that the cessation of settlements would determine prematurely the results of the negotiations for a final-status agreement. The United States believed that Israel's settlements hurt the process itself and would weaken the desire of the Palestinians and the Arab states to join it, let alone move forward with it. On the other hand, even amidst the most serious arguments (in which Jews in the United States sometimes found themselves caught between a rock and a hard place), leaders of the U.S. government reiterated their commitment to the security and integrity of Israel.

On April 22, 1992, in an appearance before the Jews of San Francisco, Dennis Ross, then the head of the political planning bureau of the State Department, and an official who played a central part in the formulation and application of the American peace policy in the Bush administration, declared that "there must not be any partition dividing Israel and the United States." Baker and Ross made clear to all Arab leaders with whom they met that they must not expect the United States to harm Israel or compel it to embrace agreement terms not consonant with Israel's desires and the network of its considerations and interests.

In this speech, Ross attested to the achievements of U.S. foreign policy, from the point of view of its treatment of Israel's needs:

- Bilateral talks, which were always satisfactory to Israel.
- The inclusion of Syria, the focal point of Arab ultranationalism, in the process.
- The negation of the Arab policy of denying Israel's existence, and its replacement with dialogue.
- The launching of the two-tracked approach.
- The holding of multilateral talks, which were designed to advance regional peace and stability while promoting understanding about a series of subjects and issues. (The official opening of these multilateral talks, in Moscow on January 28–29, constituted a major turning point.)
- Though demands and positions held by Arab states suggested otherwise, an international conference could be convened anew only with the agreement of all the sides. At one stage, Syrian president Assad had made demands in this respect couched in uncompromising, unconditional terms; it was only Baker's assertive diplomacy that led Assad not to make his demand a precondition for participation in the Madrid Conference.
- The PLO's involvement in this process was not confirmed, and there was no independent Palestinian delegation. (It will be recalled that there was instead a joint Jordanian-Palestinian delegation.)
- At Israel's insistence, the United States had even accepted the timetables envisioned by the Camp David accords, which focused on preliminary, interim arrangements in the territories.
- The Arabs had not been able to make the formal freezing of settlements a precondition for the holding of talks that derived from the Madrid Conference.

Ross emphasized that put together, these considerations demonstrated that American policy had been crafted in a manner sensitive to the needs and concerns of the state of Israel.

U.S. diplomacy and its promotion of the peace initiative managed to square the circle in the Middle East, a region heavily laden with hostility, prejudice, suspicion, extremism, and fundamentalism. The peace agreement with Egypt, which had been attained between two courageous leaders, Menachem Begin and Anwar Sadat, had been reinforced only at the end of the Persian Gulf War. The United States now searched for a way to bridge gaps, by prodding each side to accept the possibility of painful compromises that did not fulfill all of its political expectations.

In his appearance, already mentioned, before the Conference of Americans of Arab Descent on October 29, Ross was able to bear witness to the achievements of his country's foreign policy from the larger Middle East perspective. Among other things, he pointed out that the Madrid Conference had been made possible thanks to the confluence of regional and global historical events. Radicals and rejectionists had been forced to acknowledge that in view of the collapse of the Soviet Union, the military option was vanishing. The Persian Gulf War demonstrated close cooperation between the two powers and thus left the radicals and extremists in a bind. Conversely, the influence of moderates who banded together against Arab extremism grew. American credibility was proven to all, Ross declared.

Other milestones listed by this architect of the American policy included the attainment of the goal of direct negotiations on two tracks, designed to achieve a comprehensive, just, and realizable peace. A second was the basing of negotiations between the state of Israel, the Palestinians, and the Arab states on Security Council Resolutions 242 and 338, whose purpose was the realization of a genuine peace. Also, the Madrid Conference had shattered the taboo concerning direct talks, and the freeing of each side to articulate its goals, priorities, limits, and needs. It had also adopted a suitable formula for the participation of Palestinians in the negotiations. Disputes about this matter had thwarted any peace effort in the period following Camp David. The solution was a joint Jordanian-Palestinian delegation, whose members were selected exclusively from the conquered territories, did not have terrorist pasts, and were not formally linked to the PLO.

In addition, Syria, the leading patron of Arab nationalism and pan-Arabism, had joined the process. Assad's joining had encouraged other Arab states to take this path. In fact, the multilateral-track arrangement had brought wide Arab participation—twelve Arab states, including the Gulf states, Yemen, Algeria, Morocco, and Tunisia. This track had been designed to help states of the region confront sources of instability and tension, and cultivate ideas about various issues in spheres of development and economics that might be applied when comprehensive regional peace was attained. Another achievement was the conversion of the Israel-Arab dialogue to a routine matter. In this respect, the Madrid Conference was a major accomplishment. It was here that the rich, diverse web of links between Israel and the Arab states was born.

On November 12, 1991, President Bush met at the White House with sixteen leaders from Council of Presidents of Major Jewish Organizations. In the course of the meeting, the host declared that the Madrid Conference had been a turning point, that due to it Israel was now able to undertake negotiations that it had always aspired to pursue with the Arab states and the Palestinians. Virtually the entire process had developed in accord with terms Israel had made, Bush pointed out. There had been some tough moments, and these were liable to occur in the future, yet all sides had to make concessions, and Israel was not the only participant asked to give something up. The president added that his support for Israel and its security was solid as a rock. Israel had strategic importance, and the U.S. government would continue to maintain its qualitative advantage.

After the Madrid Conference but prior to the opening of the bilateral talks, Israel's ambassador to Washington, Zalman Shoval, sent briefing materials to Israel's representatives around the United States. He declared authoritatively, "The Madrid Conference is the turning point in the effort which Israel has been conducting since its establishment, the endeavor to attain peace via direct negotiations between ourselves and our neighbors." Shoval added that the peace process had resulted from the May 1987 government initiative, which Israel had promoted patiently and steadfastly.

On December 17, 1992, the heads of the Israeli delegations for the negotiations with the Arabs and Palestinians (Zalman Shoval, Uri Lubrani, Itamar Rabinovitz, Elyakim Rubinstein and myself) met with President Bush. Bush, who had recently lost the 1992 presidential election to Bill Clinton, hosted us at the White House. The meeting was arranged so that we could say farewell to him and to aides who had stood alongside the president during the political process. With Bush were James Baker, Brent Scowcroft, Edward Djeregian, Dennis Ross, and Richard Haas. The meeting lasted about half an hour, and it was warm and cordial.

Shoval, who had confronted the Bush administration during the low points that characterized relations between the two states in periods before and after the Persian Gulf War, expressed on behalf of the Israeli public his esteem for our hosts, for the historic effort they had made to advance the peace process. Even if there had been on occasion misunderstandings, some of them unpleasant or unnecessary, we believed that the process was now irreversible, Shoval declared. Recent events had indeed proven that there were extremist elements in the Palestinian camp, such as Hamas, that wanted not only to thwart the peace but to harm Israel, and, were it possible, the United States. It was regrettable that the Palestinians as a whole were not making a sufficiently great effort to curb extremism in Palestinian society by underscoring the progress that had already been made. In any case, the Israeli government, like each preceding Israeli government, would continue to pursue the process, Shoval pledged.

President Bush disclosed that he had spoken with President-elect Clinton, and that the latter would continue the policies by which the United States played the role of process promoter and catalyst.

In my remarks, I expressed my deep admiration for Bush and Baker, for their roles as initiators and sponsors of a historic process that few in the Middle East had believed to be possible. It was imperative that the same spirit continue onward, for this was the only process empowered to guarantee peace in the Middle East on the bilateral track. I added that there was considerable value in the multilateral track, via which progress, development, and innovation could be brought to the Middle East; thus we had to persist in these efforts.

When we got up to leave, the president approached me and thanked me for "the warm words," and for having depicted his acts and those of Baker and the secretary of state's colleagues in the appropriate historical context. We took leave of a U.S. government with which we had often been in dispute yet whose ability, enthusiasm, ingenuity, and vast contribution to the peace process we admired. At the time, and certainly in retrospect, I felt that Bush was a friend of Israel's. In August 1986, Bush, then vice president of the United States, had visited Israel; as director of the Foreign Ministry's North American department, I had had the pleasant duty of accompanying him to various sites. Even then, I said, I could see his good qualities and the warmth that he projected toward Israel.

8

Peace Fervor

A thread of successive Israeli efforts to talk with the Arab residents of the historical land of Israel, the Palestinians, and to establish relations of peace with Arab states that had risen up to destroy it in its infancy, can be traced throughout Israel's history. These political endeavors were characterized by various initiatives, attempts to capitalize on sundry connections, and efforts to rely on mediators and foreign states. The extent of the determination, flexibility, openness, and skill of Israel's heads of state during a particular era can be deduced from these diplomatic efforts. No facile conclusions can be drawn—the diplomacy is complex. Called upon to address this one, overarching riddle, historians will be hard pressed to analyze these endeavors on an objective basis. The problem is this: did Israel exhaust all opportunities to carry forward a peace process, or did those entrusted with its political policy falter at crucial moments, demonstrating shortsightedness, fear, and doubt?

In retrospect, one might be able to pinpoint efforts that wrought partial progress; even so, substantive advancement was continually stifled by the blight of war. Such efforts would include the cease-fire accords after the 1948 Independence War, secret meetings with Arab leaders, peace talks mediated by UN secretary general Gunnar Jaring (in which I took part in my capacity as then Foreign Minister Abba Eban's political secretary), the 1973 Geneva Peace Conference and the separation agreements attendant to this conference, and finally, the peace agreement between Israel and Egypt in 1979. From that point forward, excluding a failed peace agreement with Lebanon, the cause of peace in the Middle East went down a blind alley. Egypt remained the only state in the Arab world to forge peace with Israel, and Israeli efforts to promote the Palestinian issue on the basis of Camp David understandings went astray.

Against this backdrop of circumscribed diplomatic efforts, light can be shed on the peacemaking experiment that was the Madrid Conference. To date, Madrid was the most auspicious turning point in the history of the Israel-Arab dispute. In previous chapters, I have chronicled the sequence of events that peaked at Madrid. At play here was an unusual confluence of circumstances and personalities. Rising to the fore were a few individuals who displayed leadership ability and great emotional ardor in the quest to capitalize on passing historical circumstances and to lead the Middle East peace process forward.

The Madrid conference happened due to a fortuitous juncture of local and global events. The hopes of extremists in the Arab states shattered when the Soviet Union teetered and then collapsed. Gone was the extremists' dream of securing superpower assistance to advance their agenda; the demise of the USSR undermined those who ruled out any possibility of a peace accord between Israel and the Arab states. Also withering away fast was belief in the option of defeating Israel at war and thereby compelling it in the best possible scenario, to reconcile itself to an imposed, coercive solution. On another plane, the termination of the cold war facilitated unprecedented levels of American-Soviet cooperation in the Middle East. The Persian Gulf War in 1991 proved how close relations could be between the USSR and the United States; this cooperation left the extremists in the Arab world stranded, more at a loss than they had ever been before. In these circumstances, the world powers had an unheard-of opportunity to pursue political initiatives—which they in fact did, demonstrating an impressive measure of statesmanship and creative diplomacy. At the right historical moment, with the full support of Foreign Minister David Levy, the opportunity came to me to present Secretary of State Baker and his assistants with a political program, the two-track initiative, designed to seize the new circumstances and use them as spurs to movement toward resolution of the Palestinian issue, and beyond it, toward a comprehensive peace in the Middle East. Indeed, Baker was to mention in his *The Politics of Diplomacy* that the idea I presented became the centerpiece of the American political initiative, whose dividends have been Israel's agreements with the Pal-

estinians and with Jordan, and the negotiations for a comprehensive settlement in the region.

Baker's aide Dennis Ross remarked at one point that the transition
from the anti-Iraq coalition during the Persian Gulf War to a grouping
that could be the backbone of a peace process was extremely arduous to
effect. He and his colleagues, Ross recalled, encountered a nearly insurmountable array of doubts and objections. Many warned the United
States that its efforts would be to no avail. In this connection, the initiative that I presented to Baker, and that he eventually accepted, had tremendous import, jump-starting the stalled post–Gulf War peace effort.

Baker came to Israel on a private visit in March 1994 and gave a lecture
at Tel Aviv University's Dayan Center. Introducing him, I said that a
number of accomplishments had marked Baker's term as secretary of
state, but that as far as Israel was concerned, his greatest triumph was
laying the cornerstone for the peace process in the Middle East. His work
in our region had assured his place in history. Secretary of State Baker
had labored to fashion a framework for the process, working indefatigably to urge the sides in the dispute to talk with one another, as well
as to convene the Madrid peace conference. It was as a result of his
activity that Israel, the Palestinians, and Arab states engaged in a dialogue and negotiations. I emphasized the Madrid Conference's historic
dimensions. Baker had responded adroitly to creative ideas; he had
shown an ability to discern propitious changes in the Middle East, ones
that might lead toward new arrangements and solutions. Baker had been
acutely aware that he was confronting a region cursed by a seemingly
endless stream of war and conflict, of bloody acts of despair and wrath.
He had also gauged correctly the strengths of the state of Israel, knowing
that it would be able to repulse and thwart any attempt to deploy a
military option against it. The global transformations, coupled with the
decisive influence exerted by the large alliance formed to reply to the
Iraqi invasion of Kuwait, had become pillars, propping up Baker's initiatives in the troubled Middle East.

Once the process began, the secretary of state had maneuvered to ensure that it would not be snared by details, by relatively small matters
whose resolution could lead, at most, to fragmentary achievements circumscribed to one track only. Baker had been driven by a sense of purpose, acting as an emissary of a country that was just then taking center
stage in the world arena, its role strengthening all the time. He understood that sides in the negotiation process would have to make sacrifices

as they confronted each other's antagonistic positions and also domestic pressures.

Overcoming these hurdles, I noted, Baker had wrought fundamental changes designed to furnish comprehensive peace, on two direct tracks, between Israel and the Palestinians and between Israel and its Arab neighbors, and also on a third, multisided circuit, geared toward such regional issues as development, water, the environment, refugees, and regional security.

In those years, the thrust of the secretary of state's activity had been to soften the calcified stances adopted by the sides. He had acted to counteract the skepticism and rigidity of unbelieving states and diplomats who were not enamored with the peace process. He had enjoyed, however, the support of officials, particularly in Israel, who discerned that history was in the making and that the opportunity must not be missed. I have written that a "peace community" within Israel's government congealed around Foreign Minister Levy and myself; this group did its utmost to assist Baker's labors, particularly when his ideas applied to those who did not feel, or refused to feel, the propitious character of the times. We acted out of commitment to peace, while standing up uncompromisingly for Israel's crucial security needs and geographical requirements. In the end, we were able to embark on this quest. With the American secretary of state, we headed toward a new era, defying the odds.

Baker, and those of us who acted by his side, had known from the start that this was to be a long, serpentine, and weary road. Yet we also had faith that it would be a journey worth taking, one whose fruits would be the peace process we so ardently desired. A special framework arose that allowed the sides to share their fears and concerns, along with their hopes and aspirations. Mutual understanding ensued. Gradually, suspicion and lack of trust had dwindled, and a dialogue took root. An opportunity arose to address a slew of problems, to reduce tension, to diminish the scorn that had nourished for decades.

Speaking that day to the academics, Middle East experts, intelligence officials, and others at the Dayan Center, I recalled that at an early stage of his tenure as secretary of state, Baker had anticipated that farther down the road, Israel and the PLO were bound to meet. Like the rest of us involved in the process, he knew that the only variable still necessary for a dialogue with the PLO was an affirmative decision by Israel's government. As mentioned above, for its part, the PLO had indicated in a variety of ways, including Arafat's public declarations, that it was in favor of negotiations with Israel on the basis of mutual recognition. I disclosed to my listeners that I myself was one of those whose attention had been sought by the PLO, one of the third parties by which it tried to signal its intents to Israel. In May 1994, Israel's president Weizman had been in South Africa, to attend Nelson Mandela's inauguration as president. Together with the director general of the President's House, Arieh Shumer, I had accompanied Weizman as he met with Yasser Arafat in Capetown. I discovered that one of the PLO chairman's closest advisers had stayed in Washington at the time of the peace talks between Israel and the Palestinian-Jordanian delegation. We shook hands and became acquainted. With a mischievous gleam in his eye, Arafat's aide exclaimed, "I know you very well. Together we lived in Washington for almost two years, without ever meeting face to face."

The Madrid Conference installed a framework that facilitated a continuing, systematic negotiation. In these talks, views could be exchanged and positions examined, as the sides assessed one another's demands in the light of the changing times and of the likelihood and implications of their implementation. The Madrid formula supplied Israel with a framework for gradual, cautious negotiation; this was a process in which we were able to reassess continually our moves. This handling of the process would have been consummate and complete, had we been able to forecast which of Israel's governments would elect to condone a mixture of Arab representatives from the territories and of the PLO leadership on one and the same delegation.

In the end, it was the Rabin government that chose to deal with the PLO, on the Oslo track. It is possible that many aspects of the Oslo process that were not taken into account in advance or whose implications were not properly measured beforehand might have taken a more felicitous form had Israel chosen to persist with the Madrid formula. Yet we opted not to become fixated with such speculation, judging it to be pointless once the Oslo accords became an established fact. I doubt that the "Oslo crowd" ever pondered as a viable possibility the continuation of the Madrid framework (which had insuperable advantages), while adding PLO authorization and representation to the delegation with which we negotiated from the Madrid Conference onward. Historians undoubtedly will ponder this riddle, and their judgments will be guided and influenced by the essence and character of still-to-come stages of the political process, and of the final status arrangement that it is destined to yield.

The Madrid Conference was not the first such Middle East peace conference. The Geneva Conference, held in December 1973, preceded it. I was a delegate in Israel's contingent to this Geneva gathering and served as Abba Eban's political secretary—Eban was foreign minister and headed Israel's delegation. As a witness to both gatherings, I can say definitively that Geneva was nothing like the Madrid Conference. The Geneva Conference was summoned immediately after the Yom Kippur War. Israel turned up, tattered and blood stained, following the ordeal of the surprise war that had cost so many casualties. Eighteen years later at Madrid, Israel attended as a strong power, whose military strength and ability to withstand attacks were not open to question. The Palestinians were not represented at Geneva. In contrast, at Madrid a Palestinian contingent played a role, within the joint delegation with Jordan; without Palestinian representation, no conference could have been convened to begin with. The Soviet Union had severed relations with Israel seven years before attending the Geneva gathering; this was the first time in years that a meeting had been held between Israeli and Soviet foreign ministers, Eban and Andrei Gromyko. Ambassadors Ephraim Evron and Zev Shek, and myself, were also present.

It will be recalled that Gromyko served as the Soviet ambassador to the UN at the time of the November 29, 1947, partition resolution in favor of the establishment of the state of Israel, and that his country was the first to recognize an independent Israeli state. At Geneva, Eban offered his hand in a greeting of peace fearing that it would remain hanging in the air. Gromyko reciprocated and shook the Israeli foreign minister's hand. Seen in terms of this Russian angle, Madrid was an altogether different story. The Soviet Union came already reconciled to Israel, having a short time before renewed diplomatic relations.

The hastily assembled Geneva convention was designed to initiate a process sponsored by Secretary of State Henry Kissinger. The objective was to attain disengagement accords between Israel and Egypt, and between Israel and Syria. From the start, it was Kissinger who planned this conference; his intention was for the United States to play a kind of mediation role, as the sponsor of agreements for the disengagement of troops, and to enable face-to-face discussions between the sides.

Assad had accepted Security Council Resolutions 242 and 338, yet Syria did not attend the Geneva Conference. At Madrid, Syria was represented by a delegation headed by Foreign Minister Farouk Al-Shara.

The Geneva Conference, convened after the shock and turmoil of the Yom Kippur War, lacked preparation, or a formula conducive to the search for a comprehensive peace. The Madrid Conference reflected the major transformations that had occurred in the less than two decades between it and Geneva; there were changes in the geopolitical, strategic, economic, social, and military realms, and the Palestinian issue had risen as a recognized item on the regional agenda. The old antagonists at the Geneva Conference, who had just laid down their arms after a bloody war, convened at Madrid to bring closure to a peace process whose first cornerstone had been put in place at Camp David, in the Egypt-Israel accords.

Israel's relations with the Soviet Union and its satellites (apart from Romania) were severed in 1967. I worked then as an official in Israel's embassy in Hungary; together with the ambassador, David Giladi (a writer, journalist, and Renaissance man), Giladi's wife Helen, and the rest of Israel's diplomatic corps stationed there, I was deported to Israel. My friend, Moshe Raviv, at the time Abba Eban's political secretary, invited me to serve alongside him and the director of the foreign minister's office, Emanuel Shimoni. My assignments in the foreign minister's office, working in the proximity of the gifted Abba Eban, gave me an exhilarating exposure to policy making. This post wedded me to the fervor inherent in the peace policy and to the restless quest to promote it. Then a young, vigorous diplomat, Abba Eban cut an exemplary figure, one to be emulated by peacemakers anywhere.

Again and again, I have recalled what I had learned from the poet Yitzhak Shalev, who was my literature teacher at the Hebrew Gymnasium High School in Rehavia, Jerusalem. "Students: take a stand," he would say—in other words, do not passively allow social and national problems to dominate our lives, without taking a stand and confronting them. He was saying that to take a stand was to attempt to have influence, to help in the search for solutions. Equipped with this motto and the set of values bequeathed to us by the Gymnasium and also by the Scouts youth movement thanks to the inspirational teaching of guides like A. B. Yehoshua and Avshalom Katz, I always aspired to exert influence and promote progress whenever I was drawn close to where policy was being made and implemented. I was determined not to allow events to go by without a response, without "taking a stand"; I sought to influence the nation's decision makers as they confronted problems and issues laden with significance for Israel's future. I believed I had the right, the obligation, and the opportunity to try to influence a gamut of events, trends, and developments tied to the peace process and to the clear-cut interests of the state of Israel. In this activist spirit, when opportunity came my way, due largely to the support and encouragement of Foreign Minister David Levy, I outlined, presented, and promoted the idea of the two-track process; this plan was incorporated in the American political initiative known as the Madrid Conference, an event that bred a process capable of delivering comprehensive peace to the Middle East.

"Ask for peace, and pursue it," as the poet wrote in the Book of Psalms. Let there be no doubt: we will pursue it, until it is ours.

Appendix: Middle East Peace Conference

OPENING ADDRESSES
WEDNESDAY, OCTOBER 30, 1991

MR. FELIPE GONZALEZ, *Prime Minister of Spain*

On behalf of the Spanish Government, I want to associate myself with the warm welcome expressed to you by His Majesty the King.

We have been entrusted with the honor and responsibility of hosting in our country the Middle East Peace Conference. Thus, we follow a longstanding tradition in offering you this house as your own. Spain through her long history has known the fruits of coexistence, of tolerance, of peace among the three cultures represented here. The architecture in many corners of our soil, literature, poetry, philosophy and the sciences, still present in our libraries and which are an integral part of our identity, were once the highest expression of civilization and development in the known world. Mutual respect made that possible. Spain has also tasted the bitter results of confrontation and Al Andalus and Sefarad remained as indelible memories of happy places for many generations of men and women. That nostalgia has lived into our days. If we have known the fruits of coexistence and the bitter taste of missed opportunities, how can we not now feel the hope of an open path towards peace in that part of the world?

In the last few years our country has been immersed in a dual process of opening internally and externally. We have tried to leave behind our isolationism and learn to assume the responsibilities that we have inherited through our history, our geography and the understanding that we live in an increasingly interdependent world. Nothing in this world can be foreign to us, and least of all the destiny of a region as close now as yours, a region which has been the cradle of cultures which became interwoven in Spain, contributing to make up her identity.

We have wondered frequently if the conditions that once made possible fruitful coexistence could perhaps be repeated. A positive or a negative answer to this question would lead to hope or frustration, to peace or conflict, but I hasten to add, we have that hope and we do not want to renounce peace because new conditions exist for the two of them.

Changes in the world are taking place at lightning speed so much so that it is difficult to follow the pace of the news which keep us up to date, simultaneously, of what is happening in the farthest reaching corners of the globe. Right here we can witness this new reality. The co-sponsors of this event are two men: President Bush and President Gorbachev who until yesterday headed two blocs which were faced off ideologically and militarily and who today symbolize the search for international relations with less weapons and greater peace, with less confrontation and greater cooperation, with less violence and greater respect for the rights of individuals and of nations.

It is imperative to recall the effort, of so very many human beings who for years have worked towards this dialogue which begins today. In the last few months within the framework of the cooperation which has taken the place of confrontation it is only fair to point out the concerted effort of the Secretary of State of the United States of America and the Minister of Foreign Affairs of the Soviet Union. Their skill and their ability have made possible what is, in our opinion, most worthy of nothing: the beginning of this process.

The entire world will hang on every word uttered and of the will shown here. There is a hope which must not be dashed to the ground.

We are aware of the complexity of the process, but we Spaniards know how cooperation among cultures and the union of collective efforts can generate peaceful coexistence. Peace is the necessary condition. The region has such natural resources and human capital that in an atmosphere where conflict is substituted by cooperation the development and welfare of all the human beings living there can be guaranteed.

On the eve of 1992, a year full of events which mark past understandings and misunderstandings, which is pregnant with hope for all, we, as Spaniards, would like to continue to work with you to achieve a peace which is stable, based on justice and which can be a lasting one.

In welcoming you to our house I call upon your generosity to build peace and, for the sake of your friendship with Spain, I beg your understanding for the inevitable imperfections of our organization, which has had to work in the find of time.

I can assure you that we have all worked with great hope, moved by the spirit which you can feel on the streets, now full of traffic. If we can achieve peace, everything will be worthwhile.

We made the effort and we will continue to do everything we can to make things easier for you.

Welcome to Madrid, Welcome to Spain turned today by your presence into the capital and the homeland of peace and hope.

MR. GEORGE BUSH, *President of the United States*

Prime Minister Gonzalez and President Gorbachev, Excellencies. Let me begin by thanking the Government of Spain for hosting this historic gathering. With short notice, the Spanish people and their leaders stepped forward to make available this magnificent setting. Let us hope that this Conference of Madrid will mark the beginning of a new chapter in the history of the Middle East.

I also want to express at the outset my pleasure at the presence of our fellow co-sponsor, President Gorbachev. At a time of momentous challenges at home, President Gorbachev and his senior associates have demonstrated their intent to engage the Soviet Union as a force for positive change in the Middle East. This sends a powerful signal to all those who long for peace.

We come to Madrid on a mission of hope—to begin work on a just, lasting, and comprehensive settlement to the conflict in the Middle East. We come here to seek peace for a part of the world that in the long memory of man has known far too much hatred, anguish, and war. I can think of no endeavor more worthy—or more necessary.

Our objective must be clear and straightforward. It is not simply to end the state of war in the Middle East and replace it with a state of non-belligerency. This is not enough; this would not last. Rather, we seek peace, real peace. And by real peace I mean treaties. Security. Diplomatic relations. Economic relations. Trade. Investment. Cultural exchange. Even tourism.

What we seek is a Middle East where vast resources are no longer devoted to armaments. A Middle East where young people no longer have to dedicate and, all too often, give their lives to combat. A Middle East no longer victimized by fear and terror. A Middle East where normal men and women lead normal lives.

Let no one mistake the magnitude of this challenge. The struggle we seek to end has a long and painful history. Every life lost—every outrage, every act of violence—is etched deep in the hearts and history of the people of this region. Theirs is a history that weighs heavily against hope. And yet, history need not be man's master.

I expect that some will say that what I am suggesting is impossible. But think back. Who back in 1945 would have thought that France and Germany, bitter rivals for nearly a century, would become allies in the aftermath of World War II? And who two years ago would have predicted that the Berlin Wall would come down? And who in the early 1960s would have believed that the Cold War would come to a peaceful end, replaced by cooperation—exemplified by the fact that the United States and the Soviet Union are here today—not as rivals, but as partners, as Prime Minister Gonzalez pointed out.

No, peace in the Middle East need not be a dream. Peace is possible. The Egyptian-Israeli Peace Treaty is striking proof that former adversaries can make and sustain peace. And moreover, parties in the Middle East have respected agreements, not only in the Sinai, but on the Golan Heights as well.

The fact that we are all gathered here today for the first time attests to a new potential for peace. Each of us has taken an important step toward real peace by meeting here in Madrid. All the formulas on paper, all the pious declarations in the world won't bring peace if there is no practical mechanism for moving ahead.

Peace will only come as the result of direct negotiations, compromise, give-and-take. Peace cannot be imposed from the outside by the United States or anyone else. While we will continue to do everything possible to help the parties overcome obstacles, peace must come from within.

We come here to Madrid as realists. We do not expect peace to be negotiated in a day, or a week, or a month, or even a year. It will take time; indeed, it should take time—time for parties so long at war to learn to talk to one another, to listen to one another. Time to heal old wounds and build trust. In this quest, time need not be the enemy of progress.

What we envision is a process of direct negotiations proceeding along two tracks, one between Israel and the Arab states; the other between

Israel and the Palestinians. Negotiations are to be conducted on the basis of U.N. Security Council Resolutions 242 and 338.

The real work will not happen here in the plenary session, but in direct bilateral negotiations. This Conference cannot impose a settlement on the participants or veto agreements; and just as important, the Conference can only be reconvened with the consent of every participant. Progress is in the hands of the parties who must live with the consequences.

Soon after the bilateral talks commence, parties will convene as well to organize multilateral negotiations. These will focus on issues that cross national boundaries and are common to the region: arms control, water, refugee concerns, economic development. Progress in these fora is not intended as a substitute for what must be decided in the bilateral talks; to the contrary, progress in the multilateral issues can help create an atmosphere in which longstanding bilateral disputes can more easily be settled.

For Israel and the Palestinians, a framework already exists for diplomacy. Negotiations will be conducted in phases, beginning with talks on interim self-government arrangements. We aim to reach agreement within one year. And once agreed, interim self-government arrangements will last for five years; beginning the third year, negotiations will commence on permanent status.

No one can say with any precision what the end result will be; in our view, something must be developed, something acceptable to Israel, the Palestinians and Jordan, that gives the Palestinian people meaningful control over their own lives and fate and provides for the acceptance and security of Israel.

We can all appreciate that both Israelis and Palestinians are worried about compromise, worried about compromising even the smallest point for fear it becomes a precedent for what really matters. But no one should avoid compromise on interim arrangements for a simple reason: nothing agreed to now will prejudice permanent status negotiations. To the contrary, these subsequent negotiations will be determined on their own merits.

Peace cannot depend upon promises alone. Real peace—lasting peace—must be based upon security for all states and peoples, including Israel. For too long the Israeli people have lived in fear, surrounded by an unaccepting Arab world. Now is the ideal moment for the Arab world to demonstrate that attitudes have changed, that the Arab world is willing to live in peace with Israel and make allowances for Israel's reasonable security needs.

We know that peace must also be based on fairness. In the absence of fairness, there will be no legitimacy—no stability. This applies above all to the Palestinian people, many of whom have known turmoil and frustration above all else. Israel now has an opportunity to demonstrate that it is willing to enter into a new relationship with its Palestinian neighbors; one predicated upon mutual respect and cooperation.

Throughout the Middle East, we seek a stable and enduring settlement. We've not defined what this means; indeed, I make these points with no map showing where the final borders are to be drawn. Nevertheless, we believe territorial compromise is essential for peace. Boundaries should reflect the quality of both security and political arrangements. The United States is prepared to accept whatever the parties themselves find acceptable. What we seek, as I said on March 6, is a solution that meets the twin tests of fairness and security.

I know—I expect we all know—that these negotiations will not be easy. I know, too, that these negotiations will not be smooth. There will be disagreement and criticism, setbacks—who knows—possibly interruptions. Negotiation and compromise are always painful. Success will escape us if we focus solely upon what is being given up.

We must fix our vision on what real peace would bring. Peace, after all, means not just avoiding war and the costs of preparing for it. The Middle East is blessed with great resources: physical, financial, and, yes, above all, human. New opportunities are within reach—if we only have the vision to embrace them.

To succeed, we must recognize that peace is in the interest of all parties—war, absolute advantage of none. The alternative to peace in the Middle East is a future of violence and waste and tragedy. In any future war lurks the danger of weapons of mass destruction. As we learned in the Gulf War, modern arsenals make it possible to attack urban areas—to put the lives of innocent men, women and children at risk, to transform city streets, schools and children's playgrounds into battlefields.

Today, we can decide to take a different path to the future—to avoid conflict. I call upon all parties to avoid unilateral acts, be they words or deeds, that would invite retaliation or, worse yet, prejudice or even threaten this process itself. I call upon all parties to consider taking measures that will bolster mutual confidence and trust—steps that signal a sincere commitment to reconciliation.

I want to say something about the role of the United States of America. We played an active role in making this conference possible; both the

Secretary of State, Jim Baker, and I will play an active role in helping the process succeed. Toward this end, we've provided written assurances to Israel, to Syria, to Jordan, Lebanon and the Palestinians. In the spirit of openness and honesty, we will brief all parties on the assurances that we have provided to the other. We're prepared to extend guarantees, provide technology and support, if that is what peace requires. And we will call upon our friends and allies in Europe and in Asia to join with us in providing resources so that peace and prosperity go hand in hand.

Outsiders can assist, but in the end, it is up to the peoples and governments of the Middle East to shape the future of the Middle East. It is their opportunity and it is their responsibility to do all that they can to take advantage of this gathering, this historic gathering, and what it symbolizes and what it promises.

No one should assume that the opportunity before us to make peace will remain if we fail to seize the moment. Ironically, this is an opportunity born of war—the destruction of past wars, the fear of future wars. The time has come to put an end to war—the time has come to choose peace.

Speaking for the American people, I want to reaffirm that the United States is prepared to facilitate the search for peace, to be a catalyst, as we've been in the past and as we've been very recently. We seek only one thing, and this we seek not for ourselves, but for the peoples of the area and particularly the children: that this and future generations of the Middle East may know the meaning and blessing of peace.

We have seen too many generations of children whose haunted eyes show only fear—too many funerals for their brothers and sisters, the mothers and fathers who died too soon—too much hatred, too little love. And if we cannot summon the courage to lay down the past for ourselves, let us resolve to do it for the children.

May God bless and guide the work of this Conference, and may this Conference set us on the path of peace. Thank you.

MR. MIKHAIL GORBACHEV, President of the Union of Soviet Socialist Republics

Prime Minister Gonzalez, President Bush, Ladies and Gentlemen:

I'd also like to begin with an expression of my gratitude to our hosts, the King of Spain and the Spanish government, for their offer of Madrid as the venue for this Conference, a Conference of such importance to the entire world. It would have been difficult to select a better venue from the standpoint both of the country's prestige and authority and of the geopolitical factor, too.

I welcome here the presence of the President of the United States of America, the Arab delegations and observers, the Israeli delegation, Representatives of the European Community and of the United Nations Secretary-General. The composition of the participants, as well as the nature and objectives of this Conference, are eloquent testimony to the fact that we are participants in an event of major importance in new world politics.

The road to this point was strewn with thousands of victims and with devastations and calamities suffered by whole peoples. It was marred by hatred and atrocities, and many were the crossroads on the path that were fraught with danger of global conflagration. This conflict, the longest in the latter half of the twentieth century, bears the heavy stamp of the so-called Cold War, and it was not until an end was put to that, that ending this conflict became a tangible possibility, too.

However, enormous efforts were needed to put on track the process of reaching out towards a settlement. Those efforts reflected the tremendous potential of goodwill and the sense of responsibility of the statesmen and policymakers and of all those who became involved in this undertaking of global importance, for the region of which we speak is a region from which originate many sources of the world's millennial civilization and culture and where the vital interests of today's international community converge. It's a region inhabited by nations whose genius has furnished some of the greatest achievements of the human spirit.

I must say a few words about the role of the two powers whose presidents are now before you as co-chairmen of the Conference. It was the will of history that, without an improvement and then a radical change in Soviet-U.S. relations, we would never have witnessed the profound qualitative changes in the world that now make it possible to speak in terms of an entirely new age, an age of peace in world history. Movement in that direction has begun, and it is only in this context that we can understand the fact that a tangible hope has emerged for an Arab-Israeli settlement.

Cooperation between the two powers and other members of the U.N. Security Council was indispensable in order to stop the aggression against Kuwait and to reaffirm the viability of our new criteria in international relations. Directly after that, just as was agreed between President Bush and myself in September 1990 at our Helsinki meeting on the subject of the Gulf War, vigorous joint efforts began, aimed at achieving a Middle East settlement. All that we and the Americans have undertaken to that end signifies the right conclusions have been drawn from the Gulf War.

Our joint participation in the process of settlement was prompted by a desire to offer our good offices, not any desire to impose solutions from outside that would run counter to the national interests of states in the region. Thus, as a result of major bilateral and multilateral efforts, a signal was sent to the parties involved in the conflict, a signal of the need to negotiate, to work together towards finding a realistic balance of interests which alone may form the foundation for a durable peace.

Today we have a unique opportunity, and it would be unforgivable to miss this opportunity. Success is in everybody's interests, not only because the rights of the peoples and nations and of the individual are increasing[ly] recognized today as the universal foundation for our world order, but also for another reason of particular urgency and gravity, and that is the fact that the Middle East has become one of the most heavily armed regions in the world, where lethal weapons and nuclear technologies are building up, and where other weapons of mass destruction are also to be found.

There is justified cause for alarm. The international community is entitled to expect that this Conference will come up with decisions that will put this concern to rest. In my view, the Conference can only succeed if no one seeks any victory for one side over the other, but all seek a shared victory over a cruel past. I'm speaking of peace, rather than merely a cessation of the state of war, and a durable peace implies the implementation of and respect for the rights of the Palestinian people.

We have restored diplomatic relations with Israel. Now that deep-rooted democratic changes are taking place in our country and in the world, and now that a real process towards settling the Middle East crisis is getting underway, the absence of relations with Israel was becoming senseless. We hope and will try to make sure that this will be of benefit to the peoples of our two countries and the entire Arab world. Peace in the Middle and Near East would benefit all.

The region has vast potential. Turning to constructive pursuits, it will help not only to resolve the problems of the nations that live there, but would also become an important pillar of support for global international progress and prosperity. We must break the fetters of the past and do away with hostility, militarism, terrorism, hostage-taking, and those actions that turn people into refugees.

Our country, as a participant in the Middle East process and a neighbor that has maintained longstanding and extensive ties with the nations of the region, has a special stake in the success of this Conference. The pace we set and the way we tackle the problems that have emerged at the present stage of world development will have a strong bearing on the settlement of conflicts in the Middle East and elsewhere.

The acceleration of historical evolution when based on democracy is truly amazing. The tremendous social energy of the masses of people is being released, and typical of the way this is made manifest is the dramatic growth of national self-awareness and national consolidation, particularly where national feelings were long ignored or suppressed. This is, in general, a positive process that holds out great promise for the future. It will add greatly to the creative potential of the world community in all its diversity.

We now have a far better chance of keeping this process on a civilized course. At the micro level of world politics, there is a recognition of the complex implications of national aspirations and a willingness to put out the fires of inter-ethnic and international conflicts as witnessed in the Middle East, in Southern Africa, in Cambodia, in Korea, Afghanistan, and Central America.

Yet dangers do exist, and we're already facing such dangers. Somewhat unexpectedly, they've made themselves most strongly felt in Europe, but this entirely new international environment means that there's a much lesser temptation for any outsiders to exploit, say, the Yugoslav crisis in order to gain some advantage and strengthen their own hand at others' expense. On the contrary, the dominant tendency is to exert joint and vigorous efforts to help overcome the crisis, while respecting the right of the parties involved to decide the future destiny of their country and at the same time reminding them of their responsibility to the international community.

One may hope that crises arising in our time will not be as protracted as the one we're dealing with here. Of late, the world has been confronted by yet another crisis of tremendous proportions. What I have in mind is my own country. It became inevitable as a result of latent contradictions building up over a long period of time. A great country is going through a great transformation. It's a painful and arduous process which has brought about personal tragedies and inter-ethnic and regional conflicts. Much in the world depends on how our crisis will be resolved.

Once this crisis is overcome, our union will acquire new qualities and potential as a world power based materially on a market economy as part of the world economy, politically on democracy as part of universal democracy, and intellectually on the new thinking. We are the ones who will shoulder the main burden of achieving the recovery and prosperity of our country.

This job is for us to do. Our peoples will have to go through a difficult period of transition, but it's important that, under the new conditions created because it was our country that launched the initiative to end confrontation and to join up with the rest of the world, that the world too has not remained indifferent to our great cause. The world community is becoming increasingly aware that what is happening in the Soviet Union has a larger bearing than any regional conflict on the vital interests of the greater parts of today's world.

Today, we hear not only murmurs of approval and good wishes. We are also beginning to see practical support as well. And this is a very significant sign of the movement towards a new era, a new age. And President Bush's initiative regarding nuclear arms, with our reciprocal initiatives, constitutes a major step and a prescient symbol of this movement.

For almost half a century nuclear arms used to be the axis upon which world politics turned. The task is now by changing the nature of those politics to replace it with something completely new and more attuned with the wheels of 21st century history.

Mankind faces many peacetime challenges. All of them are formidable ones. And they include all what we call global problems: the environment, energy, food supplies, population, all the problems of development, and the total abolition of the nuclear threat, which is spreading to the edges from the former center of world confrontation.

All these challenges can only be met through joint efforts. Therefore, it is essential to fracture the logic of so many millennia, and particularly the logic of this century, persistently and patiently, to shape a new logic of interdependence, interaction, and cooperation. But this task is an extremely difficult one. We see both in our country and elsewhere, even here at this Conference, ghosts of the old thinking, sometimes unnoticed, are still present among us. When we rid ourselves of their presence we will be better able to move towards a new world order. And irrespective of our individual vision of this new order, it appears that we should now promote this objective process itself, relying on the relevant mechanisms of the United Nations, the CSCE, the European Community's modernized, old, and completely new structures of regional security and cooperation, as well as the institutions created for crisis prevention and conflict settlement.

Ladies and Gentlemen, it is for the delegations directly participating in the Conference to sort out the details of this enormous task. As cochairmen of the Conference, we will be in regular contact with our American counterparts, and we will do our utmost to find solutions for which your peoples and the entire world have long been yearning.

In my address I've mentioned the more general problems of the global process. I did this in order to emphasize once again the important international context of this Conference and of the challenge which you are facing. I wish you every success.

MR. HANS VAN DEN BROEK, Minister for Foreign Affairs of the Netherlands and Acting President of the Council of Ministers of the European Communities

On this historic day, in this beautiful capital city of Madrid, it is a privilege indeed to be speaking on behalf of the European Community and its twelve member states.

For the first time, all the parties involved in the Arab-Israeli conflict and the Palestinian question are sitting together at the conference table, confirming their commitment to a just, comprehensive, and lasting settlement. As little as a year ago, perhaps especially a year ago, most of us would have dismissed out of hand a gathering like this taking place so soon. But these are extraordinary times, holding out both challenges and promise. With their unprecedented commitment to peace the parties have met the moment of history. Let us hope that this day, as it surely must, marks a turning point in the annals of the Middle East.

Now is not the time to dwell on that history. Far from it. All too often it has been one of conflict, suspicion, and frustrated aspirations. We all know how easy it is to tap recriminations from the reservoir of bitterness that they have left. But let us today take to heart the one all-important lesson that the past has to teach. It is that this chance for peace is too precious to be wasted. It will perhaps not return in our lifetimes. There must be no turning back.

We are today setting off on a road towards a Middle East different from the one we have known. The reestablishment of legality in the Gulf encourages us all the more to look everywhere for peace based on the rule of law. There is still a long way to go, but the objective of peace is no longer a mirage shimmering between earth and sky. It has become a living reality. It lies within range.

The Twelve pay tribute to the wisdom and courage of the parties directly involved. Israel, Syria, Jordan, Lebanon, and the Palestinians. To be here today, each has in his own way surmounted difficulties, overcome ingrained reflexes and put aside doubts. It is a credit to them all that these have been transcended for the greater common objective. But it is absolutely essential that the commitment shown today is maintained, and that trust grows from it in the days and months ahead.

The Twelve welcome and attach particular significance to the participation of Egypt. The peace treaty between Israel and Egypt was an important first step. It demonstrated that commitment and courage on both sides could bring material results. Those same qualities are in evidence here today. Let us build on them.

We salute the representatives of the member states of the Gulf Cooperation Council and of the Arab Maghreb Union who are here today as observers. Their support of a peaceful settlement and their constructive role in securing the wider regional framework for peace—an area where the Twelve hope to be working closely with them—will be a much needed inspiration to progress.

The presence of a representative of the United Nations Secretary-General is an affirmation that what unites us here today are the principles and the guarantees which are enshrined in the Charter of the United Nations. In a changing world, those principles are the bedrock on which a peaceful world order stands, and it is the firm belief of the Twelve that the United Nations will have an important role to play in the coming peace process.

Last but not least, we commend the United States Administration which, in partnership with the Soviet Union, has mounted the effort to bring us together. Efforts which became all the more successful as a result of the new and constructive cooperation between the U.S. and the Soviet Union in promoting peace throughout the world. From the outset the Twelve have given their full support to the peace initiative. Secretary Baker's unswerving determination, tireless energy, and high skill have marked the Administration's pursuit of that goal. It is an outstanding achievement; it deserves to be crowned with success.

That same wisdom and courage, that same perseverance and flexibility that brought us together today must be made to prevail throughout the negotiations themselves. They are sure to be long. There may be some rough going ahead. That is why the process requires early movement and adoption of confidence building and other measures to establish trust. That is vital.

It is in this spirit that the EC and its member states, represented by its presidency, will participate in the negotiating process. We will be working closely alongside the United States and the Soviet Union. We share their overriding interest in the success of the negotiations. They can count on our constructive partnership in all the phases of the negotiating process.

The Twelve consider it of the utmost importance that the parties have committed themselves to the road map of this Conference: direct negotiations on the basis of Resolutions 242 and 338 along two tracks, between Israel and the Palestinians on the one hand, and between Israel and its Arab neighbors on the other. The political negotiations are to be underpinned by multilateral negotiations on regional cooperation in fields of mutual interest. We look forward and expect to be working closely with all the parties to ensure progress along these lines.

Bearing in mind geographical proximity, a widely shared historical heritage, intensive relations across the whole spectrum of political, cultural, economic, and humanitarian affairs with the people of the Middle East, the Community and its member states cannot but have a close interest in the future of a region with which it shares so many interests, and are resolved to share in the building of peace.

The Twelve's guiding principles throughout the negotiating process are those which have long since governed our position. They remain unchanged. These principles are Security Council Resolutions 242 and 338, the principle of "land for peace," the right of all states in the region, including Israel, to live within secure and recognized boundaries, and the proper expression of the right to self-determination by the Palestinian people. Our position on issues relating to the occupied territories, including East Jerusalem, is equally well-known. A comprehensive settlement should, in our view, encompass these principles. But we do not claim to prescribe how they should be put into practice on the ground.

What is essential now, at the beginning of this Conference, is that the way be opened to movement on substance. That, in our view, is why the early adoption of confidence-building measures is vital. They will make an essential contribution to creating the stable environment which progress in the negotiations will require. In our view a halt to Israel's settlement activity in the occupied territories is such an essential contribution. Renunciation of the Arab trade boycott of Israel is another. With regard to the situation in the occupied territories, it is important that both sides now show restraint and that Israel abide by the provisions of the Fourth Geneva Convention. We look forward to a tangible improvement in the situation in the occupied territories, even before the putting in place of interim or other arrangements.

Early movement along the parallel track of the negotiations between Israel and its Arab neighbors is equally indispensable. Progress towards a durable peace between Israel and its neighbors Jordan and Syria will be crucial to the success of the overall peace process. Much will depend on the early establishment of a basis of confidence on both sides. We cannot emphasize enough that the parties involved should negotiate—and should be seen to negotiate—on the implementation of Security Council Resolution 242 in good faith. Progress will undoubtedly contribute to further restoration of stability and sovereignty to Lebanon, and to the implementation of Security Council Resolution 425.

As we move forward through the twin-track agenda, progress there will need to be assisted and underpinned by regional cooperation that will yield the practical and visible benefits of peace. Clearly, regional cooperation cannot progress faster than movement towards a political settlement. But the political and regional agendas should go hand in hand, each one reinforcing the other.

Given its close ties with all the parties involved, the Community and its member states undertake to make an active practical contribution to progress in this important area of regional cooperation. The multilateral working groups to be established for this purpose should start their work as soon as possible.

A bold and imaginative approach is called for. We will be putting forward our own ideas. We will share with you our own experience in this regard to the benefit of all nations of the Middle East.

Building a network of mutual economic interest amongst themselves and closer cooperation with the European Community and the wider world will help the threat of conflict recede. All this will call for wider participation. That is why the Community will endeavor to associate EFTA nations, Japan, and of course the GCC states and others in a framework of closer economic cooperation. Above all, we look forward to proposals from the parties themselves. We know the ideas are there and we will very shortly be contacting the parties to discuss them.

But regional cooperation must go deeper and wider. Elements of the process set in motion by the conference on security and cooperation in

Europe could serve as an inspiration and example. It shows how a modest start can bring great results. It was during the years of the Cold War that principles for improving relations between states and between their citizens were agreed in Helsinki. These principles, and the commitments undertaken to give them effect, gradually established themselves as a code of conduct for governments, and an inspiration for the governed. Today they are universally accepted as a framework within which participating states conduct their domestic and international affairs. The CSCE also agreed [on] a series of confidence- and security-building measures, which, over time, grew into the network of arms control arrangements that has proved its worth in Europe. It is singularly lacking and badly needed in the Middle East.

Europe is of course not the Middle East but we believe that some of the lessons and experiences of CSCE could be taken on board. There is a long and difficult way to go. But in the end we hope to find ourselves in a Middle Eastern landscape that is different and new.

The most prominent features of that landscape are states that are at peace with each other, where the legitimate security needs of all have been met, where peoples give shape to their own future and a new life beckons for the region as a whole, and in particular for the Palestinians, who have been the principal victims of the Arab-Israeli dispute.

It is a landscape where new security arrangements have drastically reduced tension and are building confidence. Where networks of regional and economic cooperation reinforce the peace, and where the vast accumulation of armaments, including weapons of mass destruction, has been undone, and freed resources are made to meet the needs of citizens to pursue their well-being in security and in full enjoyment of their human rights.

These, and much besides, are the rewards that await the parties at the end of the road. That is our vision of a comprehensive settlement between Israel and the Palestinians and between Israel and its neighbors.

Commitment, good faith and perseverance. These are the essential ingredients of progress towards such a settlement. They have brought the parties here on this day. They must be sustained beyond it. In so doing, all the parties can count on the full support, encouragement and assistance to the negotiating process by the European Community and its twelve member states. We will give our best. That is the pledge I am honored to make on this historic day.

A day that marks a courageous step for each of you, and a giant leap for peace in the Middle East.

MR. AMRE MOUSSA, Minister of Foreign Affairs of the Arab Republic of Egypt

In the name of God, the Most Merciful and the Most Compassionate:

Your Excellency Mr. James Baker, Secretary of State of the U.S.A., Your Excellency Mr. Boris Pankin, Foreign Minister of the U.S.S.R., Excellencies, Heads of Delegations,

Allow me at the outset to convey to you and to the Peace Conference which you compose, a message of profound appreciation and sincere hopes from President Hosni Mubarak, of the Arab Republic of Egypt, that the convening of the Peace Conference in the Middle East would launch a genuine peace process ushering in all the peoples of the Middle East towards new vistas replacing inequity with justice, oppression with freedom, occupation with liberation, hostility with coexistence, doubts with confidence, and war with peace.

A multitude of emotions overwhelm us when we gather today in this great country, Spain, whose history witnessed long centuries of prosperous Arab culture, which achieved active and positive interaction between Latin and Arabic cultures. It laid [the] basis of a very rich cultural blend and background. This blend stands today an evidence of communication, not alienation or isolation of cultures, of the consolidation of coexistence, cooperation and peace.

We, Egyptians and Arabs, authors of history, contributors to world civilization, ancient and contemporary, unmistakably and authentically, have strongly determined to participate in the formulation of a framework of a new world, a framework of cooperation and interaction, with principles of justice, legitimacy as its texture; equality and reciprocity in rights and obligations as its structure.

The great efforts exerted to help convene this historic gathering to launch the peace process in the Middle East, represent signals, to be hopefully confirmed by the forthcoming negotiations, of the emergence of a new will, of a staunch determination by all to achieve a just, comprehensive, peaceful settlement of the Arab-Israeli conflict, the core of which is the question of Palestine.

At this crossroad of world history, when all the peoples in the Middle East look forward with hope and anticipation to this great event, we, along with millions of Arabs, and Israelis, indeed all those who genuinely advocate peace and freedom, feel profoundly indebted to the courageous, unrelenting and determined efforts of the U.S. Administration throughout the few months since March 8, when President Bush embarked on his peace initiative, with the active and consistent support of the Soviet Union. U.S. Secretary of State James Baker, through his unending highly commendable diplomatic creativity, to which I am a witness and at long last, accomplished a historic mission. The Palestinian people through their representatives took the difficult decision, so did Syria, Jordan and Israel. The decision is historic. The significance is great, it is a courageous decision to respond to the challenge of peace, a decision which we believe will be also an option for peace.

The unprecedented transformations in international relations which demolished walls of isolation, ideologies of confrontation, did lay the foundations for just settlements and achievement of peace in many troubled and conflict areas.

The evolution of history at this juncture has opened for peoples and states which have not, for different reasons, availed themselves of peace opportunities before; new, probably last, prospects for the exercise of the free will of peoples to choose their own future for the restoration of their rights, opening horizons of cooperation, mutual recognition of rights and duties, for the establishment of peace with justice that would resolve the conflicting claims in a spirit of reconciliation, accommodation and harmony through dialogue and negotiation.

The cradle of the most ancient civilizations, the birthplace of three monotheistic divine religions, Judaism, Christianity and Islam; the Middle East, was plagued for decades with wars, violence and revenge.

More than any other region in the world, it has been doomed with untold-of tragedies, full of tears, blood and human miseries. Despair, frustration, chaos and death were the haunting figure roving in all parts of these otherwise blessed territories.

The Middle East region is not perennially doomed to this fate. We believe in our collective ability to reorient the course of history, to write a new chapter for the Middle East, void of the bitter legacies of acrimony, vendetta, fears, and doubts, but instead, full of tolerance, confidence, fervor, and joint human endeavor for the sake and benefit of the future generations, Arabs and Israelis and the whole world.

Ladies and Gentlemen,
Peace was the message emanating from the East, from Mount Sinai in Egypt, from Nazareth and Jerusalem, from Mecca and Medina, those

eternal beacon houses for mankind. Peoples in the four corners of the world espoused the message of peace and echoed the call for one God Almighty. Will the sons of Abraham rededicate themselves to the divine message of peace and brotherhood? The decision is ours. We will stand accountable before our people and the peoples of the world if we fail to pass the test, and we must pass the test.

With goodwill, strong determination and positive political will, we can make 1991 the beginning of the end of a long agonizing ordeal. This is a moment of historic decision, a moment for courage, patience, wisdom, self-confidence and vision.

In history, ancient, medieval, or modern, balances of power are never eternal. At a time, could be replaced or even annulled in different contexts of time or space. History stands a most eloquent testimony to this fact. Force never resolved a conflict similar to that of the Middle East and never will, especially if it involves a multitude of factors and claims against a background of religion, history, culture and geography and when it involves more than one party.

This is the inherent morale behind the Arab-Israeli conflict. It is a conflict which defied resolution by sheer force. It is a conflict over rights, claims, counterclaims which have to be reconciled but not denied or suppressed.

To this end, Egypt, an equal and full partner in the quest for peace, will leave no stone unturned, no path uncharted, no horizons unexplored to discharge its responsibility towards its Arab and Palestinian brothers and towards the whole region until the establishment of a genuine peace in honor and dignity.

Egypt is bound by historic, cultural ties and legal obligations with its Arab brethren, and the peace relationship with Israel, which would warrant a staunch support of their legitimate demands for the implementation of U.N. Resolutions 242 and 338 and to help evolve a framework of a viable peace, security and cooperation among all countries of the Middle East parties to this conflict.

Egypt feels strongly reassured that by the sponsorship of the U.S.A. and the U.S.S.R., indeed their co-chairmanship and participation in the Conference itself, the peace process stands on a most secure, most solid launching pad. The participation of the E.E.C. constitutes an added and necessary reassurance. The positive attitudes of the E.E.C. towards the legitimate rights of the parties to the conflict invite our appreciation. The U.N. presence symbolizes international legitimacy and its Resolutions 242 and 338, the basis of the negotiation process. The principles of its

Charter form the framework under which any just and acceptable settlement could be reached.

The broadbased international participation underlines the unflinching international support for the peace process which provides the driving force behind the progress towards the attainment of its objectives.

Peace dividends will not be exclusive reward for one party nor for the parties directly involved in the process of negotiations. The whole region, the Mediterranean, Europe, the world at large will share the fruits of peace in the Middle East. They all have a high and direct stake in the just and comprehensive settlement of the Arab-Israeli conflict that should fulfill the legitimate inalienable rights for all peoples, including the Palestinian people, and in particular its rights to self-determination; a peace that should provide for the security of all states including the State of Israel through mutual recognition of rights based on equity and justice.

Egypt at one of its finest moments, 1973, called for peace. In 1977 it pioneered the march toward peace, in 1979 [it] endorsed this peace with Israel. Throughout our tireless and undaunting efforts for peace, our position has always been and will always be grounded in our commitment to international legitimacy, to the U.N. Charter and its resolutions. Today we are all the more devoted to the same principles unchanged and unnegotiable.

Ladies and Gentlemen,

Peace which we intend to establish, to consolidate and safeguard, should be built in the formula "land for peace" as reflected in Security Council Resolution 242 which unequivocally reaffirmed the inherent principle of the U.N. Charter on the inadmissibility of acquisition of territories by force, and the rights of all states to live in peace and security.

This peace is based on a number of fundamentals, basics and factors. It means right for right, obligation for obligation. Security for security, sovereignty for sovereignty. In our conviction, this and only this can fulfill the formula peace for peace.

It is inconceivable that principles long endorsed and internationally accepted would be renegotiated or reinterpreted, or outbid complete withdrawal from all Arab territories, occupied in 1967, in the West Bank including East Jerusalem, Gaza, the Syrian Golan Heights pursuant to Security Council Resolution 242 and also from Southern Lebanon pursuant to Security Council Resolution 425, is the right prelude to promote a genuine peace with justice and dignity. Arab rights to Arab territories cannot be compromised. Recognition of the legitimate rights of the Palestinian people is the prime assurance for peaceful coexistence of Israelis, Palestinians, indeed the Arabs in their respective homelands.

Arabs did not come to relinquish their rights, accepted, endorsed, and supported by rules of international law, principles of justice, U.N. Charter, resolutions and world consensus, nor did they come to concede their commitments to these principles and norms; they came to search, in good faith, with mutual trust, for a common ground for acceptable formulas on how to meet concerns, reconcile different demands, reach agreements and modalities that would secure the legitimate requirements of all parties equitably and without prejudice to the rights of any party. We call upon Israel to do the same.

Ladies and Gentlemen,

Launching this historic peace process should not be fettered with obstacles impeding its steady evolution towards a comprehensive permanent settlement. Basic fundamental requirements have to be respected and met.

First: The legal status of the Palestinian people should not be challenged. They are not just proprietors, inhabitants or residents of conquered territories. They are people with history, culture, distinct national identity worthy of all the attributes of other peoples.

Second: The West Bank, Gaza and Golan Heights are occupied Arab territories subject to the full implementation of Security Council Resolution 242. They are not also conquered territories. They are not lands promised to other peoples. They have their legitimate sovereigns. Claims not based on principles of legitimacy and international law, have no place in the world of today.

Third: Settlements established in territories occupied since 1967 including Jerusalem are illegal, and more settlements will foreclose potential progress towards real peace, cast doubts on the credibility of the process itself. They have to be stopped as they obstruct peace, undermine the groundwork for negotiations on the final status of the occupied territories and erode the will to coexist.

Fourth: The holy city of Jerusalem has its special status. It should remain free, accessible and sacred to all followers of Islam, Christianity and Judaism. The occupying power should not exercise monopoly, illegal sovereignty over this holy city. Persistence of unilateral decisions declared by the occupying power to annex the holy city lacks any validity or legitimacy. The status of the holy city should be subject to negotiations and settled by agreement on the context of legitimacy established by internationally accepted resolutions.

The Arab-Israeli dispute is in essence an Israeli-Palestinian conflict. Any breakthrough or progress depends on the settlement of the question of Palestine, in terms of rights and territories. It also requires termination of the Israeli occupation of the Syrian territories occupied in 1967 and Israeli withdrawal to Syrian international borders. Progress towards attainment of these objectives should be guided by rationality and wisdom. It should achieve justice and equity within the context of balanced rights and obligations on the basis of international legitimacy, conscious and with clear understanding of the historical developments.

Ladies and Gentlemen,

This peace conference heralds a new turning point in the history of the Middle East. It brings time-old adversaries and enemies to a meeting ground. It attempts to bridge unsurmountable gaps among former antagonists. It is an embodiment of the deep yearning of the Arab people, the Palestinians and the Israelis for peace. We hope that the Conference will resolve, with the peace process it launches, the historic conflict between the Arabs and the Israelis.

We should not fail our peoples and the peoples of the world. We should not succumb to moments of despair. We come here not to lose, but to win, together. Our dividend is peace, it is a most precious dividend, that cannot be bargained away. Millions of parents, Arabs and Israelis with their hearts broken with anguish for their lost sons, absent husbands, for their beloved ones who never returned home, are looking forward with anxious, long-waiting weary eyes.

These millions are gathered together by rays of hope. They are the corps of peace not the divisions of war, they hold and raise olive branches and address to all of us an appeal of peace and brotherhood to force open the gateway of a new history for mankind. The difficulties are great, but prospects are bright. New vistas of cooperation will be opened, new lines of communication will be established. The time has come to free the Middle East from sources of tension, weapons of mass destruction, primarily nuclear, so that resources, hitherto squandered on arms race, will be directed for development needs, common welfare and prosperity. This is a moment of truth, commitment and hope. We have opted for peace. The path is thorny, the march is tiring and the challenge is colossal. But the objective is great, noble, and worth our pilgrimage for peace.

Thank you.

ADDRESSES BY HEADS OF DELEGATIONS
THURSDAY, OCTOBER 31, 1991

MR. YITZHAK SHAMIR, Prime Minister of Israel

Distinguished Co-Chairmen, Ministers, Members of Delegations to the Conference, Ladies and Gentlemen,

It is an honor to represent the people of Israel at this historic moment; and a privilege to address this opening of peace talks between Israel and its Arab neighbors.

I would like to express our profound appreciation to our Spanish hosts for their hospitality, and for making this gathering for peace possible. In its two thousand years of wandering, the Jewish people paused here for several hundred years until they were expelled 500 years ago. It was in Spain that the great Jewish poet and philosopher, Yehuda Halevi, expressed the yearning for Zion of all Jews, in the words:

"My heart is in the East, while I am in the uttermost West."

I would also like to extend our appreciation to the co-sponsors of this conference—to the U.S., which has maintained a strong friendship with Israel in an alliance that has overcome occasional differences. And to the Soviet Union, which saved the lives of many Jews during the Second World War, and has now opened its gates to the repatriation of Jews to their ancient homeland.

The people of Israel look to this palace with great anticipation and expectation. We pray that this meeting will mark the beginning of a new chapter in the history of the Middle East; that it will signal the end of hostility, violence, terror and war; that it will bring dialogue, accommodation, coexistence and—above all—peace.

Distinguished Co-Chairmen, Ladies and Gentlemen,

To appreciate the meaning of peace for the people of Israel, one has to view today's Jewish sovereignty in the Land of Israel against the background of our history.

Jews have been persecuted throughout the ages in almost every continent. Some countries barely tolerated us, others oppressed, tortured, slaughtered, and exiled us.

This century saw the Nazi regime set out to exterminate us. The Sho'ah, the Holocaust, the catastrophic genocide of unprecedented proportions which destroyed a third of our people, became possible because no one defended us. Being homeless, we were also defenseless.

But it was not the Holocaust which made the world community recognize our rightful claim to the Land of Israel. In fact, the rebirth of the State of Israel so soon after the Holocaust has made the world forget that our claim is immemorial. We are the only people who have lived in the Land of Israel without interruption for nearly 4,000 years; we are the only people, except for a short Crusader kingdom, who have had an independent sovereignty in this land; we are the only people for whom Jerusalem has been a capital; we are the only people whose sacred places are only in the Land of Israel.

No nation has expressed its bond with its land with as much intensity and consistency as we have. For millennia our people repeated at every occasion the cry of the Psalmist: "If I forget thee, Jerusalem, may my right hand lose its cunning." For millennia we have encouraged each other with the greeting, "next year in Jerusalem." For millennia our prayers, literature, and folklore have expressed powerful longing to return to our land. Only Eretz-Israel, the Land of Israel, is our true homeland. Any other country, no matter how hospitable, is still a diaspora, a temporary station on the way home.

To others, it was not an attractive land. No one wanted it. Mark Twain described it only a hundred years ago as "a desolate country, which sits in sack-cloth and ashes, a silent mournful expanse, which not even imagination can grace with the pomp of life."

The Zionist movement gave political expression to our claim to the Land of Israel. And in 1922 the League of Nations recognized the justice of this claim. It understood the compelling historic imperative of establishing a Jewish homeland in the Land of Israel. The United Nations Organization reaffirmed this recognition after the Second World War.

Regrettably, the Arab leaders, whose friendship we wanted most, opposed a Jewish state in the region. With a few distinguished exceptions, they claimed that the Land of Israel is part of the Arab domain that stretches from the Atlantic to the Persian Gulf.

In defiance of international will and legality, the Arab regimes attempted to overrun and destroy the Jewish state even before it was born.

The Arab spokesman at the U.N. declared that the establishment of a Jewish state would cause a bloodbath which would make the slaughters of Ghengis Khan pale into insignificance.

In its Declaration of Independence on May 15, 1948, Israel stretched out its hand in peace to its Arab neighbors, calling for an end to war and bloodshed. In response, seven Arab states invaded Israel. The U.N. resolution that partitioned the country was thus violated and effectively annulled.

The U.N. did not create Israel. The Jewish State came into being because the tiny Jewish community, in what was Mandatory Palestine, rebelled against foreign imperialist rule. We did not conquer a foreign land. We repulsed the Arab onslaught, prevented Israel's annihilation, declared its independence, and established a viable state and government institutions within a very short time.

After their attack on Israel failed, the Arab regimes continued their fight against Israel with boycott, blockade, terrorism, and outright war. Soon after the establishment of Israel, they turned against the Jewish communities in Arab countries. A wave of oppression, expropriation, and expulsion caused a mass exodus of some 800,000 Jews from lands they had inhabited from before the rise of Islam.

Most of these Jewish refugees, stripped of their considerable possessions, came to Israel. They were welcomed by the Jewish State. They were given shelter and support, and they were integrated into Israeli society together with half a million survivors of the European Holocaust.

The Arab regimes' rejection of Israel's existence in the Middle East, and the continuous war they have waged against it are part of history. There have been attempts to rewrite this history which depict the Arabs as victims and Israel as the aggressor. Like attempts to deny the Holocaust, they will fail. With the demise of totalitarian regimes in most of the world, this perversion of History will disappear.

In their war against Israel's existence, the Arab governments took advantage of the Cold War. They enlisted the military, economic, and political support of the Communist world against Israel, and they turned a local, regional conflict into an international powder-keg. This caused the Middle East to be flooded with arms, which fueled wars and turned the area into a dangerous battleground and a testing arena for sophisticated weapons. At the U.N., the Arab states mustered the support of other Muslim countries and the Soviet Bloc. Together they had an automatic majority for countless resolutions that perverted history, paraded fiction as fact, and made a travesty of the U.N. and its Charter.

Arab hostility to Israel has also brought tragic human suffering to the Arab people. Tens of thousands have been killed and wounded. Hundreds of thousands of Arabs who lived in Mandatory Palestine were encouraged by their own leaders to flee from their homes. Their suffering is a blot on humanity. No decent person, least of all a Jew of this era, can be oblivious to this suffering.

Several hundreds of thousands of Palestinian Arabs live in slums known as refugee camps in Gaza, Judea, and Samaria. Attempts by Israel to rehabilitate and house them have been defeated by Arab objections. Nor has their fate been any better in Arab states. Unlike the Jewish refugees who came to Israel from Arab countries, most Arab refugees were neither welcomed nor integrated by their hosts. Only the Kingdom of Jordan awarded them citizenship. Their plight has been used as a political weapon against Israel.

The Arabs who have chosen to remain in Israel—Christian, Muslim and Druze—have become full-fledged citizens enjoying equal rights and representation in the legislature, in the judiciary and in all walks of life.

We, who over the centuries were denied access to our holy places, respect the religion of all faiths in our country. Our law guarantees freedom of worship and protects the holy places of every religion.

Distinguished Co-Chairmen, Ladies and Gentlemen,

I stand before you today in yet another quest for peace, not only on behalf of the State of Israel, but in the name of the entire Jewish people, that has maintained an unbreakable bond with the Land of Israel for almost 4,000 years.

Our pursuit of accommodation and peace has been relentless. For us, the ingathering of Jews into their ancient homeland, their integration in our society, and the creation of the necessary infrastructure are at the very top of our national agenda. A nation that faces such a gigantic challenge would most naturally desire peace with all its neighbors.

Since the beginning of Zionism, we have formulated innumerable peace proposals and plans. All of them were rejected. The first crack in the wall of hostility occurred in 1977 when the late President Anwar Sadat of Egypt decided to break the taboo and come to Jerusalem. His gesture was reciprocated with enthusiasm by the people and government of Israel, headed by Menachem Begin. This development led to the Camp David Accords and the Treaty of Peace between Egypt and Israel. Four years later, in May 1983, an agreement was signed with the lawful government of Lebanon. Unfortunately, this agreement was not fulfilled, because of outside intervention. But the precedent was set, and we looked forward to courageous steps, similar to those of Anwar Sadat. Regrettably, not one Arab leader has seen fit to come forward and respond to our call for peace.

Today's gathering is a result of a sustained American effort, based on our own peace plan of May 1989 which, in turn, was founded on the Camp David Accords.

According to the American initiative, the purpose of this meeting is to launch direct peace negotiations between Israel and each of its neighbors, and multilateral negotiations on regional issues among all the countries of the region.

We have always believed that only direct, bilateral talks can bring peace. We have agreed to precede such talks with this ceremonial conference, but we hope that Arab consent to direct, bilateral talks indicates an understanding that there is no other way to peace. In the Middle East, this has special meaning, because such talks imply mutual acceptance; and the root cause of the conflict is the Arab refusal to recognize the legitimacy of the State of Israel.

The multilateral talks that would accompany the bilateral negotiations are a vital component in the process. In these talks, the essential ingredients of co-existence and regional cooperation will be discussed. There cannot be genuine peace in our region unless these regional issues are addressed and resolved.

We believe the goal of the bilateral negotiations is to sign peace treaties between Israel and its neighbors, and to reach an agreement on interim self-government arrangements with the Palestinian Arabs.

But nothing can be achieved without goodwill. I appeal to the Arab leaders, those who are here and those who have not yet joined the process: Show us and the world that you accept Israel's existence. Demonstrate your readiness to accept Israel as a permanent entity in the region. Let the people in our region hear you speak in the language of reconciliation, co-existence, and peace with Israel.

In Israel there is an almost total consensus for the need for peace. We only differ on the best ways to achieve it. In most Arab countries the opposite seems to be true: the only differences are over the ways to push Israel into a defenseless position and, ultimately, to destruction. We would like to see in your countries an end to poisonous preaching against Israel. We would like to see an indication of the kind of hunger for peace which characterizes Israeli society.

We appeal to you to renounce the *Jihad* against Israel. We appeal to you to denounce the PLO covenant which calls for Israel's destruction. We appeal to you to condemn declarations that call for Israel's annihilation, like the one issued by the rejectionist conference in Teheran last week. We appeal to you to let Jews, who wish to leave your countries, go.

And we address a call to the Palestinian Arabs: Renounce violence and terrorism; use the universities in the administered territories—whose existence was made possible only by Israel—for learning and development, not agitation and violence; stop exposing your children to danger by sending them to throw bombs and stones at soldiers and civilians.

Just two days ago, we were reminded that Palestinian terrorism is still rampant, when a mother of seven children and a father of four were slaughtered in cold blood. We cannot remain indifferent and be expected to talk with people involved in such repulsive activities.

We appeal to you to shun dictators like Saddam Hussein who aim to destroy Israel; stop the brutal torture and murder of those who do not agree with you; allow us, and the world community, to build decent housing for the people who now live in refugee camps. Above all, we hope you finally realize that you could have been at this table long ago, soon after the Camp David accords were first concluded, had you chosen dialogue instead of violence, coexistence instead of terrorism.

Ladies and Gentlemen: We come to this process with an open heart, sincere intentions, and great expectations. We are committed to negotiating without interruption until an agreement is reached. There will be problems, obstacles, crises, and conflicting claims. But it is better to talk than to shed blood. Wars have not solved anything in our region. They have only caused misery, suffering, bereavement and hatred.

We know our partners to the negotiations will make territorial demands on Israel. But, as an examination of the conflict's long history makes clear, its nature is not territorial. It raged well before Israel acquired Judea, Samaria, Gaza and the Golan in a defensive war. There was no hint of recognition of Israel before the war in 1967, when the territories in question were not under Israeli control.

We are a nation of four million. The Arab nations from the Atlantic to the Gulf number 170 million. We control only 28,000 square kilometers. The Arabs possess a land mass of 14 million square kilometers. The issue is not territory but our existence.

It will be regrettable if the talks focus primarily and exclusively on territory. It is the quickest way to an impasse. What we need, first and foremost, is the building of confidence, the removal of the danger of confrontation, and the development of relations in as many spheres as possible.

The issues are complex, and the negotiations will be lengthy and difficult. We submit that the best venue for the talks is in our region, in close proximity to the decision-makers, not in a foreign land. We invite our partners to this process to come to Israel for the first round of talks. On our part, we are ready to go to Jordan, to Lebanon, and to Syria for the same purpose. There is no better way to make peace than to talk in each other's home. Avoiding such talks is a denial of the purpose of the negotiations. I would welcome a positive answer from the representatives of these states here and now. We must learn to live together. We must learn to live without war, without bloodshed. Judaism has given the world not only the belief in one God, but the idea that all men and women are created in God's image. There is no greater sin than to ravage this image by shedding blood.

I am sure that there is no Arab mother who wants her son to die in battle—just as there is no Jewish mother who wants her son to die in war. I believe every mother wants her children to learn the art of living, not the science of war.

For many hundreds of years, wars, deep antagonisms, and terrible suffering cursed this continent on which we meet. The nations of Europe saw the rise of dictators and their defeat after lengthy and painful struggles. Now, they are together—former bitter enemies—in a united community. They are discussing the good of the community, cooperating in all matters, acting almost as one unit. I envy them. I would like to see such a community rise in the Middle East. And I believe that, despite all differences between us, we should be able, gradually, to build a united regional community. Today it is a dream—but we have seen, in our own lifetime, some of the most fantastic dreams become reality. Today, the gulf separating the two sides is still too wide; the Arab hostility to Israel too deep; the lack of trust too immense, to permit a dramatic, quick solution. But, we must start on the long road to reconciliation with this first step in the peace process.

We are convinced that human nature prefers peace to war and belligerence. We, who have had to fight seven wars and sacrifice many thousands of lives, glorify neither death nor war. The Jewish faith exalts peace even to the extent that it considers it a synonym for the Creator Himself. We yearn for peace. We pray for peace.

We believe the blessing, of peace can turn the Middle East into a paradise; a center of cultural, scientific, medical and technological creativity.

We can foresee a period of great economic progress that would put an end to misery, hunger and illiteracy. It could put the Middle East—the cradle of civilization—on the road to a new era.

Such a goal merits our devotion and dedication for as long as it is necessary until, in the words of the prophet Isaiah, we shall be able to turn "swords into ploughshares" and bring the blessings of peace to all the peoples of our region. Let me conclude with the words of the same prophet:

"Peace, peace, both for far and near, says the Lord."

Distinguished Co-Chairmen, Ladies and Gentlemen,

Let us resolve to leave this hall with a united determination that from now on, any differences we may have will be solved only by negotiations, goodwill and mutual tolerance. Let us declare, here and now, an end to war, to belligerency, and to hostility. Let us march forward together, to reconciliation and peace.

DR. KAMEL ABU JABER, *Minister of Foreign Affairs of the Hashemite Kingdom of Jordan*

"Blessed are the Peace Makers."

The Honorable James Baker, Secretary of State of the United States of America, the Honorable Boris Pankin, Foreign Minister of the Union of Soviet Socialist Republics, Distinguished Personal Representative of the Secretary-General of the United Nations, Ambassador Edward Brunner, the Distinguished Head of the European Community Delegation, Mr. van den Broek, Foreign Minister of the Kingdom of the Netherlands, the Distinguished Observer from the Gulf Cooperation Council, His Excellency Mr. Abdullah Bisharah, the Distinguished Observer from the Maghreb Cooperation Council, His Excellency Mr. Mohammad Amamu, Distinguished Delegates, Ladies and Gentlemen,

It is with sincere appreciation that I thank the governments of the United States of America and the Union of the Soviet Socialist Republics for co-sponsoring this historic Conference. For us this occasion represents what we must strive to make, the final turning point, from a drift towards ultimate disaster for our peoples, our region, and possibly the world, to a new era of a properly constructed true peace, hope, and life. All the parties to this most chronic and tragic conflict need your continued interest and support, together with the rest of the world, so that we may attain the just peace that the peoples of the region need and deserve.

We also salute His Majesty King Juan Carlos, the guardian of Spanish democracy, as well as Prime Minister Felipe Gonzalez, the Spanish government and people, for hosting the conference in Madrid. We thank them for their gracious hospitality and warm welcome.

This is an historic moment. The challenges and the issues before us are momentous. In his speech before the National Congress in Amman on 12th October 1991, His Majesty King Hussein identified the essence of the challenge when he spoke of the possibilities of true peace and its implications for the future of the children of Abraham, father of both Jews and Arabs alike. It is worthy of note that Spain seeks to honor Arabs and Jews in 1992 in the context of the contributions of the Andalus and Sepharad. Together they generously contributed to a rich civilization, the fruits of which not only Spain, but the world and humanity, have since appreciated.

It is not impossible to hope that this Conference will herald the dawn of a new era to rectify the mistakes of the past. Perhaps the possibility of joint contribution is again at hand. Everyone must remember that God has "created mankind as nations and tribes so that they may know each other. The most noble of you, in the sight of Allah, is the most pious" (The Holy Koran, Sura 49/13). And if this Conference does anything, it must end Israel's self-righteous attitude to live by its own rules alone. This Conference is also about the credibility of international law, the United Nations Charter, and human rights.

Ladies and Gentlemen,

Jordan comes to this Conference in good faith. Our vision is not merely an end to hostility—another truce—but a comprehensive, just, and permanent peace. Our region has known nothing but instability and violence since the turn of the century. It is about time that it enjoys peace.

What is needed is not only sight but vision—vision to stand on top of the hill, not in the valley, so as to enable ourselves to look into the future and to evaluate the consequences of the absence of peace. For far too long, the peoples of the region have been locked in the groove of their own historical animosities, suspicions, and acrimony.

That is why we in Jordan register our appreciation for the endeavor of President Bush, as well as the support of President Gorbachev. It is our hope that the personal interest and support of both will remain, even increase, throughout the negotiations.

We come to this Conference standing on strong moral grounds, buttressed by a record of moderation and wise vision since the creation of our state in modern times. The most tragic conflict which we are now addressing is one of the oldest on the agenda of the United Nations, and though it may appear regional, its international dimensions are many and obvious. It is especially so against the background of the Gulf crisis in that it severely tests the credibility of the United Nations and that of the five permanent members of the Security Council. It was in the wake of the Gulf crisis that President Bush undertook to work seriously toward its resolution. We also appreciate the Soviet co-sponsorship of the effort as well as the support of the European Community. We take heart that this whole enterprise is firmly anchored in international legitimacy as embodied in United Nations Security Council Resolutions 242 and 338 based on the principle of the inadmissibility of acquisition of territory by force, and providing for the exchange of land for peace.

While it was true that most Arabs, out of a sense of outrage and feelings of injustice and betrayal, have refused since 1947 to contemplate accommodation, there were others in the Arab world who were willing to be counted for peace. Over the decades of the thirties, forties, and beyond, indeed until the present moment, the arena was abandoned to the radicals. In the clash of ideas, visions, and armies that have ensued since then, reason, often humanity itself, was pushed beyond the frontiers of choice. The situation deteriorated to the condition of a primitive state of nature, where brute force replaced civilized behavior, where might replaced right.

The Hashemite Kingdom of Jordan, which I have the honor to represent, has been, since the outset of this conflict, on the side of every effort to seriously solve it peacefully. King Hussein was actively involved in the formulation of United Nations Security Council Resolution 242, a foundation of this Conference.

Ladies and Gentlemen,

Today we have an historic opportunity for peace in a land that has not tasted it for a long time. We must remember that the extremists and the rejectionists who speak in absolute terms are still lurking in the wings. It is from there that they issue their often repeated clichés and venomous threats.

Inasmuch as peace is a good in itself, an inherent value, it is also a battle against the absolutist ideologues invoking ancient hatreds. Many think that the situation should not be resolved but left to future generations to deal with. Those of vision, however, see it differently. Considering the immediacy of the need to reach a settlement at this particular moment of world history with its interdependence between peoples and nations, King Hussein said:

> We must be involved in the drive for peace because it concerns our present and future . . . otherwise, the outcome, God forbid, will be ominous dangers.

It is for this reason that it is important to emphasize transcending the present in the search for the future. To continue to be locked in the mental straitjacket of absolutist ideologies means that there will never be a way out of the shackles of hatred.

We take to heart and with respect the words of President Bush in his 6th of March, 1991 address before the American Congress, when he said:

> I expressed my hope that out of the horrors of war might come new momentum for peace. We have learned in the modern age, geography cannot guarantee security and security does not come from military power alone . . . By now, it should be plain to all parties that peacemaking in the Middle East requires compromise.

Peace cannot, indeed must not, reflect the military balance of the belligerents now. It should, essentially, reflect the hope of a better future that will end, once and for all, our living in the midst of conflicting tragedies. It should bring us all in step with a new world that will shatter the shadows, the misery, and the fog that engulfs our lives. It was Albert Einstein who said: "Peace cannot be kept by force. It can only be achieved by understanding."

It should not be a peace at any price but an honorable peace with which we and future generations can live: a durable peace which is the product of negotiations. It must be the outcome of mutual understanding and accommodation between the parties to the conflict without sacrificing rights or deviating from the principles of international law.

Jordan's position rests on the very simple yet direct assumption that in the end, nothing is true but the truth; that a moral and just stand is ultimately more powerful than brute force. Although the world, and the Israelis themselves, know and are aware of our innocence of the crimes against the Jewish people, Israel's indignant outrage has not induced a sense of balanced justice. It has become our fate in Jordan to live with, as well as to suffer, and to contain the powerful forces of extremism. The Nazis and others unleashed the passions of injured Zionism for which the Palestinians and Jordan have paid the price.

God only knows the price we continue to pay for the sins of others. It has come to pass that our land, our culture, our people, even our very souls, as well as everything we hold dear and sacred, continue to be plundered and distorted to accommodate new realities and manufactured facts, brutally created on the ground.

And so it is that we not only ask what to do, but also welcome the present effort. The question is the more agonizing as we in the Arab world, and in Jordan in particular, contemplate our situation. In Jordan three times in four decades, we had to make room for large waves of destitute and bewildered refugees forced out of their lands and homes.

We are aware, as are our people, that in the nature of things a negotiated settlement does not represent total justice. Yet, with our traditional Jordanian moderation, rational approach, and consideration of our vision of the future, we have made consensus and balance a cornerstone of our political thesis since 1967. In the words of King Hussein:

> Peace is essential to us in leading a normal life . . . We have made it a symbol for a better life for future generations. . . . Peace has become a national objective.

That is why we think that the formula of land for peace rings more meaningfully true than any other principle or slogan. The echo of the drums of war reverberates in the heart and soul of the region. Is it not time that we, now on the threshold of the twenty-first century, bring peace to our peoples?

Ladies and Gentlemen,

Jordan enters this process from a position of moral strength, secure in the knowledge that reasonable men can reach reasonable solutions; that justice must ultimately prevail; that peace is indeed the master of all judgments, and its logic necessitates accommodation, not belligerency. Otherwise, we may truly become one-dimensional with neither soul nor spirit, driven by the primeval instincts of the political jungle, leading us to perish in perils of our own making.

We should shed the psychology of fear, get out of the shadow, and realize that states, too, like people, sometimes commit suicide because of their fear of life. More land is not more security. Occupation is against every legal principle, and the shape it has taken in the Arab occupied territories contravenes the United Nations Charter and the Fourth Geneva Convention. The building of settlements and the expropriation of land are both in clear contravention of the rules of international law.

The justice that Jordan seeks requires resort to law; law that governs the action of men, freeing them to live secure in a stable, ordered, and institutionalized universe. That alone can assure the proper division of labor and resources, and that alone can guarantee not only survival, but freedom and security. The technology of war has far out-distanced our true appreciation of its destructiveness and danger. Otherwise, how can we continue to contemplate our security in terms of missiles, nuclear, biological, and chemical weapons? Our mission must transcend the issues of mere survival to become the search for a new future.

That is why His Majesty King Hussein, in his nationwide speech of 12th October, 1991, solicited the help and support of the international community in this process:

> Our cause is not only between us and Israel but also between the world and Israel . . . between the supremacy of international law . . . and the flouting of it. . . . The whole world rejects what Israel's leadership is saying because it contravenes international legitimacy . . . Indeed, a relatively growing segment of Israelis are not too far from this world view.

The King added that our world today is "peace-oriented" and that the Arabs and the rest of the world will come together in their mutual desire and interests to find a peaceful solution.

That is one of the bases of the Jordanian position: a search for peace secure in the support of the entire Arab world, indeed, the whole world community, and in particular, the Palestinians. We and the Palestinians have a just cause which must be addressed and resolved with equity and fairness.

Our second basis for entering this peace process is our expectation that there will be no asymmetry or double standards.

The third basis of the Jordanian approach is that our cause and that of our Palestinian brethren is intricately linked by ties of history, culture, religion, language, demography, geography, as well as human suffering and national aspirations. King Hussein said:

> We would have preferred an independent Palestinian delegation, though we have no objection to providing an umbrella for our Palestinian brethren, since we are keenly aware that both Jordanians and Palestinians are besieged as the parties directly and adversely

effected by the continuation of the status quo of the Arab-Israeli conflict.

Fourth, the peace we seek must be based on United Nations Security Council Resolutions 242 and 338. The objective is real peace. We must emphasize that our understanding of Resolution 242 is that it is based on the principle of the inadmissibility of the acquisition of territory by war and the exchange of land for peace. The deliberations preceding its adoption and in which Jordan participated were based on that principle. Our position is firmly based on United Nations resolutions and international law. We are aware that Israel's creation was the result of United Nations Resolution 181 of 29th November, 1947. It is in accordance with the strength of these resolutions as well as the general principles of international law that Jordan demands the total withdrawal of Israeli forces from occupied Jordanian, Palestinian, Syrian, and Lebanese lands.

The three dimensions of the Jordanian position—the Jordanian, Palestinian, and regional—are founded on international law. Resolution 242 is a valid international instrument unanimously agreed upon by the international community. It is binding on all member states of the United Nations in accordance with Article 25 of the United Nations Charter.

Arab sovereignty must be restored in Arab Jerusalem. In the context of peace, Jerusalem will represent the essence and symbol of peace between the followers of the three great monotheistic religions. It is God's will that has made the historic city important to them all.

The illegal settlements should be removed and not augmented; the issue of Palestinian refugees and that of the displaced must be solved in accordance with the relevant United Nations resolutions. The Palestinian people must be allowed to exercise their right of self-determination in their ancestral home-land. The fulfillment of these demands is a question of the credibility of United Nations resolutions. Let me speak plainly— Jordan has never been Palestine and will not be so.

Withdrawal from Lebanon and the application of United Nations Security Council Resolution 425 is also an essential prerequisite for the establishment of a regional peace.

Fifth, the peace we seek as a result of negotiations is a permanent one, a just and comprehensive peace—that will focus on region-wide issues such as arms control and regional security, water, the environment, the fate of the Palestinian refugees and the displaced, and the economic balance among the peoples of the area through joint development programs. Peace must mean security for all, protected by all in their hearts and souls, because it is founded on justice and honor.

Sixth, our position is also predicated on our vision of a better future that will replace the present bitterness and frustration and, in the words of King Hussein:

> enable us to transform the realities into positive forces that will take us from despair to hope, from confrontation and the four decades of suffering, anxiety, and pain that accompanied it, and which left an imprint on our lives, to peace and its promise of security, stability, opportunities, and prosperity for all; from the no-war, no-peace situation and its real dangers, to a condition of certainty and ease which will enhance the creativity and hopes of the younger generation.

We seek a real peace where men, women, and children do not have to cower behind fortresses. Our quest is for an honorable peace that would enable our peoples to tear down the walls of fear and hatred, as people tore down the Berlin Wall. We want our peoples to welcome a new dawn and to enjoy the warmth of a new day, rather than the long night of darkness, which has been their fortune until now.

Ladies and Gentlemen,

It is our hope that the world appreciates and supports our position, based as it is on our liberal and peaceful Jordanian experiment in socio-economic and political development. An experiment that deserves support as it continues the Jordanian tradition of democratization, institutionalization, and the transition to political pluralism. The test, indeed the challenge of peace, is both domestic and global in that it severely exacerbates our current economic crisis, as we are compelled to absorb a third wave of returnees in the wake of the Gulf crisis.

We hope that this Peace Conference will work toward the solution of all these momentous problems leading not only to the withdrawal of Israeli forces from the Arab occupied lands, including Arab Jerusalem, but also to the delineation of Israel's permanent borders and finally real peace.

We have taken a bold step which commits us to innovative thinking that will bring peace and prosperity to the region. The parties to the conflict suffer from too many recollections of their wounded cultures. Somehow we must endeavor to bring about the change needed. We cannot continue to inhabit two different universes in this small space of land with its limited resources. Already there is too much ideological rigidity that continues to be an obstacle to sensible and rational life. For those who continue to think in absolute terms, we must emphasize that, while history may have time, men are mortal; that not only our civilizations need their wounds to be healed, but the very land, scarred by the march of armies to the drums of war, needs mending as well. There exists a limit to force and this may be the moment to heal not only the mental agony, but also to remove the physical trenches dug deep in the land. This requires patience, vision, perseverance, and wisdom deeper than mere intelligence.

Ladies and Gentlemen,
It is fitting to end this statement with a verse from the Holy Koran.

Let not a people's enmity towards you incite you to act contrary to justice; be always just, that is closest to righteousness.
(The Koran, Sura 5–8)

DR. HAIDAR ABD EL-SHAFI, Head of the Palestinian Side of the Jordanian/Palestinian Delegation

Secretary Baker, Foreign Minister Pankin, Your Excellencies, Ladies and Gentlemen,
On behalf of the Palestinian delegation, I would like to extend our warmest gratitude to our host, the Government of Spain, for its gracious hospitality, and to King Carlos and Prime Minister Gonzalez. We thank the co-sponsors of this Middle East Peace Conference for their relentless efforts in convening this Conference. A special thanks is due from our delegation to the United Nations and to the nations of Europe and Scandinavia, for their consistent and principled support for the rights of the Palestinian people.

Ladies and Gentlemen,
We meet in Madrid, a city with the rich texture of history, to weave together the fabric which joins our past with the future, to reaffirm a wholeness of vision, which once brought about a rebirth of civilization and a world order based on harmony in diversity.
Once again, Christian, Moslem and Jew faced the challenge of heralding a new era enshrined in global values of democracy, human rights, freedom, justice and security. From Madrid we launched this quest for peace, a quest to place the sanctity of human life at the center of our world and to redirect our energies and resources from the pursuit of mutual destruction to the pursuit of joint prosperity, progress, and happiness.

We, the people of Palestine, stand before you in the fullness of our pain, our pride, and our anticipation, for we have long harbored a yearning for peace and a dream of justice and freedom. For too long the Palestinian people have gone unheeded, silenced, and denied—our identity negated by political expediency, our rightful struggle against injustice maligned, and our present existence subsumed by the past tragedy of another people.

Your Excellencies, ladies and gentlemen, for the greater part of this century, we have been victimized by the myth of "a land without a people," and described with impunity as "the invisible Palestinians." Before such willful blindness, we refused to disappear or to accept a distorted identity. Our Intifada is a testimony to our perseverance and resilience, waged in a just struggle to regain our rights.

It is time for us to narrate our own story, to stand witness as advocates of a truth which has long lain buried in the consciousness and conscience of the world. We do not stand before you as supplicants, but rather as the torch bearers who know that in our world of today, ignorance can never be an excuse. We seek neither an admission of guilt after the fact, nor vengeance for past iniquities, but rather an act of will that would make a just peace a reality. We speak out, ladies and gentlemen, from the full conviction of the rightness of our cause, the verity of our history, and the depth of our commitment. Therein lies the strength of the Palestinian people today, for we have scaled the walls of fear and reticence and we wish to speak out with the courage and integrity that our narrative and history deserve.

The co-sponsors have invited us here today to present our case and to reach out to "the other" with whom we have had to face a mutually exclusive reality on the land of Palestine. But even in the invitation to this Peace Conference, our narrative was distorted and our truth only partially acknowledged. The Palestinian people are one, fused by centuries of history in Palestine, bound together by a collective memory of shared sorrows and joys and sharing a unity of purpose and vision. Our songs and ballads, our folk tales and children's stories, the dialect of our jokes, the images of our poems, that hint of melancholy which colors even our happiest moments, are as important to us as the blood ties which link our families and clans.

Yet the invitation to discuss peace, the peace we all desire and need, comes to only a portion of our people. It ignores our national, historical, and organic unity. We come here wrenched from our sisters and brothers in exile to stand before you as the Palestinians under occupation, although we maintain that each of us represents the rights and interest of the whole. We have been denied the right to publicly acknowledge our loyalty to our leadership and system of government, but allegiance and loyalty cannot be censored or severed. Our acknowledged leadership is more than just the democratically chosen leadership of all the Palestinians people; it is the symbol of our national identity and unity—the guardian of our past, the protector of our present, and the hope of our future. Our people have chosen to entrust it with their history and the preservation of our precious legacy. This leadership has been clearly and unequivocally recognized by the community of nations, with only a few exceptions who had chosen, for so many years, shadow over substance.

Regardless of the nature and conditions of our oppression, whether the dispossession and dispersion of exile or the brutality and repression of the occupation, the Palestinian people cannot be torn asunder. They remain united, a nation wherever they are, or are forced to be.

And Jerusalem, ladies and gentlemen, that city which is not only the soul of Palestine but the cradle of three world religions, is tangible even in its claimed absence from our midst at this stage. Its apparent, though artificial, exclusion from this Conference is a denial of its right to seek peace and redemption, for it too has suffered from war and occupation. Jerusalem, the city of peace, has been barred from a peace Conference and deprived of its calling. Palestinian Jerusalem, the capital of our homeland and future state, defines Palestinian existence—past, present and future—but itself has been denied a voice and an identity. Jerusalem defies exclusive possessiveness or bondage. Israel's annexation of Jerusalem remains both clearly illegal in the eyes of the world community and an affront to the peace that this city deserves.

We come to you from a tortured land and a proud, though captive, people, having been asked to negotiate with our occupiers, but leaving behind the children of the Intifada, and a people under occupation and under curfew, who enjoined us not to surrender or forget. As we speak, thousands of our brothers and sisters are languishing in Israeli prisons and detention camps, most detained without evidence, charge, or trial, many cruelly mistreated and tortured in interrogation, guilty only of seeking freedom or daring to defy the occupation. We speak in their name and we say: set them free.

As we speak, the tens of thousands who have been wounded or permanently disabled are in pain: let peace heal their wounds. As we speak, the eyes of thousands of Palestinian refugees, deportees, and displaced persons since 1967 are haunting us, for exile is a cruel fate: bring them home. They have the right to return. As we speak, the silence of demolished homes echoes through the halls and in our minds: we must rebuild our homes in our free state.

And what do we tell the loved ones of those killed by army bullets? How do we answer the questions and the fear in our children's eyes? For one out of three Palestinian children under occupation has been killed, injured, or detained in the past four years. How can we explain to our children that they are denied education, our schools so often closed by army fiat? Or why their life is in danger for raising a flag in a land where even children are killed or jailed? What requiem can be sung for trees uprooted by army bulldozers? And, most of all, who can explain to those whose lands are confiscated and clear waters stolen, the message of peace? Remove the barbed wire, restore the land and its life-giving water.

The settlements must stop now. Peace cannot be waged while Palestinian land is confiscated in myriad ways and the status of the Occupied Territories is being decided each day by Israeli bulldozers and barbed wire. This is not simply a position; it is an irrefutable reality. Territory for peace is a travesty when territory for illegal settlement is official Israeli policy and practice. The settlements must stop now.

In the name of the Palestinian people, we wish to directly address the Israeli people with whom we have had a prolonged exchange of pain: let us share hope instead. We are willing to live side by side on the land and the promise of the future. Sharing, however, requires two partners willing to share as equals. Mutuality and reciprocity must replace domination and hostility for genuine reconciliation and coexistence under international legality. Your security and ours are mutually dependent, as entwined as the fears and nightmares of our children.

We have seen some of you at your best and at your worst, for the occupier can hide no secrets from the occupied, and we are witness to the toll that occupation has exacted from you and yours. We have seen you anguish over the transformation of your sons and daughters into instruments of a blind and violent occupation—and we are sure that at no time did you envisage such a role for the children whom you thought would forge your future. We have seen you look back in deepest sorrow at the tragedy of your past and look on in horror at the disfigurement of the victim turned oppressor. Not for this have you nurtured your hopes, dreams and your offspring.

This is why we have responded with solemn appreciation to those of you who came to offer consolation to our bereaved, to give support to those whose homes were being demolished, and to extend encouragement and counsel to those detained behind barbed wire and iron bars. And we have marched together, often choking together at the nondiscriminatory tear gas or crying out in pain as the clubs descended on both Palestinian and Israeli alike. For pain knows no national boundaries, and no one can claim a monopoly on suffering.

We once formed a human chain around Jerusalem, joining hands and calling for peace. Let us today form a moral chain around Madrid and continue that noble effort for peace and the promise of freedom for our sons and daughters. Break through the barriers of mistrust and manipulated fears. Let us look forward in magnanimity and in hope.

To our Arab brothers and sisters, most of whom are represented here in this historic occasion, we express our loyalty and gratitude for their life-long support and solidarity. We are here together seeking a just and lasting peace whose cornerstone is freedom for Palestine, justice for the Palestinians, and an end to the occupation of all Palestinian and Arab lands. Only then can we really enjoy together the fruits of peace: prosperity, security and human dignity and freedom.

In particular, we address our Jordanian colleagues in our joint delegation. Our two peoples have a very special historic and geographic relationship. Together, we shall strive to achieve peace. We will continue to strive for our sovereignty, while proceeding freely and willingly to prepare the grounds for a confederation between the two states of Palestine and Jordan, which can be a cornerstone for our security and prosperity.

To the community of nations on our fragile planet, to the nations of Africa and Asia, to the Muslim world, and particularly to Europe, on whose southern and neighborly shores we meet today: from the heart of our collective struggle for peace, we greet you and acknowledge your support and recognition. You have recognized our rights and our government, and have given us real support and protection. You have penetrated the distorting mist of racism, stereotyping, and ignorance and committed the act of seeing the "invisible" and listening to the voice of the silenced. The Palestinians, under occupation and in exile, have become a reality in your eyes and, with courage and determination, you have affirmed the truth of our narrative. You have taken up our cause and our case, and we have brought you into our hearts. We thank you for caring and daring to know the truth—the truth which must set us all free.

To the co-sponsors and participants in this occasion of awe and challenge, we pledge our commitment to the principle of justice, peace and reconciliation based on international legitimacy and uniform standards. We shall persist, in our quest for peace, to place before you the substance and determination of our people, often victimized but never defeated. We shall pursue our people's right to self-determination, to the exhilaration of freedom, and to the warmth of the sun as a nation among equals.

This is the moment of truth; you must have the courage to recognize it and the will to implement it for our truth can no longer be hidden away in the dark recesses of inadvertency or neglect. The people of Palestine look at you with a straightforward, direct gaze, seeking to touch your heart, for you have dared to stir up hopes that cannot be abandoned. You cannot afford to let us down, for we have lived up to the values you espouse, and we have remained true to our cause.

We, the Palestinian people, made the imaginative leap in the Palestine National Council of November 1988, during which the Palestine Liberation Organization (PLO) launched its peace initiative based on Security Council Resolutions 242 and 338, and declared Palestinian independence based on Resolution 181 of the United Nations, which gave birth to two states in 1948: Israel and Palestine. In December 1988, a historic speech before the United Nations in Geneva led directly to the launching of the Palestinian-American dialogue. Ever since then, our people has responded positively to every serious peace initiative and has done its utmost to ensure the success of this process. Israel, on the other hand, has placed many obstacles and barriers in the path of peace to negate the very validity of the process. Its illegal and frenzied settlement activity is the most glaring evidence of its rejectionism, the latest settlement being erected just two days ago.

These historic decisions of the Palestine National Council wrenched the course of history from inevitable confrontation and conflict towards peace and mutual recognition. With our own hands, and in an act of sheer will, we have molded the shape of the future of our people. Our parliament has articulated the message of a people with the courage to say "yes" to the challenge of history, just as it provided the reference, in its resolutions last month in Algiers and in the Central Council meeting this month in Tunis, to go forward to this historic Conference. We cannot be made to bear the brunt of other people's "no." We must have reciprocity. We must have peace.

Ladies and gentlemen, in the Middle East there is no superfluous people outside time and place, but rather a state sorely missed by time and place—the state of Palestine. It must be born on the land of Palestine to redeem the injustice of the destruction of its historical reality and to free the people of Palestine from the shackles of their victimization. Our homeland has never ceased to exist in our minds and hearts, but it has to exist as a state on all the territories occupied by Israel in the war of 1967, with Jerusalem as its capital, in the context of that city's special status and its non-exclusive character.

This state, in a condition of emergence, has already been a subject of anticipation for too long. It should take place today, rather than tomorrow. However, we are willing to accept the proposal for a transitional stage, provided interim arrangements are not transformed into permanent status. The time frame must be condensed to respond to the dispossessed Palestinians' urgent need for sanctuary and to the occupied Palestinians' right to gain relief from oppression and to win recognition of their authentic will. During this phase, international protection for our people is most urgently needed, and the *de jure* application of the Fourth Geneva Convention is a necessary condition. The phases must not prejudice the outcome; rather they require an internal momentum and motivation to lead sequentially to sovereignty. Bilateral negotiations on the withdrawal of Israeli forces, the dissolution of Israeli administration and the transfer of authority to the Palestinian people cannot proceed under coercion or threat in the current asymmetry of power. Israel must demonstrate its willingness to negotiate in good faith by immediately halting all settlement activity and land confiscation while implementing meaningful confidence-building measures. Without genuine progress, tangible constructive changes and just agreements during the bilateral talks, multilateral negotiations will be meaningless. Regional stability, security and development are the logical outcome of an equitable and just solution to the Palestinian question, which remains the key to the resolution of wider conflicts and concerns.

In its confrontation of wills between the legitimacy of the people and the illegality of the occupation, the Intifada's message has been consistent: to embody the Palestinian state and to build its institutions and infrastructure. We seek recognition for this creative impulse which nurtures within it the potential nascent state. We have paid a heavy price for daring to substantiate our authenticity and to practice popular democracy in spite of the cruelty of occupation. It was a sheer act of will that brought us here, the same will which asserted itself in the essence of the Intifada, as the cry for freedom, an act of civil resistance, and people's participation and empowerment. The Intifada is our drive towards nation building and social transformation. We are here today with the support of our people, who have given itself the right to hope and to make a stand for peace. We must recognize, as well, that some of our people harbor serious doubts and skepticism about this process. Within our democratic, social, and political structures, we have evolved a respect for pluralism and diversity, and we shall guard the opposition's right to differ within the parameters of mutual respect and national unity.

The process launched here must lead us to the light at the end of the tunnel, and this light is the promise of a new Palestine—free, democratic, and respectful of human rights and the integrity of nature. Self-determination, ladies and gentlemen, can neither be granted nor withheld at the whim of the political self-interest of others, for it is enshrined in all international charters and humanitarian law. We claim this right; we firmly assert it here before you and in the eyes of the rest of the world, for it is a sacred and inviolable right which we shall relentlessly pursue and exercise with dedication and self-confidence and pride.

Let us end the Palestinian-Israeli fatal proximity in this unnatural condition of occupation, which has already claimed too many lives. No dream of expansion or glory can justify the taking of a single life. Set us free to reengage as neighbors and as equals on our holy land.

To our people in exile and under occupation, who have sent us to this appointment laden with their trust, love, and aspirations, we say that the load is heavy, and the task is great, but we shall be true. In the words of our great national poet, Mahmoud Darwish: "My homeland is not a suitcase, and I am no traveler." To the exiled and the occupied, we say: You shall return and you shall remain and we will prevail, for our cause is just. We will put on our embroidered robes and kufiyyas and, in the sight of the world, celebrate together on the day of liberation.

Refugee camps are no fit home for people who had been reared on the land of Palestine, in the warmth of the sun and freedom. The hail of Israeli bombs, almost daily pouring down on our defenseless civilian population in the refugee camps of Lebanon, is no substitute for the healing rain of the homeland. Yet, the international will had ensured their return in United Nations Resolution 194—a fact willfully ignored and unenacted.

Similarly, all other resolutions pertinent to the Palestinian question, beginning with Resolution 181, through Resolutions 242 and 338, and ending with Security Council Resolution 681, have, until now, been relegated to the domain of public debate, rather than real implementation.

They form the larger body of legality, including all relevant provisions of international law, within which any peaceful settlement must proceed. If international legitimacy and the rule of law are to prevail and govern relations among nations, they must be respected and, impartially and uniformly, implemented. We, as Palestinians, require nothing less than justice.

To Palestinians everywhere: today we bear in our hands the precious gift of your love and your pain, and we shall set it down gently here before the eyes of the world and say—there is a right here which must be acknowledged, the right to self-determination and statehood; there is strength and there is the scent of sacred incense in the air. Jerusalem, the heart of our homeland and the cradle of the soul, is shimmering through the barriers of occupation and deceit. The deliberate violation of its sanctity is also an act of violence against the collective human, cultural, and spiritual memory and an aggression against its enduring symbols of tolerance, magnanimity, and respect for cultural and religious authenticity. The cobbled streets of the Old City must not echo with the discordant beat of Israeli military boots; we must restore to them the chant of the muezzin, the chimes of the church bells, and the prayers of all the faithful calling for peace in the City of Peace.

From Madrid, let us light the candle of peace and let the olive branch blossom. Let us celebrate the rituals of justice and rejoice in the hymns of truth, for the awe of the moment is a promise to the future, which we must all redeem. The Palestinians will be free, and will stand tall among the community of nations in the fullness of the pride and dignity which by right belongs to all people. Today, our people under occupation are holding high the olive branch of peace. In the words of Chairman Arafat in 1974 before the U.N. General Assembly: "Let not the olive branch of peace fall from my hands." Let not the olive branch fall from the hands of the Palestinian people.

MR. FARES BOUEZ, Minister of Foreign Affairs of the Republic of Lebanon

Mr. James Baker, Secretary of State of the United States of America, Mr. Boris Pankin, Minister of Foreign Affairs of the Soviet Union, Excellencies, Heads of Delegations, Ladies and Gentlemen,

I have the pleasure, in the name of the President of the Republic of Lebanon, His Excellency Mr. Elias Hrawi, and on behalf of the Government of Lebanon, to extend my deepest thanks to Spain, to His Majesty the King, to His Majesty's Government, and to the Spanish people for hosting this Conference on this land steeped in history.

I would also like to convey my thanks to the Spanish authorities and administration for their meticulous organization and for the effective arrangements which they have successfully implemented in a very short space of time, responding thereby to the unanimity of all concerned to hold this Conference in this beautiful capital, Madrid.

Such unanimity and warm greeting are but a proof of the trust placed by the world and by us in this great country, the seat of a rich civilization of which visible evidence abounds.

This unanimity embodies everyone's desire that Spain be the place where the hopes of the peoples of the world converge and that the triumph over instinct, the upholding of right, justice and reason, and the search for peace be the loftiest standards of civilization.

This Conference held under the title of Peace is, without any doubt, of paramount importance and can become possibly the most important gathering since the Second World War.

Peace is the aspiration of humanity, the end sought by peoples the world over, the purpose for which all religions, philosophies and ideologies strive.

Conscious of the importance of this Conference, it is our duty to express our deep gratitude to the United States of America and the Soviet Union for their unstinting efforts to hold this Conference.

We also appreciate the efforts made by states and other parties who supported the convening of the Conference and are sincerely contributing to its success.

Our praise is due to the efforts pursued by Presidents George Bush and Mikhail Gorbachev to convene this Conference and for the time they devoted to it in spite of numerous other problems in the world.

I would like to mention particularly Minister Boris Pankin, who followed and lent his support to the efforts aimed at holding the Conference, and to Secretary James Baker, who devoted his exceptional skills and capacities to the achievement of this major accomplishment, thus demonstrating rare determination and ability.

I would like also to extend my thanks to Prime Minister Felipe Gonzalez for his valued speech, and the European Community for being here with us and for its firm position which was expressed by Minister van den Broek, Acting President of its Council of Ministers.

Lebanon, a country which believed in the message of peace, tolerance, and coexistence, a country which practiced openness and understanding and nurtured the exchange of ideas and knowledge, welcomes this historic opportunity to let peace prevail in a region whence religions, laws, and civilizations emanated and which gave birth to thought and philosophies, witnessed the pharaohs and the advent of Abraham, Jesus Christ, and Mohammed, the sons, companions, prophets, and imams. Pyramids, sanctuaries, temples, churches, mosques were erected, to which Jerusalem, Bethlehem, Mecca and Najaf bear witness.

It is a land where civilizations interacted, the Sumerian, Phoenician, Pharaonic, Babylonian, Greek, Byzantine, Ottoman and Arab, and where the outlines of temples intermingled with the pillars of sanctuaries and the engravings in churches.

This is where the history of the world and its conscience lie.

It contains for every man, wherever he may be, an element of his identity. It is the patrimony of humanity and we are but guardians of its sanctuaries and protectors of its heritage. From here springs our glory. We are its custodians as generations go by. Lebanon is proud of its Arab identity which binds it to countries with which it has a common history, language, culture and destiny.

Ladies and Gentlemen,

Today we have come from a land small in size, modest in terms of population, not particularly endowed with natural resources, but large in the aspirations of its people, rich in civilization, great in terms of its contribution to the world to whom it gave the alphabet, also culture and knowledge.

We have come to you today from a land which was and still remains a beacon of science to the world in all its dimensions, such as the Beirut Roman school of law, Justinium and Papinium, and up to our universities, our writers, our poets, and our thinkers to this day.

We have come to you today from a land whose sons have crossed seas and deserts towards the five continents and distant lands, where they integrated into other societies, formed friendships with their fellow men, built, and prospered.

We have come from a land coveted by greed, where doctrines and policies went into conflict, where cultures and philosophies collided, so much so that it was said that the country had vanished forever.

Wars tore it asunder, wars waged by others on its soil. For 16 years our country bled. Some said it had died. The number of mourners increased. The concept of lebanization was born to mean countries agonizing and peoples being torn apart. Here is Lebanon, like the phoenix, rising from its ashes, belying those who betted on its demise and played the card of its annihilation.

Here is Lebanon today in spite of the deep wounds and the bitter trial, returning to the family of nations, reaffirming that it is too strong to be liquidated and too large to be struck off the map or forgotten, more steadfast than a mere transitional or temporary state. Here it is to stay and to watch the ramparts of the will of its sons rebuff wave after wave. It is here in spite of all predictions, calculations, pessimistic analysis as if it alone knows that its fate is to live and its mission to continue.

The message, if at all, of the Lebanese war is that the Lebanese formula will not fade away because it is founded upon inevitability of conviviality.

Ladies and Gentlemen,

You have heard a great deal about Lebanon. No doubt you know that this small country has practiced and lived the great human experiment which the international community is about to enter into.

You know that all divine religions, their sects and ramifications exist in Lebanon, which presented an ideal opportunity for all ideas and doctrines, be they political, philosophical or social, to meet and interact. The prevailing climate of democracy and individual and social freedom was the real guarantee enabling one to live and to practice these experiences. From this viewpoint, we in Lebanon are in a position to enrich the concept of the new world order and to consolidate its foundations. This we say in the light of our bitter experience, which has shown that the various ideas, doctrines and religions cannot but live together.

The concept of the new world order, although not clearly defined as yet, would derive benefit from our experience and will be based on the unshakable realities of the societies it seeks to encompass on the necessity of coexistence.

Having paid the price of the international and regional conflicts which were reflected on our soil, we have set out on the path to internal peace and have succeeded in carrying out a number of essential and important tasks, thereby surprising everyone. The challenge and the dream came together. We first set up a government of national unity which adopted and applied the Taif agreement. We also introduced a number of Constitutional amendments to ensure a wider and more globally based political participation of all the components of the Lebanese formula. The state undertook to dissolve the militias and collect their weapons, artificial barriers which had split areas, sects, and parties were dismantled and the Lebanese were assimilated again into society, thus rejecting the separation which had been forced upon them.

The State then started rebuilding its national, security and administrative institutions, the army regained its unity and began to deploy, spreading the authority of the Lebanese State on most of its territory, thus paving the way for Lebanese sovereignty to be exercised on Lebanese soil.

All this took place in a brief span of time with modest means, compensated only by the support of some of our brothers and friends. Lebanon proved once again it was capable of overcoming its trials and tribulations and astonish[ing] the world. Miracles are easy when destiny is at stake. The State did all it could on the homefront and frustrated a number of claims, such as: Lebanon cannot be unified or cannot take a national decision. But our great endeavor will not totally succeed as long as there are pending questions which go beyond our internal borders and touch upon regional as well as international factors.

Events have shown that Lebanon is whole and cannot be fragmented. The South and the North, the Bekaa, Beirut and the mountains are all part of it. Deprived of any of its areas, it would lose a vital limb, bleed forever, struggle and vent its rage on every part of the world. This rage often turning into resistance against occupation.

Violent acts increased, their victims were to be found among the Lebanese and non-Lebanese alike. This violence, though painful at times, was nothing but an anguished expression of passionate determination to let justice prevail.

Ladies and Gentlemen,

Events have proved that South Lebanon, in particular, can detonate a conflagration of the entire situation, that its sons would express their wrath as long as they have to suffer the yoke of occupation, and as long as United Nations resolutions and international laws which guarantee a solution to the problem are ignored and not respected.

This occupation and the accompanying events and developments have cost Lebanon and the world dearly.

Every country has, one way or the other, paid the price of Israeli occupation of the South.

Ladies and Gentlemen,

Lebanon was and still is a peace-loving country, co-founder of the United Nations Organization, president of one of the sessions of the General Assembly, and contributor to the establishment of several international organizations, namely, the International Court of Justice, of which it was a member. It also took part in the drafting of the International Covenant of Human Rights.

Lebanon adheres to international legitimacy, and abides by U.N. Security Council and General Assembly resolutions as well as the rules of international law.

Lebanon calls for a new international order, where principles of law, rejection of aggression, and peaceful settlement of disputes prevail.

Lebanon attaches great importance to the implementation of Resolution 425, since the Armistice Agreement of 1949 still governs the situation with Israel. Article 8 provides "that this agreement shall remain in force until both parties reach a peaceful settlement."

It is for all these reasons that Lebanon has sought and still seeks to apply Security Council Resolution 425 of 19 March 1978, which calls for strict respect for the territorial integrity, sovereignty and political independence of Lebanon within its internationally recognized boundaries.

It also calls upon Israel to cease its military action against Lebanese territorial integrity and withdraw forthwith its forces from all Lebanese lands.

The resolution decided to establish immediately an interim force for South Lebanon under the authority of the United Nations for the purpose of confirming the withdrawal of Israeli forces, restoring international peace and security, and assisting the government of Lebanon in ensuring the return of its effective authority in the area.

Although Resolution 425 met obstacles which prevented its immediate, total, and unconditional implementation, in keeping with the letter of its text, due to the persistent refusal by Israel to implement it, these have only redoubled Lebanon's insistence on its literal application.

Lebanon views the implementation of this resolution as a challenge to and a test of the sincerity of the international community, which must demonstrate seriousness in complying with its own resolutions and in finding the necessary elements to implement both letter and spirit of that document.

The implementation of this resolution would show clearly that the international community does not apply double standards, that what is true of its compliance with international law and its respect of the sovereignty exercised by independent states on their territory extends to all regions and all cases without any discrimination.

I must, in this respect, remind you that Lebanon was the first Arab country to condemn the aggression on Kuwait. Lebanon never faltered one instant throughout the crisis. Its position was based on the principle of the sovereignty and independence of states, even though Lebanon found it difficult to apply international law by force to a fraternal Arab country, albeit an aggressor.

The Lebanese government, who wishes this Conference total success, would like to assure you that it will spare no effort to have Resolution 425 implemented, whatever path this Conference may follow and whatever its final results may be. We have notified the two co-sponsors of this Conference, the United Nations [sic] and the Soviet Union, that our acceptance of the invitation to attend was predicated on this position. Here I would like to praise the numerous friendly countries which have supported our position, namely the United States of America, which has notified us in writing of its firm position, which is that the total implementation of Resolution 425 does not depend upon a comprehensive solution in the region nor is it linked to it, even though such a solution would enhance peace and stability in Lebanon.

Resolution 425 is a separate and complete resolution, comprising an inherent detailed mechanism for its implementation. It is in no way linked to any of the efforts being pursued to apply the international resolutions related to the question of the Arab territories occupied in 1967, namely, Resolutions 242 and 338.

We wish these efforts to come to a successful, rapid, and total conclusion, but as we do so, we reiterate that Lebanon is concerned above all with the total liberation of its territory. Lebanon accepts no substitute to Resolution 425, and expects that the search for peace and the emerging signs of the new international order will contribute towards eliminating the obstacles which stand in the way of its implementation and will overcome once and for all the procrastination experienced in enforcing it.

Upon implementation of Resolution 425, Lebanon will firmly undertake to control the security on its internationally recognized borders and will preempt any security breaches, thereby removing any justification for acts of resistance against the occupation.

The borders themselves are covered by Resolution 425, which is based on the Armistice Agreement of 1949. They are internationally recognized and can in no way be the subject of negotiations.

Ladies and Gentlemen,

Lebanon is situated in the Middle East. It has embraced the region's thoughts, beliefs, creeds, and philosophies. It has also suffered from the conflicts which have swept it. More than others, the Lebanese are aware, their country being at the crossroads of East and West, where land meets sea, that there can be no real peace if peace is not comprehensive and does not encompass all its peoples and parts.

Peace will be enjoyed by no one in the region if volcanoes are still erupting on our borders, if peoples are still oppressed and rights are still violated.

Lebanon, co-founder and active member of the League of Arab States, is committed to the Arab cause and in particular to the cause of the Palestinian people, its rights to self-determination, to return to its land, to free the Arab occupied territories, and to establish a just peace in the region.

Lebanon is keen to ascertain its solidarity with the Arab position calling for the implementation of Security Council Resolutions 242 and 338, which form the basis for this Conference in the sense of the formula "land for peace." The pursuance of the settlement policy will definitely have an adverse effect on all peace efforts in the region. As for the Palestinian problem, which is at the heart of the Middle East conflict, its global and just solution would allow the region to enjoy what it deserves in terms of stability, security, and tranquility.

This applies particularly to our country, Lebanon, which has paid the highest price because of the expulsion of the Palestinian people from its homeland. Lebanon itself was the target of two large-scale Israeli invasions in 1978 and 1982, which have taken an enormous toll in human life and property. I regret to remind you that Israeli attacks on my country, Lebanon, have not ceased, but rather continued until yesterday and are perhaps being carried out now as I speak to you. Lebanon, with its small territory not exceeding 10,450 square kilometers, with its social, political, and economic structure and its modest natural resources, was able, with difficulty, to shelter displaced Palestinians while awaiting the settlement of their cause. But Lebanon will not be able to provide them with the basic necessities of a decent life, nor include them without suffering a negative impact on its internal situation. This would, in turn, lead to conflict and struggle in order to satisfy basic social, economic, and even political requirements on its land. This is why Lebanon cautions against any attempt to solve the Palestinian problem by settling the Palestinians on a narrow strip of land where a large population is living within a delicate and sensitive balance. There the struggle for survival would become dangerous, it will not give Palestine back to its people and would lead to the very loss of Lebanon. Settlement projects ignore the fact that peoples belong to their land and are attached to it. In this region of the world, the land is the source of identity, love for the homeland is an article of faith, and authenticity is rooted in the land.

The land for the Lebanese, Palestinian, and Arab peoples is intimately linked to their identity, heritage, authenticity and origin. Relinquishing this will forever be in the minds of these peoples a justification for rancor, frustration and revolt.

The situation is further exacerbated when citizens are uprooted from their homeland, their birthplace, under various unrealistic slogans, cut off from their environment, their culture, the soil they tilled, their achievements, to be forced in their hundreds of thousands to leave wide expanses of land and faraway continents in order to be settled on a narrow bank of territory which is the object of contention and fighting, a country they did not know and to which they are not realistically linked. By this I mean the Soviet citizens who are being pushed into emigration and are being uprooted from their natural environment.

Ladies and Gentlemen,

The time has come for the Middle East to become part of the New World Order. The time has come for the peoples of this region of the world to know what peace and a happy life can mean.

The time has come for this region where religions, civilizations, cultures and peoples coexisted in peace to find its authenticity.

The time has come for individual and collective energies to be set free in order to serve development and prosperity.

The time has come for the peoples of the region to become an active component of the international order rather than being a burden for it and a source of anxiety for its members.

The time has come for this region to be the rule of international law rather than its exception.

The time has come for this region to be again a bridge between continents instead of being a barrier to their coming together.

The time has come for the peoples of the region with their authenticity and their heritage to rediscover and to play their historic role in reaching out for human horizons and shaping their future.

The time has come for the peoples of this region to free themselves from the ruthless state of permanent mobilization which was imposed on them and which has undermined their natural development and wasted their potential on wars and armies.

The time has come for the peoples of the region to provide the means of their own development rather than rely on precarious and transient foreign sources for survival.

The time has come for all to see that the balance of power is transient and can be altered.

The time has come to seize upon historic opportunities and to replace sterile assessments with healthy analysis.

The peoples of the region, we assure you, are faced today with an historic opportunity which will not always present itself. Before them lies the chance to come out of their introversion, a chance brought about by exceptional, favorable, and rare circumstances as well as considerable efforts and perhaps even fate.

The conflict was so long and so acute that people became accustomed to the logic of strife and discord and enclosed themselves in it. Any venture for peace by any leader deserves to be valued, praised and supported in the face of refusal by rejectionists and outbidding of profiteers. Were we to lose this rare opportunity and were we to fail to respond to those who decided to seize upon it and chose to resist the easy temptation of extremism, the propension to aggression and to give in to instincts, we shall have to bear the responsibility of history and future generations will hold us to account. The alternative to success in our attempt to reach peace through this Conference is lurking behind the door. It lies in the conviction which will spread in the area that peace is impossible and openness sterile. It lies in the belief which will spread in the region that the failure of this historic endeavor will close the door to any new venture in the foreseeable future.

It lies in the conviction which will prevail in that part of the world that political, religious or sectarian extremism is the only way to resist oppression and injustice.

Ladies and Gentlemen,

Let us stand behind the rational and the wise, let us foil the stakes bid on despair, rancor, and hatred.

Lebanon has emerged form the hell of overlapping wars waged on its soil. Lebanon is recovering its health, sovereignty, and historical role. Lebanon is committed to the success of this Conference and to upholding justice. Lebanon would simply like to say to you the following:

No to the balance of terror.

Yes to the concerted forces of peace.

No to injustice and imbalance.

Yes to the triumph of peace.

May God guide our steps and inspire us.

Thank you.

MR. FAROUK AL-SHARA, *Minister of Foreign Affairs of the Syrian Arab Republic*

Distinguished Co-Chairmen, Ladies and Gentlemen,

I would like to begin my statement at this opening session of the Peace Conference by addressing my deep thanks to His Majesty, King Juan Carlos, and to the government and people of Spain for hosting this historic Conference and for all the facilities and care they have offered participating delegations. On behalf of my country, Syria, its President, Government and people I would like to express our deep appreciation to this friendly country, Spain, with which we enjoy deep-rooted historic, human and cultural ties, whose manifestations are still alive and bright to this very day.

I would also like to express my thanks to the co-sponsors of the Conference, the United States of America and the Soviet Union, for the determination they have demonstrated to convene this Conference at the date proposed by Presidents George Bush and Mikhail Gorbachev.

In this context, I would like to express my appreciation for the great efforts of President Bush supported by President Gorbachev, which were the pre-eminent factor in imparting to the Peace Process unprecedented momentum and seriousness. Consequently, this Conference cannot be considered a ceremonial event, as one of the participating parties had wanted. Rather, it is an international event which has aroused interest in the entire world.

In addition, I cannot fail to recall the sustained personal efforts of Secretary of State James Baker during his eight visits to our region, particularly the important, lengthy and frank talks he held in Damascus. These talks, by their seriousness and the positive atmosphere which surrounded them, have, indeed, helped to make convening of this Peace Conference possible.

It must be emphasized at this point that the role of Europe in the Peace Process is both important and vital. Europe is geographically close to our region. Security in one region cannot fail to affect that of the other while both share common interests.

The role of the United Nations, regardless of the status allotted it in this Conference, remains important; as long as the objective of the peace process is to reach a comprehensive, just and peaceful settlement within the framework of international legitimacy and on the basis of United Nations resolutions; and as long as the results reached by the parties are to be sanctioned by the Security Council.

The convening of this Peace Conference in this beautiful country, Spain, evokes boundless symbols, meanings and images. The peoples of the entire world, not only the peoples of our region, are buffeted by conflicting feelings towards this Conference, feelings fluctuating between success and failure, between optimism in achieving peace and the pessimism of a regression to conflict and confrontation. It is no exaggeration to state that the continuing intransigent Israeli position, which is bereft of any justification, is the one that places the world on the brink of incalculable dangers and prevents the region from enjoying peace.

The Arabs, throughout their long history, have always advocated peace, justice and tolerance. Their history, both ancient and modern, abounds with evidence of this fact. The Jews, and Oriental Jews in particular, know better than anyone that they have lived among Muslim Arabs throughout history wherever they coexisted without ever suffering any form of persecution or discrimination, either racial or religious. Rather, they have always lived in grace and dignity, participating in all walks of life. The Jews have never known security, tolerance and equality approximating the security, tolerance and equality they have enjoyed in the lands of Arabs and Muslims. Anyone perusing the pages of history today will realize the blatant contrast between this tolerance and full equality with which the Arabs treated the Jews for hundreds of years, on the one hand, and the persecution, injustice and discrimination inflicted on the Arabs—particularly Palestinian Arabs—languishing under Israeli occupation, on the other.

Suffice it to recall—if only the reminder were heeded—that had Israel's political orientation since 1948 been humane, millions of Arabs: Palestinians, Syrians and Lebanese, would not have been uprooted from their homes; nor would they have been denied—until today—their right to return. Had Israel's policies not been settler-colonialist, Palestinians languishing under Israeli occupation since 1967 would not have been denied all their fundamental rights, foremost among which is their right to self-determination. It is that very right that the Palestinians—children, women and the elderly—have steadfastly expressed through their peaceful Intifada during the past four years as seen and heard by the entire world. The continuing denial of the right of self-determination of the Palestinian people will lead this people to believe that resorting to violence alone is the most viable means of achieving that right.

The list of evidence of inhuman Israeli practices is long and documented. These are practices which were condemned by dozens of resolutions adopted by the United Nations. These are practices of which the Israelis are tacitly cognizant. They are known to many a fair-minded historian and journalist in the West, although some do not dare address these practices frankly and unequivocally for reasons which are regrettably not known to wide sections of European and U.S. public opinion. First among these reasons is that Jewish extremists both inside and outside Israel harass those writers and journalists and jeopardize their livelihoods and future. If they happen to be Christian they are accused of being anti-Semitic. But if they are Arabs and Muslim it is easier to accuse them—without any evidence whatsoever—of terrorism and the intention of destroying Israel. Contrary to every law and norm, the burden of proof in the minds of these extremists is incumbent on the accused. Thus the innocent becomes a suspect in the eyes of a large sector of Western public opinion. The aggressors who have usurped the land of others by force thus become the advocates of peace, whereas the victims of aggression who demand the return of their occupied land and their usurped rights become terrorists and destructive war-mongers.

Distinguished Co-Chairmen,

We have never carried the banner of war and destruction. Syria has consistently called for the achievement of comprehensive and just peace on the basis of United Nations resolutions. We have always emphasized our sincere intention and serious desire for peace. At the height of the October war President Hafez al-Assad said:

> We do not revel in death and destruction. Instead, we are repulsing death and destruction. We are not aggressors and we have never been, but we have and continue to repel aggression. We do not wish death on anyone, but we are protecting our people from death. We love freedom and wish it both for ourselves and for others.

Peace and the usurpation of land of others cannot coexist. For peace to be stable and durable it must encompass all parties to the conflict on all fronts. Developments in our region have proved this fact. Israel exploited the signing of its peace with Egypt in 1979 to then proceed to annexing Jerusalem in 1980, the Golan in 1981 and invading Lebanon in 1982. It is clear that Israel perpetrated this series of aggressive acts at a pace that exceeds the pace of its withdrawal from the Egyptian Sinai.

In the aftermath of each act of aggression the Security Council was called upon to convene and resolutions were unanimously adopted; Resolution 476 declaring the annexation of Jerusalem as null and void; Resolution 497 declaring the imposition of Israeli laws in the Golan as being null and void and with no international legal validity, and Resolution 425 calling for unconditional Israeli withdrawal from Lebanon.

However, as was the case with Resolutions 242 and 338, these resolutions were not implemented at the time due to Israeli rejection and intransigence and due to the atmosphere of the Cold War between East and West. Now, as the Cold War has come to an end, as the spirit of confrontation and competition between the United States and the Soviet Union has given way to a new stage of reconciliation and cooperation, and as the Peace Conference has convened, the peoples of our region and of the world at large await the implementation of these resolutions at the earliest date through serious and productive talks.

It is noteworthy to point out in this context that Security Council Resolutions 242 and 338, on the basis of which the Peace Conference is being convened, were adopted as a compromise among the permanent member States of the Security Council. As it is well known, the majority of these States have been sympathetic to Israel since its creation. Hence, the implementation of these two resolutions should not be the subject of new bargaining during bilateral negotiations. Rather, they should be implemented in all their provisions and on all fronts. Resolution 242 emphasizes in its preamble the principle of "the inadmissibility of the acquisition of territory by war." This means that every inch of Arab land occupied by the Israelis by war and force: the Golan, the West Bank, Jerusalem and the Gaza Strip must be returned in their entirety to their legitimate owners. International public opinion is aware more than ever before—and especially following the Gulf Crisis—that double standards are no longer acceptable in this age, that the principles of international law, not the law of the jungle, must be respected, and that United Nations resolutions, not brute force, must be applied.

At last, the States of the world have come to realize that Israel alone resists the efforts for peace with all the influence it can muster. It is Israel which perpetuates its occupation of the territories of others by force. All have come to realize that Israel follows a futile and obsolete ideology based on expansion, the building of settlements and the uprooting of Arabs from land in which they had lived for centuries in order to replace them with new immigrants who have never lived in this region.

In this regard, Syria would like to remind the co-sponsors of the Conference, and through them the international community, that Israeli occupation of Syrian and Palestinian territories has resulted in uprooting approximately half a million Syrian citizens from the Golan who have to date not been able to return. The occupation has also resulted in the presence of over a quarter of a million Palestinian refugees in Syria who are denied the right to return to the homeland of their fathers and forebears in Palestine.

The claims invoked by Israel for the migration of world Jewry to it at the expense of the native Arab population are not sanctioned by any legal or humanitarian principle. If the entire world were to adopt such claims it would have to encourage all Christians to emigrate to the Vatican and all Muslims to holy Mecca.

It is a contradiction in terms that Israel refuses to implement United Nations Resolution 194 of 1948 which provides for the return of all Palestinian refugees to their homes and for compensation to those who do not wish to return, under the pretext that there is not enough land. Yet, at the same time, Israel continues to induce hundreds of thousands of new Jewish immigrants to settle in this very land and to abandon their lands of origin such as the Soviet Union, which extends over one sixth of our planet's land mass.

We believe that the time for inconsistencies and empty pretexts whose only aim is to justify the perpetuation of occupation and annexation has now passed. We believe that all parties, both aggressors and victims, now stand at the threshold of a historic opportunity—which may not come about again—an opportunity to end long decades of destructive conflicts and to establish a durable, comprehensive and just peace that would deliver the region from the vicious circle of war and usher in a new era in which the peoples of the region may devote themselves to its prosperity and development.

In order for a just peace to be established no Arab land must remain under Israeli occupation, nor can the right of the Palestinian people to self-determination remain denied.

If the objective is truly for the peoples and the States of the region to coexist; to enjoy security, peace, and prosperity; to place their plentiful energies and resources at the service of their economies and development . . . how can such a desirable objective logically be realized without eliminating occupation and restoring legitimate rights?

The Arabs have given much for peace. They have openly declared that they desire peace. They merely demand the enjoyment of the fundamental rights guaranteed by the Charter of the United Nations to all peoples and which have been recognized by the international community and the world at large for every people.

Alone among all States of the world Israel insists on maintaining its hold on the Arab territories which it occupied by force under the pretext of security; as if geographic expansion can guarantee security in this age of scientific and technological advancement. Were the world to emulate this Israeli logic how many wars and conflicts will arise between neighboring states under that pretext?

The Arabs have responded to the call of the co-sponsors of the Conference in appreciation of their efforts and serious endeavor to work towards a just and comprehensive peace in the region.

However, Israel would be gravely mistaken were it to interpret this Arab response as a license for it to perpetuate its intransigent stands within the Conference or any of its committees. Israel would also be doing itself an injustice—more so than to others—if it were to take lightly the peace process or the unanimous international wish to reach a just and comprehensive settlement to the Arab-Israeli conflict in accordance with the criteria of international legitimacy as well as the spirit and letter of the Charter of the United Nations and its resolutions.

Despite Syria's numerous reservations concerning the format and terms of reference of this Conference, the Syrian Arab delegation has come here to attempt to reach a comprehensive, honorable and just peace to all aspects and fronts of the Arab-Israeli conflict. Our delegation has come carrying inexhaustible reserves of good will, a genuine serious desire for a just peace and determination to help enable this peace process succeed and reach its noble objective. That determination is only equalled by a no lesser determination to reject any attempt to exploit the current peace process to legitimize that which is illegitimate and unacceptable according to the United Nations, its Charter and resolutions; or to obtain any gains—however small—which would mirror the abhorrent injustice of aggression or which would reward the aggressor.

This firm Syrian position whose every element is anchored in the principles of international legitimacy and resolutions of the United Nations deems it imperative for Israel to withdraw from every inch of the occupied Syrian Golan, West Bank, Jerusalem, the Gaza District and the South of Lebanon. This position also deems it imperative to safeguard the legitimate political and national rights of the Palestinian people, foremost among which is their right to self-determination. The building of settlements in the occupied Arab territories is an illegal action; it is considered null and void and it stands as a major obstacle in the way of peace. Thus, it is imperative that the settlements be removed. The continuation of settlement activity in the Arab occupied territories, particularly since the peace process has commenced, is tangible evidence that Israel does not want to reach genuine peace.

Distinguished Co-Chairmen,

Syria's acceptance of President Bush's initiative which is based on Security Council Resolutions 242 and 338 and the principle of "land for peace" has opened the way to the peace process—as has been acknowledged by all. Our presence as participants in this Conference embodies our desire to achieve comprehensive and just peace. Our agreement to undertake bilateral talks is clear indication of our serious contribution to building a genuine and comprehensive peace in the region.

However, concern for the success of the peace process requires that multilateral talks which do not fall within the framework of Resolution 242 not be initiated until substantive and concrete achievement has been made in bilateral negotiations which would confirm the elimination of the major obstacles on the road to peace. That is because Israel—as everyone knows—is not interested in implementing Resolutions 242 and 338 on the basis of the principle of "land for peace." Israel is interested only in entering into negotiations on economic cooperation with the States of the region while perpetuating its occupation of Arab territories. This is in contradiction with the objective on which the convening of this Conference was based.

Distinguished Co-Chairmen,

We have come for an honorable and just peace based on international law and legitimacy. We have not come for a false peace which reflects the conditions imposed by the aggressor and the yoke of occupation.

We have come for a genuine peace encompassing all the fronts of the Arab-Israeli conflict and not for a peace which would address one aspect of the conflict to then merely cause new conflicts and tensions in the region.

Proceeding from our belief in such a peace we confidently and resolutely declare our determination to work towards a comprehensive, just and peaceful settlement to the Arab-Israeli conflict which would liberate the land, and guarantee the national rights of the Palestinian people as well as security for all.

Were the Peace Conference to succeed in achieving these objectives, which are the focus of world expectations, it would herald a new dawn in our turbulent region and the beginning of a new era of peace, prosperity and stability.

CLOSING REMARKS
FRIDAY, NOVEMBER 1, 1991

MR. YITZHAK SHAMIR, *Prime Minister of Israel*

Distinguished Co-Chairmen Ladies and Gentlemen,

Let me first apologize, as I have to leave this hall immediately after my statement, together with some of my colleagues, in order to return to Israel before sunset, in time for the advent of our holy day of rest. I trust no one will see in this a sign of disrespect.

Let me also express again our thanks and appreciation to our Spanish hosts and to the co-sponsors for putting so much effort in making this conference possible.

For two days, we have sat in this hall, armed with a lot of patience, to listen to what our Arab neighbors have to say.

We have heard much criticism and many charges. We can respond to each and every charge, to every misrepresentation of history and fact—and there were quite a few—and we can refute every contention. We, too, can cite morality, justice, and international legality in our favor.

But is this what we have come here for? Such futile exchanges and rebuttals have been taking place during the last forty-three years at the U.N. and in countless international gatherings. They have not brought us one inch closer to mutual understanding and peace. This is precisely why we have persistently called for direct, face-to-face talks. Nevertheless, we came here out of goodwill, hoping there might be a change, a turn for the better in tone and content, that would lead us to a new and more promising chapter. And we have not given up this hope.

Let me therefore make just a few remarks, not for the sake of polemics, but to shed light on a few facts.

Syria's representative wants us and the world to believe that his country is a model of freedom and protection of human rights, including those of the Jews. Such a statement stretches incredulity to infinite proportions. The ancient Jewish community in Syria has been exposed to cruel oppression, torture, and discrimination of the worst kind. Most of the Jews fled the country over the years and the few thousand left are living in perpetual terror. Anyone who tries to cross the border is incarcerated in prison, beaten and tortured, and his family exposed to punishment and constant fear. But not only are the Jews the victims of the Syrian regime. To this day, Syria is the home of a host of terrorist or-

ganizations that spread violence and death to all kinds of innocent tar-
gets, including civil aviation, and women and children of many nations.
I could go on and recite a litany of facts that demonstrate the extent to
which Syria merits the dubious honor of being one of the most oppres-
sive, tyrannical regimes in the world. But this is not what we have come
here for.

To the Lebanese people, our neighbors to the north, we send a message
of sympathy and understanding. They are suffering under the yoke of
Syrian occupation and oppression and are denied even the capacity to
cry out in protest. We bear no ill-will to the courageous and suffering
Lebanese, and we join them in the hope that they will soon regain their
independence and freedom. We have no designs on Lebanese territory,
and in the context of a peace treaty and the removal of the Syrian presence, we can restore stability and security on the borders between our
two countries.

In many respects, we have a situation of *de facto* non-belligerency with
the Kingdom of Jordan. We sincerely believe that a peace treaty with
Jordan is achievable. In the context of such a treaty, we will determine
together the secure and recognized boundaries, and lay the foundation
for a relationship of mutual cooperation and neighborly relations. Both
countries stand to gain from a relationship of peace and we hope to
achieve it through direct, bilateral negotiations.

I listened attentively to the statement of the Palestinian Arab spokesman in the joint Jordanian-Palestinian delegation. The Palestinian Arabs
are our closest neighbors and in many respects, their lives are intertwined with ours. This is one more reason for the importance we attach
to an accommodation with this community.

The Palestinian Arab spokesman made a valiant effort at recounting
the sufferings of his people. But let me say, that twisting history and
perversion of fact will not earn them the sympathy which they strive to
acquire. Was it not Palestinians who slaughtered a major part of the
Jewish community of Hebron, without any provocation? Was it not Palestinians who rejected every peace proposal since the beginning of the
century and responded by violence? Was it not Palestinians who produced a leader who collaborated with the Nazis in the extermination of
Jews in the Holocaust? Was it not the Palestinians who called their Arab
brethren in 1948 to come and help them destroy the Jewish State? Was
it not the Palestinians who rejoiced and danced on the roofs when Iraqi
Scud missiles were falling on Tel Aviv? Have they forgotten that more
Palestinians were killed by their own brethren in a few recent years, than

in clashes with Israeli security forces? Even to this very day, under conditions which you describe as occupation, is it not a fact that any Jew who strays into an Arab village risks his life, but tens of thousands of Palestinian Arabs walk freely in every town and village in Israel and no one molests them?

We have presented the Palestinians a fair proposal, one that offers them a chance to improve their lot immensely. I appeal to them to accept our proposal and join us in negotiations.

Ladies and Gentlemen,

We have come here to seek together the road that would lead us to peace and accommodation, rather than to engage in a match of charges and counter-charges. Peace is not just words or a signature on a piece of paper. Peace is a frame of mind and a set of actions that are the opposite of hostility, and create a climate of mutual trust, tolerance and respect.

With an open heart, we call on the Arab leaders to take the courageous step and respond to our outstretched hand in peace. Yesterday, I extended an invitation to come to Israel for the first round of peace negotiations and begin a sincere exchange that would lead to agreement. We hope you will accept our invitation. We will readily reciprocate. I am sure I speak for every man, woman and child in Israel, who join me in the hope that, after all, this gathering will be registered in history as a turning point, away from hostility and forward to coexistence and peace.

Thank you.

DR. KAMEL ABU JABER, Minister of Foreign Affairs of the Hashemite Kingdom of Jordan

Mr. James Baker, Secretary of State, Mr. Boris Pankin, Foreign Minister

The Jordanian position is based on sound moral grounds, adhering to principle, adhering to provisions of international law, United Nations resolutions, international legitimacy and the guarantees of the five permanent members of the Security Council, particularly the two co-sponsors. We had hoped that this would induce a sense of balance especially since we emphasized the need to structure a negotiated settlement based on an institutionalized, legal framework. Instead, it appears as if time stood still as far as Israel is concerned. We had hoped and still do, that the spirit of Madrid would cause a change of heart and attitude leading to the development of a substantive position. What we heard, however, was in fact a further retreat into the old ideological molds, clearly designed to distract, worse, derail the process.

Sadly enough, what we heard was a reiteration of past positions, emphasizing yet another retrenchment, another retreat from the spirit of compromise. Positions clearly designed to obfuscate not only historical annals to fit a particular prejudice, but worse still to push the other side to climb behind the rigid ideological trenches it has been attempting to scale. Surely, the Israelis must have known that when they arrived in Palestine it was not an empty territory. It was inhabited by the ancestors of the Palestinians. Even then it was already called "the land of milk and honey."

It is not our aim now, nor has it been when we first outlined our position, to indulge in an historical debate. We too have our own vision of history and our tale to tell. And while there is soft elegance in our culture there is also fierce durability that even now has an opinion about the bold stand we have taken. We had hoped that we will get out of our past, not in the spirit of denying it—never—but in the hope of looking towards the future: a better, brighter future for the children of the region. We hoped that all the participants will capture the present historic moment, and live up to it, instead of a process of selective rewriting of history.

The core of the present Arab-Israeli conflict revolves around the occupied territories. To say that "... the issue is not territory" is a gross reduction of the truth. We have come here prepared to make peace within the context of a comprehensive and just peace settlement. The time has come for Israel to recognize the right of self-determination of the Palestinian people on their own territory, their ancestral homeland. No amount of denying the fact will make it disappear.

The negatives embodied in the Israeli address were in stark contrast to the willingness on the Arab side to negotiate an honorable settlement. Again Israel said: no to Palestinian self-determination, no to withdrawal from the West Bank, including Arab Jerusalem; no to withdrawal from the Gaza Strip, the Golan Heights, Jordanian territory as well as the Lebanese South. Bluntly and publicly Israel effectively declared its intention to maintain its illegal position and continue its settlement program.

We hoped that the time may have come for Israel to overcome the heavy burden of its past wounds and to follow a path leading towards a better future. Instead it continues to cling to yesterday, nursing its mental and physical wounds. We have avoided negativism as well as code words designed to irritate, hoping to take a first step towards bridging the great divide. We had hoped to silence the call of the wild and the absolutist rhetoric.

We emphasized our vision of an honorable, durable and comprehensive peace with which we and our children can live with. We too need to look ourselves in the mirror with pride and we will. That is we based our position on 242 and 338 while we emphasized our recognition, even these were less than ultimate justice.

Jordan is irrevocably committed to the noble cause of peace and we stand ready now, as we have always been, to pay our fair share for its realization. But, let me say it again, we are not seeking peace at any price. Far from it. We are seeking justice, fairness and legality.

Israel can have either land or peace, but it cannot have both. It can have the true security that comes from a negotiated *political* solution. Force alone will never provide security. Only when accepted by its neighbors, as part of the region, not merely in it.

Let me reiterate Jordan's position, which rests on the simple and valid principle of "land for peace." That is why we call on Israel to abide by United Nations Security Council Resolutions 242, 338, and 425 pertaining to the occupied territories, the Syrian Golan Heights and Lebanon.

Israel's refusal to abide by these resolutions undermines the credibility of the world body and seriously raises the issue of asymmetry and double standard in applying international law.

The Palestinians must have and exercise the right of self-determination on their own soil. That is why the immediate halting of the establishment of settlements is an essential prerequisite of a comprehensive regional settlement.

Not only Israel is in need of security, but every country in the region too. Considering the imbalance in the military equation, it becomes obvious that the Arab side is the part in more need of security guarantees.

Ladies and Gentlemen,

We have not come to Madrid, the venue of this historic international conference, simply to debate, discuss, or score points against each other. We came here with the intention of seriously considering the elements of a comprehensive peace settlement. Our approach remains constructive, and our faith and confidence in the seriousness and commitment of the co-sponsors is unshakable.

It may be very well that Israel wants peace, but it wants the Arabs alone to pay the price. Again we find it necessary to emphasize that the issue is territory: an exchange of land for peace that carries with it the promise of a brighter future going far beyond mere existence.

In firmly and clearly calling for an honorable and lasting settlement, we had hoped to move the region from the past into a promising future. Instead we find that Israel still has both its feet firmly planted in the past.

DR. HAIDAR ABD EL-SHAFI, Head of the Palestinian Side of the Jordanian/Palestinian Delegation

Secretary Baker, Foreign Minister Pankin, Your Excellencies, Ladies and Gentlemen,

We wish first to congratulate the co-sponsors for succeeding where so many have failed before. The fact of the Conference itself convening is no negligible feat, but a tribute to sheer persistence, tenacity and hard work. For this, we extend our appreciation.

Ladies and Gentlemen,

For this historic Conference to succeed, requires, to borrow a literary phrase, a "willing suspension of disbelief—the predisposition and ability to enter alien terrain where the signals and signposts are often unfamiliar and the topography uncharted. This solemn endeavor on which we are embarking here in Madrid demands of us a minimal level of sympathetic understanding in order to begin the process of engagement and communication. For this interdependent age demands the rapid evolution of a shared discourse that is capable of generating new and appropriate perceptions of the basis of which forward-looking attitudes may be formed and accurate road maps drawn.

Failing this, time will not spare us and our peoples will hold us accountable. Thus, we have the task, rather the duty, of rising above static and hard-set concepts, of discarding teleological arguments and regressive ideology, and of abandoning rigid and constricting positions. Such attitudes barricade the speaker behind obdurate and defensive stances, while antagonizing or locking out the audience.

Eliciting instant responses through provocation and antagonism would, admittedly, generate energy, but such energy can only be short-lived and ultimately destructive. Energy with direction, real momentum, emerges from a responsible and responsive engagement between equals, using recognizable terms of reference regardless of the degree of disagreement.

In all honesty, we, the Palestinian delegation, came here to present you with a challenge—to lay our humanity before you and to recognize yours, to transcend the confines of the past, and to set the tone for a peace process within the framework of mutuality, expansiveness, and acknowledgement. We deliberately refused to limit the options before us to one or to fall into the trap of reductive entrenchment with a rigid either-or argument. Ladies and Gentlemen, peace requires courage to make and perseverance to forge.

In his opening speech, President Bush sent a strong message, not just to the participants, but to the world as a whole—a peace pledge with the dual signs of "fairness and legitimacy" as necessary components. We were gratified, for the Palestinian peace initiative is firmly grounded in these two principles. Most speeches which followed reaffirmed them and sought to demonstrate seriousness of intent. The Israel statement, however, remained the exception, imprisoned in its own anachronistic and antagonistic rhetoric, incapable of responding to the tone and implications of the occasion.

But the days of domination, of manipulative politics are over, and the emergent realities of our contemporary world are consecrating the principles of moral politics and global harmony as the criteria and measures of value.

We further find it incomprehensible how Israel can violate with impunity the integrity of the process and the consensus of the participants. United Nations Security Council Resolution 242 and the principle of "territory for peace" constitute the terms of reference and the source of legal authority for the Conference and negotiations, as stated in the letters of invitation. The positive response of the Palestinian people was primarily in recognition and appreciation of this commitment. The essence of 242, as formulated in its own preamble, is "the inadmissibility of acquisition of territory by war," thus containing within it an internal and binding definition which renders it incapable of being variously or subjectively interpreted or applied. We came here to realize its implementation, not to indulge in exegesis or semantics or to be party to its negation or extraction from the peace agenda. This is not only an Arab and Palestinian requirement; it is also a demand of the international community and a test of validation for the new era in global politics.

The same terms articulated in 242 apply to East Jerusalem, which is not only occupied territory, but also a universal symbol and a repository of cultural creativity, spiritual enrichment, and religious tolerance. That today an apartheid-like pass system bars many Palestinians from entering our holy city is both painful and provocative. The gates of Jerusalem must be open. Palestinian Jerusalem is the vehicle of our self-definition and the affirmation of our uninterrupted existence on our land.

Ladies and Gentlemen, the issue is land, and what is at stake here is the survival of the Palestinian people on what is left of our olive groves and orchards, our terraced hills and peaceful valleys, our ancestral homes, villages, and cities. International legitimacy demands the restoration of the illegally-occupied Arab and Palestinian lands to their rightful owners. Israel must recognize the concept of limits—political, legal, moral, and territorial—and must decide to join the community of nations by accepting the terms of international law and the will of the international community. No amount of circumlocution or self-deception can alter that fact.

Security can never be obtained through the acquisition of other people's territory, and geography is not the criterion for security. The opposite is actually true. Retaining or expanding occupied territory is the one sure way of perpetuating hostility and resentment. We are offering the Israeli people a unique chance for genuine security through peace: only by solving the real grievances and underlying causes of instability and conflict can genuine and long-lasting stability and security be obtained.

We, the people of Palestine, hereby offer the Israelis an alternative path to peace and security: abandon mutual fear and mistrust, approach us as equals within a two-state solution, and let us work for the development and prosperity of our region based on mutual benefit and well-being. We have already wasted enough time, energy, and resources locked in this violent embrace of mutual destruction and defensiveness. We urge you to take this opportunity and rise to meet the challenge of peace.

Settlements on confiscated Palestinian land and the expropriation of our resources will surely sabotage the process launched by this Conference, for they are major obstacles to peace. They constitute a flagrant violation of Palestinian rights and the Fourth Geneva Convention. All settlement activity and confiscation of Palestinian land must stop, for these measures constitute the institutionalized plunder of our people's heritage and future.

The Palestinians are a people with legitimate national rights. We are not "the inhabitants of territories" or an accident of history or an obstacle to Israel's expansionist plans, or an abstract demographic problem. You may wish to close your eyes to this fact, Mr. Shamir, but we are here in the sight of the world, before your very eyes, and we shall not be denied. In exile or under occupation, we are one people, united despite adversity, determined to exercise our right to self-determination and to establish an independent state, led by our own legitimate and acknowledged leadership. The question of all our refugees will be dealt with during the permanent status negotiations under the terms of United Nations Resolution 194.

We have already declared our acceptance of transitional phases as part of this process, provided they have the logic of internal coherence and interconnection, within a specified, limited time frame and without prejudicing the permanent status. During the transitional phase, Palestinians must have meaningful control over decisions affecting their lives and fate. During this phase, the immediate repatriation of the 1967 displaced persons and the reunion of separated families can be carried out.

We have also expressed the need for protection and third party intervention in the course of bringing about a settlement under such conditions of disequilibrium between occupier and occupied. For peace, as a state of civilization between societies, real peace between peoples, cannot precede the solution of the problems which are at the core of the conflict. It is the solution which opens the door to peace, and not the other way around.

On these grounds, we hereby publicly and solemnly call upon the co-sponsors of the Conference, directly or through the United Nations, to place the whole of the Occupied Palestinian Territories under their trusteeship pending a final settlement. The Palestinian people are willing to entrust you with the protection of their lives and lands until a fair and legitimate peace is achieved.

They are the same people, our Palestinian people, who have celebrated the occasion of this Conference by offering olive branches to the Israeli occupation soldiers. Palestinian children were decorating army tanks with this symbol of peace. Our Palestinian people under occupation and in exile were here with us during the past three days, in our minds and hearts, and it is their voice that you have heard.

To the co-sponsors and to the international community that seeks the achievement of a just peace in the Middle East, you have given us a fair hearing, you cared enough to listen, and for that we thank you.

MR. FARES BOUEZ, Minister of Foreign Affairs of the Republic of Lebanon

Messrs. Co-Chairmen, today ends the opening phase of the Madrid Conference to which we have come with an open mind and the keenness to contribute to the establishment of peace based on justice, international legitimacy, and the United Nations resolutions.

It is with great satisfaction that we listened to the statements of the co-sponsors, Presidents George Bush and Mikhail Gorbachev. They emphasized the basic principle guiding this Conference—namely, compliance with international law, the inadmissibility of the acquisition of territory by force, and the safeguarding of the right of peoples to live in security and with self-determination.

The Lebanese delegation also listened with much interest to the statements of all the other parties called upon to negotiate to bring about the desired peace.

Therefore, we would like to make the following observations.

Firstly, the holding of this Conference was an indispensable first step towards achieving the objective of peace for which this Conference indeed took place. A just, lasting, and comprehensive peace in our region, based on international legitimacy and the United Nations resolutions.

Secondly, we consider the various points in the statements of Presidents George Bush and Mikhail Gorbachev, and particularly, those pertaining to the establishment of peace, based on justice and fairness. We consider them to be viable means for peace and stability in our region.

Thirdly, we believe that the statement made on behalf of the European Community is a balanced and much appreciated contribution to the genuine efforts for the fulfillment of the aims of the Conference. We noticed with satisfaction that Lebanon was singled out in a paragraph which supported the implementation of Resolution 425.

Fourthly, having listened to the other statements, a clear difference emerged between Arab positions, which sought to overcome hate [between] countries and the residue of the past in order to open a new page in regional relations founded on wisdom and reason, and that of an Israeli position which maintained its traditional ideas and allegations which have been clearly proven to run counter to the peace process in the region.

The statement of the Israeli delegation was not only lacking a declaration of acceptance of the principle of this Conference, embodied in the

United Nations resolutions, and the principle of "land for peace"—which have been unanimously agreed to by the organizers of this Conference and its participants. It also pursued its falsifications and denigration of international legitimacy and the United Nations Charter and resolutions.

We had hoped that the Israeli delegation would share our conviction that the success of this Conference depends on the will of all parties to seek peace and the need to demonstrate this will by taking specific measures in the field that would bring about mutual trust.

We are still awaiting a clear demonstration of that will on the part of the Israeli delegation by declaring its commitment to the implementation of Resolutions 242, 338, the United Nations Charter, and in particular, the right of peoples to self-determination so as to make this right attainable by all, and especially at present, attainable by the Palestinian people.

Our attention was drawn, in the Israeli Prime Minister's statement, to his attempt to annul the United Nations resolutions and question their legitimacy, although Israel itself would not have come into existence if it were not for a Security Council resolution granting the Jews a part of Palestine.

Moreover, if that were Israel's attitude towards the U.N. resolutions, then what would be the meaning of holding this Conference, which is based on Security Council Resolutions 242 and 338?

I would now like to turn to Lebanese—the national Lebanese issue.

Lebanon has demanded, and reiterates its demand before you today, for the immediate, complete, and unconditional withdrawal of all of Israel from all the Lebanese territories, pursuant to Security Council Resolution 425 of 19 March 1978.

However, it is surprising that the head of the Israeli delegation should speak of peace without taking one single step towards achieving it. On the contrary, Israel continues to aggress Lebanon and rejects the implementation of Resolution 425.

Is Israeli escalation in southern Lebanon, which has accompanied this Conference, the best response to the umbrella of principles and values which govern this gathering?

Desirous of peace, Lebanon has made giant strides to recover.

It, therefore, declares before you its undertaking to preserve security throughout its territory, especially in the south, as soon as Israel complies with Resolution 425 and withdraws its forces beyond the Lebanese international boundaries according to international provisions.

The Lebanese delegation can only emphasize once again that Resolution 425 should be applied today, and not tomorrow, since this would provide an incentive for the Peace Conference to succeed and would pave the way for the settlement of the region's problems.

Sixth, we wish to stress the need to think about the future, and to arrive at a conception for the development of the region which would carry with [it] the foundations of construction, social justice, and economic welfare.

However, we would also like to stress our belief that it is more important, and more constructive, to negotiate the present rather than the future.

Let us focus therefore, and agree, on our present to enable us to prepare for our future.

How can we consider distributing their (inaudible) before we shrug off our shoulders the burden of adversity so that the proclamation may enhance the prospect of peace, the status of Jerusalem, a halt to settlement, and respect for the principle of land for peace.

Therefore, we say that to pave the way for multilateral negotiations we need to make significant progress in bilateral negotiations.

Finally, we have noticed in the Israeli writer's reply that Israel is attached to withdrawing from Lebanon and does not have any ambitions in Lebanese territory. Therefore, we wonder why Israel continues to occupy Lebanon, why it continues to incite violence in Lebanon, why it continues to denigrate the dignity of our people.

The independence of Lebanon, as though it was Israel's obsession begins with the south. And as long as the south is under the yoke of occupation, [the] independence of Lebanon will not be complete.

Israel, in fact, had brought with it all the contradictions in the world. Israel knows very well that Syria came to Lebanon supporting legitimacy and consolidating unity.

Lebanon's relationship with Syria does not accept Israel's interference or even Israel's intention to link its presence in Lebanon to the presence of Syria.

Finally, Israel's attempt to link its withdrawal from Lebanon with any other element or factor carries with it a clear rejection of Resolution 425, which should be implemented unconditionally.

Thank you.

MR. FAROUK AL-SHARA, Minister of Foreign Affairs of the Syrian Arab Republic

I wanted to read a statement which I had prepared to reply to the speech made by the head of the Israeli delegation which he made yesterday. But the head of the Israeli delegation, who has just left, paying no heed to this historic Conference and to the peace process, has taken a different course from the chief subject on whose basis the Conference is held, which is the achievement of just, comprehensive, and lasting peace in an area which has not known security, stability, and well-balanced development for long decades.

Yesterday some Western journalists said the Syrian speech was perhaps tough, and I told them it was not tough. Rather it gave facts and realities as they are, and I challenged some of them when I said I shall find it strange if the Israeli delegation can find one single paragraph to answer to. This challenge was not out of place, because I never accused Israel of anything that is not in it, and thus the head of the Israeli government could not reply to any word or expression by which I described the Israeli policy in our region.

Today, I find it necessary to make clear some facts because those, for us, for the co-sponsors of the Conference and for the international community, more realistic? A Palestinian who still remembers his house, who may even have the key to his house, or talk about the return of Jews who were there two thousand years before. This is a difference between forty and four thousand years, which was discussed by the head of the Israel government. He talked about freedom of worship. We all know, through the media, and Arab media, that they encourage Israeli extremists to destroy sacred places, the act of arson against the holy al-Aqsa Mosque, their attempt to destroy the al-Aqsa Mosque and they claim they try those people.

Israeli control over Jerusalem is not a guarantee for any of the three religions, or for the city to remain holy with its spiritual places eternal, to remain the city of peace, so long as it is under Israeli control and under the feet of their soldiers.

Mr. President,

I had wanted to concentrate on peace for which we have come. But before this let me show you an old picture of Shamir, when he was 32 years old. The caption says—it is distributed in Europe. At the time he was 32 years old. Height 165 cm., then the other details which you all know. This picture was distributed because he was wanted. He himself confessed he was a terrorist. He confessed he practiced terrorism and participated in murdering U.N. mediator Count Bernadotte in 1948, as far as I remember. He kills peace mediators and talks about Syria, Lebanon, terrorism. I cite another example: Israel in 1954 hijacked a Syrian civilian aeroplane, and downed a Libyan civilian aeroplane.

The problem is that I don't have enough time to talk about Israel's terrorist practices which needs volumes, not only a quarter of an hour. But I would like to briefly say that Israel hijacked a Syrian civilian aeroplane in 1954 with passengers on board between Cairo and Damascus. Israel downed a Libyan plane in 1973, as I remember, and killed over one hundred civilian passengers. Israel hijacked a Syrian plane six or seven years ago which was carrying a Syrian political delegation. Had Syria not hastened to file a complaint with the Security Council, the plane would not have been released.

Yesterday I gave our perception of terrorism and we believe he could not respond to any word in it. I don't want to disturb you with more details. If anyone wants more, they can refer to it.

He says the 1967 war was defensive. In their media they say the Arabs attacked Israel in 1967. They insult historians. I would like to say one final word. Regardless of who occupied, or who started the war in 1967, the text of the resolution is clear, Mr. President, that it prohibits the acquisition of other people's land by war. This land must be returned.

Finally, and simply, Mr. President, we have come here for peace. We declare with confidence and resolution our determination to work for just and comprehensive peace that liberates lands, and guarantees rights and security for all parties. We would find it strange if the Israeli side declined to continue the bilateral talks or create excuses to prevent their continuation in Madrid.

I am sorry, Mr. President, I took a longer time but I have to clarify those facts.

Thank you.

MR. AMRE MOUSSA, Minister of Foreign Affairs of the Arab Republic of Egypt

Co-Chairmen, distinguished delegates, our meeting here during the past three days in these fabulous surroundings and warm hospitality, graciously provided by our Spanish hosts, has been described as historic and momentous. I have been reflecting upon the real meaning of the Conference. As I looked across this T-shaped Conference table and listened to the different views of the parties, I asked myself, are we on the threshold of a new era in the Middle East, as indeed we should be? The answer is in the affirmative, for whatever the positions of one party or the other, we cannot and we should not continue arguing, trading accusations and recrimination. Old arguments and archaic strategies should be left at the wayside the moment we leave this Conference.

We have listened especially today to some passionate speeches which manifest once again how acute the conflict in the Middle East is and how the change in attitudes, change in content, is badly needed. And I address Israel mainly. Speeches such as the one we heard today does not help the process of peace. This is not the language of peace. We came to negotiate. We came to talk to each other about the future, and we have a responsibility to do everything possible to make this endeavor succeed. Arab nations have come here to achieve peace with Israel. Her status is not questioned, nor in doubt. Israel, we hope, has come to find peace with the Arabs, including and in particular with the Palestinians, a matter which entails by necessity the respect of their rights in territory and in self-determination. This is a *sine qua non* for peace.

The co-sponsors have committed themselves to continue working together rather than against each other in the Middle East. This is a very important fact and very positive point. Our meeting here, Ladies and Gentlemen, must [*inaudible*]. Misrepresentation of facts must stop. Wild dreams of expansion must come to an end. Illegal acts, such as building settlements, should be frozen. More than anything else, and as never before, this Conference places an awesome responsibility on the parties to demonstrate that peace has a chance and that coming here was not in vain.

This solemn quest for peace must be pursued, its full potential realized. In the next few days and in the weeks and months to come, different forms of negotiation shall hopefully commence. In the process, there will be continuing difficulties, moments of tension. But we must continue our search for peace, a just and fair peace, not peace at any price, but peace based on legality, on Resolution 242 and 338. Peace at the end must prevail.

Egypt, a nation that has been at the forefront, both in war and in peace, a nation with deep Arab roots and peaceful relations with the Jewish state, knows more than anyone else in the Middle East the agony of war and the virtue of peace; from this unique perspective, an unparalleled experience, at least so far, Egypt shall continue to support the legitimate rights of all the nations in the region and participate in laying down the foundation for [a] stable, secure and prosperous Middle East. Egypt shall fulfill her role in the upcoming negotiations in order to ensure peace in the Middle East and address regional problems, in particular the arms race and the problem of the proliferation of arms of mass destruction, especially nuclear weapons.

Our common objective must be a consensus on how to coexist as equals. This will no doubt entail many difficult decisions for all sides. We must learn to reconcile ourselves with reality. There cannot be peace if we allow our dreams to cloud our vision. There can only be genuine peace with all its implications when Israel chooses sincerely to live with the Arabs and the Palestinians, respecting their legitimate rights and ending the occupation of Arab lands.

Israel also has rights, and the Arab side has demonstrated readiness to respect those rights, as stipulated in Resolution 242 and 338. There is no escape from Resolution 242 or 338.

We have a long road ahead of us. All of us have a contribution to make in ensuring that we march on. Confidence that all parties are sincerely pursuing peace will have to be continuously reinforced. We may need to reassure one another at each hurdle that there have been no regressions from the achievements of this Conference in Madrid. Palestinian suffering must be alleviated. Many other confidence-building measures must be implemented.

Peace is not a luxury nor an option. Peace is an imperative. We must overcome our differences, and we shall overcome our differences.

Thank You.

MR. BORIS D. PANKIN, Minister of Foreign Affairs of the Union of Soviet Socialist Republics

Distinguished Ministers, Distinguished Participants in the Conference, Ladies and Gentlemen,

The Madrid forum is in its third day. And all these days I have had the impression—as probably most of all us present here—that, despite all the odds, in the Palacio Oriente all of us seem to be the creators of, and participants in, the turning point in the modern Middle East history. Foreign Minister Amre Moussa asked a question on this score and I say—seem to.

The Madrid Conference may be become a turning point in the destiny of the entire region. The people of the Middle East, who for decades have been suffering from wars and lack of security, are the victims of occupation, have been expelled from their homes and have become the victims of terrorism, now see the chance of a peaceful settlement.

Humanity, it seems, has now realized that it is vitally important to overcome hostility, alienation, and confrontation. The search is gaining strength for new approaches to solve decades-old problems and to find solutions on the basis of a balance of interests.

I realize the immensity of the task we face. Yet, I am convinced that we have the possibility to fulfill the mission that history has entrusted us—to make the favorable wind of change become a reality in the Middle East. We know how much we can achieve if we meet each other halfway.

The road to Madrid was difficult and complex. For the representatives of Israel and Arab states to get together it was necessary to overcome hurdles that sometimes seemed insurmountable. It required bending every effort, thorough work and an intensive search for unorthodox solutions and realistic compromises in many countries. Each Middle East participant in the Conference had to mobilize the potential of the good will and to put aside numerous stereotypes and taboos. Yet, we managed to travel part of the road, and for [the time] being it is, indeed, only part of the road.

Let me remind you that the Soviet Union has always been in favor of convening a Middle East forum, which would give an impetus to the search for solutions in our region. The opportunity to embark on the road of practical implementation of that idea has surfaced after the Gorbachev-Bush summit in Helsinki last year. The Soviet Union and the United States have taken mutual obligations to act together in the interests of a [comprehensive] settlement in the Middle East.

Naturally, the interaction and cooperation of the two great powers has become a major factor that has made it possible to convene the Madrid Conference. The Soviet Union and the United States have always been in contact at all preparatory stages of the Conference and acted as partners, complementing each other's efforts. The final preparatory phase of the Conference called for especially intensive efforts and their putting into effect.

Let me note that the efforts of the European Communities have played a significant role at all stages. West European countries have a considerable potential for a constructive contribution to organizing the cooperation and good-neighborly relations among the countries of the region. We welcome the participation of the representative of the European Communities in this Peace Conference.

The convening of the Conference itself is a major breakthrough, our common success. But it is important that it does not evade us, that the efforts we have made are not in vain. We find ourselves today at a very important stage of turning to direct bilateral and multilateral negotiations. The three days of the Conference have not shaken my hope that this stage can be overcome.

Taking the floor among the last speakers I have a significant advantage over those who spoke from this rostrum before me, and I would like to use this advantage to share my vision of the results of the three days of work in this hall. Despite the fact that at times the emotions ran extremely high, the statements by the heads of delegations, in my opinion, were focused on the fundamental problems of concern to the peoples of the Middle East. The broad range of views which surfaced in the course of initial and, so far, indirect discussions does not overshadow the common feature in the positions of all the parties—the desire to have a durable and just peace in the Middle East and to solve the most difficult problems that have turned this region into the global powderkeg.

It is true that many, if not all of us, have their own ideas of the model of international relations in the Middle East that envisages peace and unity, justice and security. Those models of the Middle East settlement may differ in some details, sometimes even in important ones. That is inevitable for it is impossible to deny differences in historical experience, traditions, or propensities. However, there can be no doubt that all models thought by their authors as workable should proceed from the same principle—the need to find a balance of interests.

Echoing the words of President Gorbachev, let me give a short description of our vision of major points of the peace process.

First, the negotiations should lead Arabs and Israel to an historical compromise that may help leave behind the psychological, territorial, and national disputes presently dividing the parties.

All states and peoples of the Middle East should gain the right and the possibility to live in peace and harmony, within internationally recognized borders, which are secure for all of them. Nobody can be singled out and, moreover, nobody can be excluded—neither Palestinians nor Israel.

The formula of the historic compromise between Arabs and Israel contains the central notion and the main purpose of the settlement. Its implementation is designed to become a kind of a beacon in search and at the same time the core of future agreements on the establishment of a just, comprehensive and durable peace. That goal, of course, cannot be achieved without mutually acceptable agreements—both on the territorial aspects of the conflict and on its central element—the Palestinian problem.

In the final analysis there can be no doubt that Resolution 242—which forms the basis of this Conference—contains the principle of "territory for peace." This principle is applicable to "all the fronts"—the West Bank, the Gaza Strip, and the Golan Heights.

The return of those lands to their legitimate owners will turn interstate borders into bridges of communication and remove the main obstacle in the way of eliminating the state of war and establishing peace.

Second, the settlement process should put an end to the several-decades-old tragedy of four millions of Palestinians. The Palestinian problem is the original source of explosions which have repeatedly blown up the situation in the region and shaken the entire planet.

Clearly the Palestinian problem has grown in complexity which cannot be removed overnight. Statements by the participants in the Conference have shown once more that the solution to this problem should probably pass through various stages before a definitive settlement is reached. However, there can be no doubt that Palestinians have the right to self-determination enshrined in the U.N. Charter as a natural and inalienable right of any people. It is essential to ensure the required responsibility and good will on both sides in holding negotiations on how that right is to be implemented given the specific situation in the West Bank and the Gaza Strip. I believe that the negotiating option suggested by the co-initiators of the peace process opens up possibilities for realistic solutions to this problem taking into account the interests of both Palestinians and Israel.

Third, it is necessary to find an adequate solution to the problem of Jerusalem, acceptable to all. This city is the crossroads of religious interests of the peoples of the entire world, which go far beyond the Middle East. I think that the search for a common denominator in the positions of the parties will be a long and thorough process requiring tolerance and prudence in this extremely delicate and sensitive issue. Indeed, every believer—Moslem, Jew, or Christian—looks up to holy mosques, temples, or synagogues. Their feelings should be taken care of in a very thorough way.

Fourth, it is necessary to ensure the implementation of Security Council Resolution 425 as regards Lebanon.

Fifth, the unfolding difficult movement toward peace and security in the Middle East cannot ignore comprehensive cooperation in the region. Only the living fabric of trust and mutual understanding substantiated by close ties and joint development can ensure genuine security for all and everybody.

The process of reaching Middle East accord gets under way at a point in time when mutual trust in the region is unfortunately at a very low point. Difficult and vast [are the] problems to be solved to begin movement toward a durable and just peace.

I mean above all the uncontrolled arms race. The Middle East is a sorrowful testimony to the situation when unlimited storage of lethal arsenals not only continuously depletes material resources of states but also cultivates a dangerous militarized thinking, turning the entire region into a minefield of sorts. The tragic example of consequences of uncontrolled superarmament are the well-known events in the Gulf.

In other words, the alarm has gone off. And we welcome the fact that in the Middle East all parties get to think of the practical steps to limit the armaments in the region.

There are numerous other common regional problems in the Middle East which can be tackled only through joint efforts. For example, people of the Middle Eastern countries know better than many others how precious water is for man. Acting in isolation, it would impossible to save water resources for future generations.

Neither can we ignore the problem of terrorism, which haunts every Arab or Israeli family. The inhuman practice of using hostages remains, so to say, a bomb threatening the process of the Middle East settlement.

The threat of destroying the environment does not know any borders. Let me recall that during the Gulf crisis the threat of the ecological disaster transcended the borders of the conflict zone itself.

Finally, it is impossible to imagine [a] peaceful future for the Middle East without a broad, equal, and mutually advantageous economic cooperation. Divided by mistrust, conflicts and confrontation the region will not be able to integrate into the context of the development of the modern world, where openness and broad interaction are gaining strength. Should not that encourage states of the region to join their efforts together?

All of the above are problems to be solved at the negotiating table—provided we want hostility and mistrust to give way to an historic compromise between Israel and Arabs, and eventually, maybe, to building a common Middle East home.

Ladies and Gentlemen,

Our plenary sessions are about to end. The parties have stated their positions. We now come to the stage of direct negotiations, of elaborating bilateral and multilateral agreements designed to ensure a comprehensive settlement in accordance with Resolutions 242 and 338 of the U.N. Security Council. Let us be realistic. This Conference only offers a chance to come to a settlement. We should be very careful about that opportunity and try not to let emotions run high in the negotiating process. I call upon representatives of all the parties to show at the table maximum constructiveness and preparedness to take into account the interests and concerns of each other. This is the most reliable way to mutually acceptable solutions, tested by ages of world diplomacy.

That is why it is important after the plenary sessions to turn to the discussion of specific issues in the bilateral working groups. We are convinced that this should be started here, in Madrid, without losing the pace we have developed.

The multi-faceted and complex nature of the Middle East peace process urgently requires a timely shift to the discussion of organization of multilateral negotiations. The nature and contents of the future agreements should, of course, be determined by the parties involved themselves. This is an immense responsibility of the parties to the negotiations.

At present, just as the human being needs air to breathe, gestures from both sides testifying to good intentions are badly required. Undoubtedly, a most convincing demonstration of preparedness to a serious dialogue would consist in stopping the settlement activity in the occupied territories. I think that in this case Arab countries could take adequate steps in response.

I would like to assure you that as a Co-Chairman, the Soviet Union intends to assist actively in the creation of an atmosphere favorable to reaching agreement. I am sure that this will be facilitated by the relations of partnership we have established with the other Co-Chairman—the United States of America—as well as by the trust expressed to the co-chairmen by all the participants in the negotiations during these three days of discussions.

Provided the situation unfolds in this manner, these three days in Madrid will be inscribed in the history of the Middle East as the point of departure in forming a qualitatively new period—a period of lasting and durable peace.

In our view, this state of the region will make it possible to ensure to the peoples of the Middle East a future worthy of their great past and of their role in the development of human civilization. The region which has given to the world the first alphabet and three world religions, outstanding achievements in mathematics, astronomy, and medicine, priceless masterpieces of culture, architecture, and literature, the region which has long been a most important crossroads of trade, that region instead of being an arena of hostility, alienation, and terrorism will turn into an arena of broad and fruitful international communication, cooperation, and peace.

Ladies and Gentlemen,
There is a good symbol and sign in the fact that the Middle East Peace

Conference has been convened in Spain—the country where the European and Eastern civilizations have met and become harmoniously intertwined in their impressive achievements.

It is my agreeable duty to thank sincerely the host country, the leaders of Spain—His Majesty King Juan Carlos I, Prime Minister Felipe Gonzalez, and Minister for Foreign Affairs Francisco Fernandez Ordoñez for the readiness to host the Conference, excellent organization, and traditional Spanish hospitality.

Ladies and Gentlemen,
The Ecclesiast said that there is [a] time to destroy and [a] time to build. I am deeply convinced that in the Middle East [the] time has come for building. So let us do everything we can to bring this about through successful bilateral and multilateral negotiations.

MR. JAMES A. BAKER III, Secretary of State of the United States of America

Distinguished Colleagues, Ladies and Gentlemen,
Over the last eight months, many people in the region have exerted great efforts and contributed in many ways to make this Conference and negotiations possible. All of you in this hall fall into that category. But there are some who are not here now, individuals who have made essential contributions to the process, without which in my view this Conference would not have happened. In this regard, I want to pay tribute:

- To President Mubarak of Egypt, who was a confidant, advisor, friend and advocate for this process from the very beginning.
- To King Fahd of Saudi Arabia, who demonstrated by word and deed that new opportunities for Arab-Israeli peace existed after the Gulf War, and who personified this new approach in the Arab world.
- To President Assad of Syria, whose assurance to me that Syria had made an historic choice and decision in favor of peace, and whose early commitment to this process, both proved to be vital.
- To King Hussein of Jordan, whose courage, leadership and willingness to commit publicly and quickly in support of this process transformed the dynamics in the region.
- To Prime Minister Shamir of Israel, whose steady determination and strong leadership proved essential in reaching agreement to

convene this Conference and to launch direct bilateral negotiations for real peace between Israel and its neighbors.

- To Foreign Minister Levy of Israel, who was determined to develop an active and meaningful peace process and who worked
  creatively to overcome obstacles in our path.
- To President Hrawi of Lebanon, who has worked to re-establish
  central authority in his war-ravaged country, which is a necessary
  step toward peace in the region.
- To Palestinians with whom I met, like Faisal Husseini and Hanan
  Ashrawi, whose personal courage in the face of enormous pressures has created the possibility of a better life for Palestinians.

Even in a period of dramatic and far-reaching change around the
world, this Conference stands apart. Fourteen days ago, President Bush
and President Gorbachev invited Israel, the Arab states and Palestinians
to this Peace Conference and to direct negotiations that follow. In response to that invitation, Israel, Jordan, the Palestinians, Syria and Lebanon agreed to attend the Conference and to participate in the direct
negotiations. In addition, the European Community, Egypt, Saudi Arabia, Kuwait, Bahrain, Oman, the United Arab Emirates, Qatar, Tunisia,
Morocco, Algeria and Mauritania agreed to participate in this process.

This Conference demonstrates vividly the end of the Cold War and
the flowering of U.S.-Soviet partnership in resolving regional conflicts.
Where we once competed, we now cooperate. Where there was once
polarization, there is now coordination. What was once unthinkable—
the United States and the Soviet Union co-sponsoring a process of peace
in the Middle East—became a reality this week.

Our work—making peace through negotiations—has just begun. As
we look at the challenges ahead, it is worth noting and learning from
what we have already accomplished.

- For decades, agreement on whether to negotiate eluded the par-
  ties. This weekend, direct, bilateral negotiations aimed at com-
  prehensive, genuine peace will start.
- For decades, agreement on what to negotiate eluded the parties.
  This weekend, negotiations should begin on the accepted basis of
  United Nations Security Council Resolutions 242 and 338.
- For decades, agreement on how to negotiate eluded the parties.
  This weekend, negotiations will begin on two tracks and in
  phases; and in a few weeks, those parties who wish to participate
  will convene to organize multilateral negotiations on a wide

range of issues that affect the well-being of all peoples in the region.

These are not mere platitudes. During these eight months of diplomacy, though the parties sometimes fell back on old slogans and outmoded code words, they also came to understand the need to engage concretely and pragmatically to resolve problems. I said often that the parties would probably stake out maximum positions, especially as they got closer to negotiations.

This is not surprising, especially in a public forum. The key, however, is to get beyond the rhetoric and into the direct negotiations.

A basic tenet of American thinking is that negotiations are the best way to resolve disputes and achieve peace. Negotiations do not guarantee peace. But without negotiations, there is no way to produce genuine peace and no mechanism to develop understandings that can endure.

The United States is willing to be a catalytic force, an energizing force, and a driving force in the negotiating process. Our involvement in this process will be rooted solidly in the core principles enunciated by President Bush last March. They will remain the cornerstone that guides our participation in the negotiating process.

The U.S. is and will be an honest broker. We have our own positions and views on the peace process, and we will not forego our right to state these. But, as an honest broker with experience—successful experience—in Middle East negotiations, we also know that our critical contribution will often be to exert quiet, behind-the-scenes influence and persuasion.

Let no one mistake our role as an honest broker to mean that we will change longstanding U.S. policy positions; and let no one mistake our policy positions as undercutting our determination to help the parties reach fair and mutually acceptable solutions to problems. As President Bush and I have both said this week, it is not our policies that matter; it is those of the parties. They are the ones that must negotiate peace.

This week, the parties provided insight into their thinking about a negotiated settlement. They outlined three broad requirements in the search for peace:

- First, we heard a yearning for peace—the wish of peoples in the region to live in a mutually satisfying relationship with neighbors, a relationship characterized by peace treaties, economic relations, cultural ties, and political dialogue.
- Second, we heard an emphasis on land—the desire of peoples in the region to exercise authority and political governance over ter-

ritory they consider part of their national, political, historical or religious patrimony.

- Third, we heard a need for security—the requirement of people to live free of fear, and the obligation of governments to do their best to protect their citizens.

What the parties in fact said this week is that these core issues—land, peace, and security—are inseparable elements in the search for a comprehensive settlement.

The parties have made clear that peace by itself is unachievable without a territorial solution and security; that a territorial solution by itself will not resolve the conflict without there also being peace and security; and that security by itself is impossible to achieve without a territorial solution and peace. The process on which we are embarked can work only if all issues are put on the table, and if all issues are satisfactorily resolved.

One key issue is the style of negotiations. Today, the Soviet Union and the United States are on the same side of the table—literally and figuratively—in striving for global peace and the resolution of regional conflicts. Today, and in the future, we will work together in pursuit of a Middle East settlement.

The United States, at the highest levels, will remain intimately engaged in this process. We expect to be available to the parties throughout this process. The United States and the Soviet Union are prepared to participate directly in the negotiations themselves, with the consent of all parties.

We will do our part. But we cannot do your part as well. The United States and the Soviet Union will provide encouragement, advice, recommendations, proposals, and views to help the peace process. Sometimes, you will be satisfied with our views, sometimes frustrated. Sometimes, we will support your positions and sometimes not. Sometimes we will act quietly and behind the scenes, and sometimes we will make known our views and positions in public. None of this, however, will relieve you—the parties—of the obligation of making peace. If you won't do it, we certainly can't. As I have said from the beginning of this effort, we cannot want peace more than you, the parties most directly affected by its absence.

Parties in this process cannot reasonably be expected to operate outside their political environment; but they should be expected to educate, shape, guide, and lead politics and opinion. Leaders in the region have taken difficult and courageous decisions to get to this Conference and to negotiations. More difficult and more courageous decisions will be required to settle this conflict.

Let me say a word about the venue of the bilateral negotiations.

As you know, the invitation sent to the parties on October 18 contained the terms of reference for this peace process, terms of reference that had been meticulously negotiated and agreed. This invitation specified that direct, bilateral negotiations would begin four days after the opening of the Conference. But there was never agreement regarding the location for those bilateral negotiations.

The parties have not yet been able to agree on where to hold these negotiations. It is the view of the co-sponsors that the direct, bilateral negotiations should start in Madrid as soon as possible. It is the intention of the co-sponsors to continue to consult with the parties with a view to fulfilling the requirements of the invitation on this subject.

From the perspective of the co-sponsors, and indeed from the perspective of most of the rest of the world, it would be very difficult to understand how a party could now refuse to attend bilateral negotiations simply because of a disagreement over the site of those negotiations.

Finally, I want to note that a meeting will take place in several weeks among those parties who wish to participate in multilateral negotiations to organize those negotiations. These talks will focus on issues of critical interest to many parties in the region. They will be a complement to the bilateral negotiations. I am pleased that the multilateral negotiations have already gained widespread support and interest both in and outside the Middle East.

This week, many have focused on the need for steps that would build confidence and trust. The United States continues to believe that confidence-building measures are important for the process and for the parties themselves.

I want to be perfectly honest, standing here as I am before colleagues with whom I have spent many, many hours since last March. The unwillingness of the parties to take confidence-building steps has been disappointing. You have dealt successfully with formulas and positions. You have agreed on terms of reference that are fair and equitable. You have launched a process of negotiations that can succeed. But you have failed to deal adequately with the human dimension of the conflict.

As I travelled through the region, I witnessed terrible scenes of human tragedy, suffering, and despair. Innocent civilians caught in the crossfire of a conflict they wish would end. Refugees and displaced persons wandering across the vast expanses of time. Mothers and fathers, afraid of the future that awaits their children. And children, being schooled in the lessons of animosity and conflict, rather than friendship and accommodation.

Formulas, terms of reference, and negotiations are not enough. Support for a negotiating process will not be sustainable unless the human dimension is addressed by all parties. A way must be found to send signals of peace and reconciliation that affect the peoples of the region. Don't wait for the other side to start; each of you needs to get off the mark quickly. You should know best what is needed.

Through negotiations and through these and other steps, you can demonstrate respect for the rights of others. You can express understanding of the fears of others. You can touch the people—the women, men, and children—who are the victims of the Arab-Israeli conflict. We can only succeed at the table if we find ways of reaching out to one another away from the table.

The challenges have been great, and the obstacles have been many, on the road to peace. Your decisions over these eight months of intensive diplomacy have created a new baseline of realism and commitment to peace. This Conference has been vital in breaking down the barriers of communication, and in establishing for all to see that Arab and Israeli leaders can meet face to face.

In closing, let me speak to each of you personally and directly.

For over four decades, the world waited for this week. Peace-loving peoples everywhere tried time and again to get you—the makers of this intractable conflict—to join together to discuss your differences. This week, here in Madrid, you finally have met and held such a meeting.

This has been a start—a good start—an historic start that has broken old taboos—an important start that opens further opportunities.

But it is only a start—and that's not enough. You must not let this start become an end.

When you walk out these doors, you carry with you great responsibilities. You carry with you the responsibility to your peoples to seek peace. You carry with you the responsibility to the world to build a comprehensive and just peace. You carry with you the responsibility to yourselves to break with the past and pursue a new future.

For if you do not seize this historic opportunity, no one will blame anyone outside your region.

You now shoulder the destiny and challenge of making peace, as you enter direct negotiations with your neighbors. The continuation and success of this process is in your hands. The world still looks to each of you to make the choice for peace.

MR. HANS VAN DEN BROEK, Minister for Foreign Affairs of The Netherlands and Acting President of the Council of Ministers of the European Communities

Mr. Co-Chairmen,

I would like to take this opportunity in the first place to commend our

Co-Chairmen in convening this historic opening Conference where we see all parties around the table for the first time, which anyhow is historical. I believe indeed that this is no more than a beginning, a very important beginning. Having listened to all the contributions, I indeed am convinced how much we need a step-by-step process accompanied by confidence-building measures from the very beginning.

The greatest problem to overcome in the initial phase in the negotiating process, as far as I can see it, is overcoming mistrust and creating further solid foundations for meaningful negotiations in good faith. Many elements have been put on the table, many valuable incentives have been given by various delegations. Others have been accused of being too much withholding and looking too much to the past. We believe that bridges can be built and bridges have to be built. The European Community has very traditional and longstanding bonds with the Middle East and with all the parties alike. The European Community and its member states are not partisans in the favor of the one viewpoint or the other but are partisans for legality. We are partisans for peace including security and justice for all without exceptions. We will continue to stand ready to assist this cause for any party that calls on us and we will remain in close and constant consultation with the co-sponsors in order to see that we further the process by cohesive action and coherent action.

Mr. Co-Chairmen, the Middle East that finds peace with itself can be a blessing not only for its own people, not only for its own environment, but for the world as a whole. It has a lot to offer and it has a lot to gain. And we are firmly determined to help the Middle East to achieve this goal. And as I have indicated in the initial address the day before yesterday, the European Community is fully prepared not only for a constructive partnership but also for a concrete partnership. We feel that parallel to the bilateral negotiations also multilateral negotiations should be started up in due course; not at the expense of the political process but in parallel with the political process and emphasizing that all the parties are masters of their own decisions and can decide when results achieved in the multilateral process should be put into effect, but identifying the splendid opportunities that are there when peace is achieved. The possibilities of cooperation in the region and the contribution that the European Community can bring in concrete [form], we believe could be identified already at an early stage, thus giving an additional incentive to all the parties to reach a political solution which eventually will allow for peace but also for economic development and prosperity for all. I pledge on behalf of the European Community and its twelve member states a full assistance and readiness along the process for all those parties that so desire.

Thank you very much.

Index

Abrams, Dan, 41
Achille Lauro, 18
Agriculture, 149
Akaba-Eilat Gulf, 137
Algeria, 159, 167
Allen, Woody, 3
Alluf, Muwaffaq, 141
Alterman, Natan, 153–54
American Israel Public Affairs
   Committee (AIPAC), 6
American Jewish community, 1
Anani, Jawad al-, 142
Anar, Nadav, 115
Anderson, Sten, 41
Aphek, David, 51, 115
Arab economic boycott, 111
Arad, Moshe, 48
Arafat, Yasser, 41, 47–48, 59, 86,
   98, 131
Aram, Shimon, 9
Arens, Moshe: aid request and, 89;
   Arafat and, 41; Asia and, 40;
   Baker and, 19, 21; Egypt confer-

ence and, 30–31, 38; Lavi project and, 38; leftist views and, 39;
Palestinian delegates and, 26, 35;
party change and, 139; PLO
and, 41–42; U.S. framework
proposal and, 28; U.S.-Israeli relations and, 39, 40
Arms control, 60, 153
Ashrawi, Hanan, 105, 121, 133,
141
Asia, 40
Assad, Hafez, 55, 76, 99, 159, 166,
176
Association of American Arabs,
159

Baker, James: administration
change and, 168, 169; assurances letter and, 113; Ben-
Aharon and, 86; Benelux
paradigm and, 150; compromise
bridge and, 100; conference location and, 109, 137; delegate

About the Author

EYTAN BENTSUR is Director-General of the Israeli Ministry of Foreign Affairs.